D0072241

ST. MAXIMUS THE CONFESSOR

THE ASCETIC LIFE
THE FOUR CENTURIES ON CHARITY

ΛΟΓΟΣ ΑΣΚΗΤΙΚΟΣ
ΚΕΦΑΛΑΙΑ ΠΕΡΙ ΑΓΑΠΗΣ

Ancient Christian Writers

The Works of the Fathers in Translation

EDITED BY

JOHANNES QUASTEN, S. T. D.
Catholic University of America
Washington, D.C.

JOSEPH C. PLUMPE, Ph.D.
Pontifical College Josephinum
Worthington, O.

No. 21

REF
BR
60
·A35
no. 21

ST. MAXIMUS THE CONFESSOR

THE ASCETIC LIFE
THE FOUR CENTURIES ON CHARITY

TRANSLATED AND ANNOTATED
BY

POLYCARP SHERWOOD, O.S.B., S.T.D.

St. Meinrad Archabbey

Professor of Patrology
Pontifical Institute of St. Anselm, Rome

NEWMAN PRESS

New York, N.Y./Ramsey, N.J.

69321

Nihil Obstat:

J. Quasten
Cens. Dep.

Imprimatur:

Patricius A. O'Boyle, D.D.
Archiep. Washingtonen.
die 23 Feb. 1955

ALL RIGHTS RESERVED

Library of Congress
Catalog Card Number: 55-8642

ISBN: 0-8091-0258-7

PUBLISHED BY PAULIST PRESS
Editorial Office: 1865 Broadway, New York, N.Y. 10023
Business Office: 545 Island Road, Ramsey, N.J. 07446

PRINTED AND BOUND IN THE UNITED STATES OF AMERICA

auctoribus vitae
filius

CONTENTS

CONTENTS

ST. MAXIMUS THE CONFESSOR

THE ASCETIC LIFE
THE FOUR CENTURIES ON CHARITY

ΛΟΓΟΣ ΑΣΚΗΤΙΚΟΣ
ΚΕΦΑΛΑΙΑ ΠΕΡΙ ΑΓΑΠΗΣ

INTRODUCTION

Maximus, a disciple at the same time of two great diverse spiritual tendencies, that associated with the Pseudo-Denis and that stemming from Origen, endeavored to compose them in his own thought and life. To him is due at once the transmission of the Origenist spirituality and the first serious reasoned criticism of the Origenist myth;[1] to him is due a further and definitive diffusion among the orthodox of the *Corpus Dionysiacum* and the refutation of Monenergism sheltered by a famous text of Denis; a Neoplatonic mystic, he did not hesitate to use Aristotelian concepts and logic in the refutation of Monothelite errors. As a monk, then, nurtured on the same spiritual fare as the Monophysites—Denis and Origen—he had the acumen while retaining the fulness of this spirituality not only to reject the Monophysite position but to elaborate the orthodox doctrine of two natures in its ulterior consequences of two wills and operations.[1a]

Yet it is not only in the speculative and doctrinal realms that Maximus fixes our attention.

A simple monk (for he was neither priest nor superior), Maximus was the inspirer of several anti-Monothelite councils in Africa and played a great part in the Lateran Council of 649;[2] thoroughly a subject of the emperor, he knew how to maintain the Church's liberty in the face of the imperial ecclesiasticism; a thorough Byzantine by cultural formation and attachment, he consistently placed unity of faith, even though it be with the less-cultured Latins, above the narrower unity of language and rite.

It is the one man of God and of His Church underlying this series of contrasts that I would try to sketch in the following pages. Previous writers have treated Maximus under one or the other of these aspects—as polemic theologian, as ascetic author, as champion of the Holy See, as exegete, as philosopher; even von Balthasar in his *Kosmische Liturgie* considers only the structure of Maximus' thought. It is then the whole Maximus that I would endeavor to present.

In two passages of his earlier works Saint Maximus himself gives a key to his whole life and activity, which it will be well to set at the head of this sketch of his life and doctrine. First he speaks in his introduction to the *Difficulties from Denis and Gregory*[3] of their sanctity, of their God-given wisdom, so much so that they 'possess the living Christ above all, or better, Christ has become the soul of their souls, manifest in all their deeds and words and thoughts.' Such is the basis of his adherence and reproduction of the doctrine of the Fathers. Again in the second part of the same work, dealing with the relations of body and soul at conception, he writes:

> The holy Fathers and teachers clearly proclaim, rather the truth that speaks and is spoken through them, that together with the descent of God the Word at conception instantaneously by means of a rational soul the Lord Himself, God the Word, was united to the flesh. . . .[4]

Here Maximus alleges not only the authority of the Fathers but that of the very fact itself: *the truth that speaks.* These passages indicate, I think, the cardinal attitudes of his life and thought: fidelity to the Spirit-animated tradition and to the revealed fact—the mystery of the God-man.

If then Maximus is called theologian, as sometimes he

has been, it is rather in the sense that St. John the Evangelist is called theologian than that in which St. Thomas Aquinas receives the title. For the coherence of Maximus' thought, which not all would allow,[5] does not derive from the systematization of the Church's teaching in function of some humanly-posited principle or philosophy,[6] but from a vision of the divine things in the light of the Incarnation of the Son of God, in the light therefore of that mystery by which alone we know the Father and our salvation. Having thus grasped the significance of Gospel and Tradition, in a word, of Christ, it is not essential that the conceptual furniture for expressing this understanding of Christ be everywhere the same—so long as it be apt for its function and pressed to fulfil it.

Maximus has in fact used extensively the writings of Evagrius of Pontus, of Denis the Mystic, of Origen; how much he is indebted to the Cappadocians, especially Gregory of Nyssa, and to Cyril of Alexandria, has not been studied; nor yet the imprint left on the turn of his doctrine not only by his constant opposition to Monophysite errors but by his profound sympathy with the innate trend of their thought, the emphasis on, and the exaltation of, the *one* Christ our God. It was in fact to defend this unity of Christ that he unceasingly maintained the distinction of the natures, human and divine, alike after as before the union.

The *Life and Combat* of St. Maximus was written some twenty years after his death, at the time of the sixth ecumenical council (680–81).[7] It gives us little precise information in addition to the six contemporary documents which have come down to us. These documents have all been studied, completed, and analyzed by Devreesse.[8] The other source of our knowledge of Maximus are his

writings.[9] The letters especially and some of the other
occasional pieces give valuable information. Grumel has
made some use of them in his notes on the life of St.
Maximus.[10]

I. LIFE

Born in 580, Maximus received his formation and
schooling during the years of Gregory the Great's pontificate. The education thus received was common to all the
youths who looked forward to the imperial service, the
Church, or simply to affairs. It comprised the usual gram-
mar, rhetoric, and philosophy. Under philosophy was
included the quadrivium (arithmetic, music, geometry,
astronomy) and philosophy itself. This philosophical instruction was based chiefly on the works of Plato and
Aristotle, along with the commentators.[11]

It would have been therefore in the impressionable
years of youth that Maximus made his first acquaintance
alike with Aristotle and the Neoplatonists. For it was the
commentaries of Proclus, Iamblichus, and the like that
accompanied the texts of the masters.

It is worth noting this first contact with Neoplatonic
thought; for it would seem that the love of the supernal
world there first imparted flowered not only in Maximus'
monastic vocation but in the whole of his theological
activity as defender and interpreter of Denis the Mystic
and of Gregory the Theologian.

Before, however, he was to start out on the monastic life,
Maximus was to attain one of the highest positions at the
imperial court—namely that of first secretary to Heraclius,
who came to power in 610. It was doubtless during the
years of his schooling and imperial service that he formed

those close friendships with men of the court that his later correspondence permits us to appreciate.

His time of service with the emperor was not long. Probably about the year 613-14 Maximus withdrew to a monastery, that of Chrysopolis (now Scutari) on the Asiatic shore across from Constantinople. His biographer is probably right in saying that his love for the life of solitude (the hesychastic life) prompted him to leave the court.

In this life too he made quick progress. By the year 618 he already had a disciple, the monk Anastasius, who was to be with him to the end.

THEOLOGICAL POSITION AT THE OUTSET

Only some six or seven years (624-25) after Anastasius had become his disciple, Maximus must have left his first monastery at Chrysopolis for that of St. George at Cyzicus (now Erdek).[12] His earlier writings, with but one possible exception (Ep 6), are to be assigned to this stay. It was from here that he wrote the first surviving letters to John the Chamberlain, among which is that magnificent encomium on charity, of which Combefis says: *vere maximum agit Maximus.* Surely this little treatise is worthy of the highest praise, yet it betrays a point of view in the spiritual life and a terminology which could only be favorable to the Monenergistic and Monothelite heresies. Thus in eulogy of our union with God he writes:

> As we all have one nature, so we are able to have with God and with one another but one mind (γνώμη) and one will, being in no way at odds either with God or with one another.[13]

This illustrates, as well as any one passage can, how apt for confusion such terminology was, and indicates equally

well a spirituality which places the summit of holiness in
the unity of wills. I have been brought to think that this
spirituality was in large measure common property not
only among the Byzantines but also among the Monophysites. This being true, it will not be difficult to understand the caution with which Maximus proceeded in
taking up a clear-cut opposition to Sergius and Pyrrhus in
their feelers for compromise with the Monophysites.

In any case it was also at Cyzicus and in discussion with
Bishop John that the *Ambigua* were conceived. In these he
makes a similar statement about one will of God and the
saints, which afterwards he felt bound to retract.[14]

Though, then, this larger group of *Ambigua* were written
down only after Maximus had arrived in Africa, yet they
were thought out in his talks with the bishop.[15] It is clear
even from a cursory reading that it is not the Monophysites or Monenergists which gave them anxiety, but the
Origenists. This is a refutation of Origenism, especially of
the doctrine of the henad, with a full understanding and
will to retain what is good in the Alexandrian master's
doctrine—a refutation, perhaps, unique in Greek patristic
literature.[16]

A careful and full analysis of this whole block of questions is necessary for establishing or disproving the homogeneity of Maximus' thought. Given a self-consistent
thought-structure in these *Ambigua*, one would be justified
in understanding the two Gnostic Centuries,[17] so predominantly Origenistic, in the light of this structure. In
fact this Origenistic influence is so strong[18] that von Balthasar speaks of a real Origenistic crisis in the Confessor's
thought and conjectures his supposed stay at Alexandria
in 633 as the occasion of this crisis.[19]

Now the texture of Maximus' refutation of Origen in

the *Ambigua* seems to me sufficiently coherent. We may then point out some of the relations that obtain between the two Centuries in question and the other works of Maximus.

First of all, the two Centuries seem to be a literary unity, not the work of a compiler.[20] Von Balthasar has drawn attention to the many similarities between the Centuries and the *Questions to Thalassius* and *to Theopemptus*. I for my part would draw particular attention to the intimate relations which bind the contrary motifs of the Centuries with the *Ambigua*. Of the contrary motifs by far the most noteworthy are the initial group of ten.[21] This ten is obviously a unit[22] and as clearly a forceful summary of the anti-Origenist doctrine of the *Ambigua*.

Its position at the beginning of 200 predominantly Origenist chapters is highly significant. Maximus, basing himself on the *Ambigua*, is giving, as it were, the metaphysical framework in which the Origenist and Evagrian sentences are to be understood. They are to be understood in the context he gives, not that of their original authors.[23]

If such an interpretation of Maximus be tenable, he then appears not as suffering an Origenist crisis, but as deliberately endeavoring to give the assimilable elements in the Alexandrian master's thought a secure place in monastic tradition. The success of this effort is another and a quite distinct question.

The *Ambigua*, then, though composed later in Africa, were conceived and thought out in discussions with the bishop of Cyzicus. Judging from the extent of the *Ambigua* and the relations of abbot and spiritual son obtaining between the bishop and Maximus, his stay at Cyzicus must have actually been of some duration. I should say at least a year, with the expectation that it should be permanent.[24]

The advance of the Persians on Constantinople in the spring of 626, as Msgr. Devreesse has pointed out,[25] will have occasioned the dispersal of the monastery of St. George at Cyzicus and sent Maximus further on his way to Africa.

PROGRESS TO AND ESTABLISHMENT IN AFRICA

On this journey there are two possible stopovers—Cyprus and Crete. Maximus himself relates that once he had been in Crete, that the Severian bishops then held a dispute with him.[26] This notice tells us two things: the stay in Crete was more than a passing call; Maximus was already known as a theologian and defender of the Chalcedonian faith. Doubtless it was during this stay that he made the acquaintance of the bishop of Cydonia, the third principal town in Crete,[27] to whom later he writes at his correspondent's request.

For a stop in Cyprus we have no similar direct statement of Maximus, but may only infer it from the fact of his correspondence with the Cypriote Marinus[28] and from a possible acquaintance with the bishop Arcadius.[29]

When did Maximus finally arrive in proconsular Africa? The end of Epistle 8, as published by Devreesse,[30] makes it clear that he was at Carthage at least by Pentecost of 632. I think, however, his actual arrival should be set back a few years before that date. This will depend on Maximus' relations with Sophronius. Now it is known that Sophronius, at Alexandria in June of 633, was elected patriarch of Jerusalem in 634. Hence the relations which bound the two men together would have to have been formed before that date, 633. Sophronius and Maximus dwelt in the same African monastery while Sergius the patriarch and his fellows (among whom was Pyrrhus) were fabricating Monenergism.[31] This monastery was called *Eucratas,*[32] Sophronius' surname.[33] Of this community Sophronius was apparently the head, for Maximus refers to him as teacher and *abbas.*[34] All seem agreed that Sophronius was largely responsible for awakening Maximus to a sense of danger in the new heresy. What the extent of that influence was, is still to be determined.[35] In any case the relations of master and spiritual guide which Maximus gives to Sophronius in his own regard demand some length of time for their formation. Tentatively, then, let us assign Maximus' arrival in Africa to the years 628–30.

The group of letters to the bishop of Cyzicus, 28–31, 8, all express Maximus' desire to be restored to the bishop's community of St. George's Cyzicus. Perhaps the group of four were written in the first years of his exile and Epistle 8 when the master he had found in Sophronius was already on his way to the east. In any case at the end of Epistle 8 he still prays to be brought back,[36] though doubtless with the same readiness to bear the separation with the help of their prayers as he expresses in Letter 31.[37]

However, about this time—632, 633—I suppose that Maximus came to accept his exile as a permanent thing. In the extant correspondence there is no further mention of returning to the east. From one letter, the 25th, it also appears that he had in Africa a superior to whom he must excuse himself. This Conon, of whom we know nothing further, succeeded perhaps Sophronius in the direction of the exile Byzantine community near Carthage.

It is during the first years of this African stay that Maximus composed the two great works which have come down to us complete—the *Questions to Thalassius* and the earlier, larger *Ambigua.*

RELATIONS WITH IMPERIAL GOVERNORS

In the years that follow there are three elements in Maximus' life: his continuing monastic life, his relations with the imperial governors of Africa, his activity against Monophysitism and the rising heresies, Monenergism and Monothelitism.

Of this first there is little one can say, for it has no external history. Yet it is well to realize that Maximus remained a monk and a contemplative to the very core throughout all the subsequent controversies and polemics. To be convinced of this it is enough to read the remarks with which he prefaces his great polemic work *Ad Marinum*.[38]

Of the governors there are two with whom Maximus was intimately connected: Peter the Illustrious and George.

Peter, *strategos* of Numidia, was ordered in the year 633 to proceed to Egypt.[39] To this same Peter we find Maximus addressing a little treatise against the doctrine of Severus. Peter has just informed him of the safe conclusion of a sea voyage and of the return to their heresy of some ill-converted Monophysites. Peter must be at Alexandria after the Pact of Union of June, 633. Finally Maximus refers Peter to Sophronius who, he says, is able to supply all the deficiencies of the letter.

The next letter we have to Peter is to recommend to him the newly-converted Alexandrian deacon Cosmas, that he may in case of necessity use his good offices with the 'God-honored pope.'[40] The reference is doubtless to Cyrus of Alexandria, and Peter is still or again in that town.

Finally we find Peter again in Africa where he had occasion to be concerned over the title accorded there to the ex-patriarch Pyrrhus, *most holy*. Maximus' reply is an impassioned review of the whole Monothelite question.[41]

Maximus' relations with George were perhaps closer; at least we know more about them because of the disaster in which his term as eparch ended. Only one letter is addressed to George, a letter of encouragement in time of trial.[42] The whole affair Maximus reports to his friend at court, John the Chamberlain.[43] The story briefly is this. George had endeared himself to the whole population by his care of widows and orphans, by his solicitude for the persons displaced by the Mohammedan conquests, by his zeal for the Chalcedonian orthodoxy. Not least was he solicitous for his fellow Byzantines and the exile monks of the Eucratas monastery. In November, 641, a certain Theodore arrived, bearing letters supposedly from the empress-regent Martina, ordering George to set at liberty some Monophysite nuns. When this was noised among the people, there was a great commotion and the empress' good name for orthodoxy was gravely compromised. Therefore, to preserve her reputation and to quiet the people, George, having consulted Maximus, declared the letters spurious. Shortly after this incident George was recalled to Constantinople.

This recall can scarcely be a result of the Theodore incident; there is not the time for a courier to have gone to Constantinople and to have returned. If such were the case, Martina's fall from power, in the autumn of 641, would certainly have been known in Africa and reflected itself in the correspondence seeking George's return; but there is no such indication. It seems therefore much more probable that George and Maximus were right in declaring the Martina letters spurious.

However that may be, the Africans, especially the Byzantines, were left in great uncertainty as to the outcome of this recall for their beloved eparch.

In all his relations with public officials Maximus appears as their counselor and above all as solicitous for their orthodoxy in regard, almost exclusively, to Monophysitism.

MONOTHELITE CONTROVERSY: THE 'PSEPHOS'

This constant polemic against Monophysitism as such without suggestion of the developing heresies, Monenergism and Monothelitism, brings us face to face with the problem of the rise of Maximus' opposition to these heresies. Father Grumel gives the impression that Maximus was very slow in entering the lists against Monothelitism. The letter to Peter about Pyrrhus' title *most holy* (written 643–44) he terms the first openly anti-Monothelitic document from the Confessor's hands.[44]

This is rather late, ten years after the Pact of Union of Alexandria; and all the more surprising when Maximus himself in the dispute with Pyrrhus[45] assigns the first steps of Monenergism to the letter of Sergius, patriarch of Constantinople, to George Arsas asking for patristic texts in favor of one energy. This was in the year 617.[46]

There cannot be question here even of sketching the rise of these heresies; the outlining, however, of the genesis of Maximus' attitude towards them can scarce be omitted. The remarks then that follow must suppose some knowledge of the former.[47]

Without doubt the anonymous biographer throws the hardened position of controversy back many years before its time when he relates that the rising heresy was a chief motive for Maximus in leaving the imperial service.[48] This certainly was not the case. The first clear indication of his diffidence or rather non-acceptance of Monenergism is found in the later *Ambigua*, showing the influence of

Sophronius' synodicon of 634,[49] and in his reply to Pyrrhus (Ep 19) which is subsequent by but a little to Cyrus' Pact of Union and Sergius' judgment against the disputed terminology—one operation, two operations in the Lord.

This is the first evidence come down to us; it is amply sufficient.

Of these documents the letter to Pyrrhus is of greater importance.[50] Pyrrhus had written Maximus, relating the action of Sergius in regard to the openly Monenergistic Pact of Alexandria and seeking his support for the Sergian policy.

The judgment (psēphos) of Sergius, to which Maximus refers,[51] has come down to us. Grumel has given as the text of this psēphos a passage from Sergius' letter to Honorius.[52] He seems, however, to have overlooked a passage a few paragraphs above in the same letter which is textually repeated in the Ecthesis of 638.[53] Now it is known that the Ecthesis was no more than the psēphos promulgated over the imperial signature.[54] I believe therefore that we have the very text of the psēphos in the passage just indicated.

The Pact of Union had patently admitted one operation. The psēphos forbade mention either of one or two operations of Christ, it being alone permissible to refer to the only-begotten Son Jesus Christ operating what is divine and human, as proceeding from the one Incarnated Word of God. So far so good; there is nothing in this overtly heterodox. But why this restriction? The psēphos goes on: Some are scandalized because to speak of one operation seems to imply denial of the two natures which Our Lord possesses—an objection scarce worthy of attention. On the other hand many are scandalized, because the phrase 'two operations' is not found in the Fathers and implies two contrary wills in Our Lord.

This latter part of the *psēphos* is clearly tendentious; but as these pros and cons are presented not as a matter of precept but only as a matter of accessory opinion, one could let them pass.

What, then, is Maximus' attitude toward this document? Sophronius in his synodicon had avoided the proscribed terminology, while forcefully combatting the underlying doctrinal tendency. Maximus similarly accepts the *psēphos*, but according to his own doctrinal interpretation. The reason for his great praise of Sergius is precisely this, Sergius' rejection of the Alexandrian novelty, that is, the Monenergistic Pact of Union. This *psēphos* maintains the right doctrine in the face of this error.[55] He then proceeds to state what is this right doctrine. When he comes to speak of the Incarnation, he is most explicit. Sergius in writing to Honorius, and later, Pyrrhus in his dispute with Maximus,[56] assign all suffering and passion to the humanity of Christ alone and then correspondingly all operation to the Godhead. Maximus seems to have such a thought in mind when in this letter he stresses with exceptional vigor the exchange of properties (*communicatio idiomatum*), writing: 'He works humanly what is divine . . . and divinely what is human.'[57] It is only a few lines further on that he enunciates the principle governing the whole question:

> That which is made up of diverse things without mixing them, by a natural bond of union, both preserves their component natures unchanged and conserves undiminished their (several) component powers for the completion of a single work.[58]

Here we find not only the distinction of two natures

maintained, but likewise that of the consequent powers. Unity is found in the work done, not in the doing. The distinction of operations is not here explicitly affirmed (it is necessarily implied); perhaps because there was a real confusion of terminology, which gave specious justification to the tendentiousness of the *psēphos* and about which Maximus is careful to seek further explanations.[59]

Maximus then with great dexterity affirms the orthodox doctrine in this question, while still observing the *psēphos*, an authoritative document; he avoids offending the official party while making it clear that the favored Monenergism is scarcely acceptable unless the term *operation* is explained.

This is precisely the weak point. It was above all Sergius' tergiversations on the meaning of the will that chiefly turned Maximus against him.[60] This testimony of Maximus on the progress of his opposition to Sergius is trustworthy, for he gave it in the presence of Pyrrhus who was in a position to object to any misstatement or exaggeration. Now the death of Sergius (December 9, 638) followed but a couple of months on the publication of the *Ecthesis*. Maximus therefore must have taken his stand, but not thereby inaugurating an active polemic, against Sergius' doctrine quite apart from the open controversy precipitated by the publication of this document.

This is more than mere surmise. We have still a letter of Maximus written after Honorius' death (October 12, 638) but before news of the *Ecthesis* reached him, that is, before the spring of 640.[61] In this tome to Marinus of Cyprus[62] after a consideration of two passages from the Fathers, seeming to favor Monenergism or Monothelitism, Maximus treats of Honorius' letter to Sergius. Here he corroborates his own interpretation of Honorius in a perfectly orthodox and dyothelite sense with the reports of the

2

affair that his friend Anastasius had secured for him in Rome.[63]

There can be no doubt whatsoever that a letter such as this was intended for a more numerous audience than its immediate recipient. Nor can there be any doubt, in view of the final reference to Marinus' bishop[64] as a defender of the 'one spotless, orthodox faith,' that Maximus was quite aware he was taking sides in a controverted question.

In the east therefore, and consequently also for Maximus, the issue was well joined before the *Ecthesis*. Between Rome and Constantinople, however, it was the *Ecthesis* that brought the question to a head.

Monothelite Controversy: the 'Ecthesis'

The *Ecthesis* was in substance but the *psēphos* of 634 republished, but this time over the emperor's signature. *In substance*, for the accompanying matter manifests a clear development in the sense of Monothelitism. The very speaking of two wills is represented as beyond the daring of Nestorius; he spoke of two sons, but also of identity of will. Therefore, the document goes on, 'let us confess one will of Our Lord and true God Jesus Christ,' that there be no chance of conflict between the human nature and the divine Word.[65]

This document came to the knowledge of the Roman authorities on the return of Severinus' apocrisaries sent to Constantinople to obtain the imperial approval of his election to the Roman See. These apocrisaries were sufficiently astute to obtain imperial approval for Severinus without committing him to the *Ecthesis*. This took time. It was not till the spring of 640 that they returned to Rome with the *Ecthesis*; for Severinus was

consecrated only May 28, 640.[66] That Severinus condemned the *Ecthesis* before his death a few months later
(August 2, 640) is not certain.[67]

Maximus received knowledge of the *Ecthesis* about the
same time as Severinus. His friends at Constantinople informed him of all the attempted bargaining with the
pope's apocrisaries and sent him a copy of the document
only after these same ambassadors had left Constantinople.
We learn of this only from Maximus' letter to Thalassius.
Unfortunately, there remains only the first part of the
letter; Maximus' comments on the *Ecthesis* did not serve
Anastasius' purposes, he did not therefore preserve them
for us.[68] Maximus' first reaction to the *Ecthesis* then we
can only infer from the approving way in which he
recounts the apocrisaries' accomplishment of their mission.

The next, surely dated group of letters that we have are
those pertaining to the recall of George, belonging to the
fall of 641 and early 642.[69] The 12th letter only need
detain us here. Why does this letter enter into detail about
the Monophysitism of Severus while giving no indication
of the Monothelite controversy? One cannot suppose, as
we have just seen, that Maximus was unaware of the controversy or failed to see its importance. The explanations
must be sought elsewhere, in the peculiar circumstances
which called forth this letter.

The *Ecthesis* had anathematized Severus.[70] But now the
whole tenor of the letter brought by Theodore manifested
a decided favoring of the Severians. Even supposing
Theodore to be an impostor, the suspicion necessarily
hangs on that the danger at Constantinople was not from
the defenders of the *Ecthesis*, whose then chief, Pyrrhus,
Maximus may have already known to have been deposed
(September 29, 641), but from Severian Monophysitism.

In a word, this was definitely not the occasion for speaking of the *Ecthesis* and its doctrine.

CRISIS: THE AFFAIR OF PYRRHUS

The year following Heraclius' death (February 11, 641) was one of change at Constantinople. At Rome John IV took definite action against the *Ecthesis*;[71] yet it was not he but his successor Theodore who was to bring the matter finally to a head.

There have come down to us three documents[72] of Theodore which inform us of this affair at the outset of his pontificate (consecrated November 24, 642). It was not so much the rejection of the *Ecthesis* that is noteworthy, but its being reckoned as a work of Pyrrhus (Sergius is not mentioned). Further, Pyrrhus is considered personally. Theodore is frankly perturbed that this author of Monothelitism has been deposed, not for his heresy but merely on account of the people's dislike for him. Theodore therefore insists that he be canonically deposed for his heresy.[73] Two special points are made: (1) that the emperor should see to it that Pyrrhus be sent to Rome; and (2) that it is entirely out of place to call one in Pyrrhus' position of a deposed patriarch by the patriarchal epithet, *most holy*.[74]

Here it is that the papal exhortations and request find a faithful echo in Saint Maximus. He had been asked by Peter the Illustrious about the title to give Pyrrhus who had come there after his fall. Maximus replies at length, reviewing the whole history of the heresy. In direct answer to Peter's question he declares such a title wholly inapplicable so long as Pyrrhus remains separated from the Church, that is, equivalently, from the Roman See. He is therefore urged to make his peace with the pope of Rome and thus with the whole Church.[75]

This being the case, it is reasonable to suppose that Maximus was in touch with the Roman court, whose lead in the attitude to be taken to Pyrrhus he followed to the letter. There remains, however, an explanation to be found for the agitated tone of the whole letter and the vehemence with which he speaks of Pyrrhus. For this latter business it is enough to recall how Pyrrhus had been Martina's adviser at the time of the affair of George, a great schemer for the new theology, and how finally he had come to that Africa where Maximus was himself the great defender of orthodoxy. For Maximus, Pyrrhus must have been a most undesirable refugee; yet there he was, and in addition expecting the patriarchal style—quite enough to try Maximus' patience.

If then we have read the evidence aright, this vehement letter to Peter is not the first openly anti-Monothelite document from Maximus' pen, as Grumel supposes;[76] but the first time when he passes from a purely theological consideration of the question to the concrete arena of ecclesiastical life and personalities. The first datable (640) anti-Monothelite writing is Maximus' defense of Honorius in TP 20, which we have discussed above.[77] There are in addition a number of patently dyothelite opuscula which may only be dated from the fact that they expressly defend two wills in Christ.[78]

From the time of Maximus' letter to Peter about Pyrrhus (643) to the great dispute of July, 645, between the monk and the ex-patriarch, we have no surely dated document. The dispute, however, has come down to us in its entirety as it was noted down at the time of the discussion and later copied at Rome before Pyrrhus had gone back on his profession of faith.[79] The sessions were carried on in the presence of the patrician Gregory and of numerous bishops.

The impression this victory made on the African bishops and the impulse it gave to anti-Monothelite controversy is not small. The following year three councils were held in Africa to treat of the Monothelite question. Letters were written to Pope Theodore, to the emperor, and to the patriarch Paul.[80]

Maximus could scarcely have had anything directly to do with these councils as it was in that year that he reached Rome, as did Pyrrhus.[81]

About the time of this conference Maximus composed his chief controversial work, addressed to his friend the priest Marinus. It is a remarkable piece of writing[82] from several points of view. The fragments that have been preserved contain some of the finest analyses of the acts of the will that have come down to us. This and the careful exposition of the relation of the wills of saints to the divine would fully justify von Balthasar's dating: 'certainly not before the Roman stay,'[83] if he had meant: certainly not before the fully developed controversy, that is, before 645 and the dispute at Carthage. Such a date could not well be questioned. The inference, however, that it was written in Rome is far less sure. In fact it can reasonably be argued that it was written in Africa (at Carthage?) about the time of the dispute.

The reason is the apparent reference to this polemic opus in a datable and placeable letter addressed to the same Marinus, priest of Cyprus. I refer to the epistle on the procession of the Holy Spirit and the orthodoxy of Honorius, excerpted by Anastasius.[84] Here Maximus refers to the 'notebooks I have sent . . . about the soul and other chapters.'[85] This reference can easily enough be understood of the first polemic work. There in fact we find first of all the careful analysis of the acts of the soul, after which come various chapters on topics related to the controversy.[86]

This opuscule, TP 10, may be dated between the years 642–46, with greater probability for the later years.[87] If this be so, the great work to Marinus will necessarily be of about the same time.

Of this latter work perhaps the most remarkable trait is the introduction. In this close-packed paragraph Maximus manages to condense the whole of his ascetic and mystical doctrine. The very terminology recalls his early ascetical and anti-Origenist works.[88] The mainspring of all spiritual seeking is in full evidence—the insatiate desire of God;[89] likewise the insistence on the union of *theoria* and *praxis*. This summary, then, he places at the head of his chief anti-Monothelite treatise, without his feeling or without there, in fact, being any discrepancy or discord between the introduction and the body of the treatise. This is as much as to say that Maximus felt his doctrine, ascetic and dogmatic, to be a coherent whole. This connection of the two aspects of doctrine Maximus himself indicates in the second paragraph in which he outlines the questions to be dealt with.

After the dispute of July, 645, or early the following year Maximus left Africa for the center of Christianity. It may be that he travelled thither with or about the same time as Pyrrhus. We may only gather from the *Relatio motionis*[90] that Maximus was in Rome in the year 646 along with Pyrrhus.

It was not long, however, that Pyrrhus remained in Rome or faithful to Rome. His reversion to Monothelitism, whatever may have been its motives,[91] was occasion of not a little bitterness. Shortly after this relapse Maximus reviews and refutes the Monothelite heresy in a letter to the Sicilian monks, apparently during a sojourn there. He felt it necessary to defend the orthodoxy of his former correspondence with the ex-patriarch.[92]

ROMAN ACTIVITY

From this time on till his imprisonment Maximus remained in Rome or its vicinity. The biographer mentions this period as that of Maximus' most intense activity[93] in defense of orthodoxy, whether by conversations, by treatises, or by letters. Some of the incidents of this Roman stay have been preserved for us in the acts: thus his conversation with a certain Gregory, sent by the emperor, on the emperor's alleged sacerdotal prerogatives.[94]

Among the literary works is to be noted the tome to Stephen of Dora. This was written in Rome against the *Ecthesis*. It must then be of the year 646/7, before the edict of 647, the *Typos*.[95] The tome is evidence of Maximus' activity. It contains 29 citations from the Fathers and heretics relative to the disputed question. When was this *florilegium* gathered together? Was it Maximus' own personal work? What relations does it have with the later and fuller *florilegium* of the Lateran Council?[96]

These questions do not concern us directly, yet the few references to *florilegia* in the writings of Maximus and of Sergius are indicative of the slowness with which the orthodox reaction to the imperial heresy developed. In the early approaches with dissident Christians Sergius was ready with a *florilegium*, aside from the forged 'libellus Menae.' Thus in 619 he sent a *florilegium* to George of Arsas.[97] In 633 Maximus was unable to send Peter anti-

This effort is made the next year. A court bishop comes to interrogate him; Maximus prevails in the discussion which ends in hopeful anticipation. The emperor, however, is willing to show Maximus all honor on the sole condition of his adhering to the *Type*. With this second failure, Maximus was left in the hands of the soldiery, some of whom maligned him as being impious towards the Mother of God. Yet here again the Confessor won the people and the clerics to him so that they accompanied him so far as they might on the road of his exile.

The place of this second exile was at Perberis, like the first at Bizya, also in Thrace. Here Maximus remained six years.

For the emperor the chief culprit in the whole affair was Pope Martin. He had died September 16, 655, shortly after Maximus' first trial. But so long as other opponents of his religious policy were recalcitrant, the emperor would not remain content. Thus in 662 Maximus and the two Anastasius, the disciple and the apocrisary, were recalled to Constantinople for a further, definitive trial and punishment. This time the accusation no longer had any political tinge. The three remaining most notable exponents of the orthodox doctrine in the east were summoned before a Monothelite council, where, together with Martin and Sophronius, they were anathematized and then turned over to the civil officer there present for the execution of the sentence—the mutilation of those members by which they had propounded the dyothelite doctrine. Their tongues and right hands amputated, therefore, they were taken about the city, exposed to the scorn of the populace, before being shipped off to their exile in Lazica, on the south-east shore of the Black Sea.[107]

Arrived there the 8th of June, 662, they were at once

separated, each dispatched to his individual place of exile.

Maximus, already broken with age and abusive treatment, died the 13th of August, 662;[108] in spirit he was still and yet remains a strong, pure light of faith and charity, of orthodoxy and contemplation.

II. DOCTRINE

What then was the Confessor's concept and view of Christianity for which his whole life and death had been but a constant witness? We can say with perfect truth that it was the same as ours. He himself told his examiners at the Process: 'I have no private teaching, but the common doctrine of the Catholic Church.'[109] Yet such an answer would completely evade the question that has but now been asked. What is wanted is to know the concrete contour and form which this common doctrine took in the teaching of St. Maximus. Here we must say at once that his whole system is ascetical and mystical;[110] yet it is equally necessary to explain the import of these terms as applied to our author. For in fact these terms apply not so much to the content of his writings as to the point of view from which they are written. Revelation, Scripture, the Fathers, philosophy, and other human knowledge is all laid under contribution in so far as it may serve to advance man towards his end. Neither theological nor philosophical speculation simply as a development of truth has any place in St. Maximus. He considers everything in its actual, existent state, that is, as saturated with the unique end of creation—deification.[111] 'Because of this the whole arrangement of created things exists, they abide and were brought into being from nothing.'[112]

Our sketch then of Maximus' doctrine will fall into three divisions: on God, on man, on man's deification. This division follows, in a way, Maximus' own thought. God is at once the principle and end of all things, who provides the means for attaining to Himself. Therefore the concept of God commands the whole. Of equal importance is the concept of human nature and of man's actual condition. These then provide the elements for the doctrine of salvation and deification. Man's becoming God is considered only as the result of God's becoming man; the mystery of Christ therefore stands at the very heart of the Maximian synthesis, is that synthesis.[113]

a. GOD

God's nature. The utter simplicity of God and His goodness are the most salient characteristics of the divine essence. God is good, is goodness itself. The good, which is God, is the end of the whole life of virtue, of the practical life.[114] Thus charity, which God is, and the good are placed in close relation; for charity is the supreme virtue of the practical life and that which deifies most of all. It is in fact because God is by nature good and passionless that He loves all men equally; it is in imitation of Him that man must practice the same even-handed charity towards all.[115] It is here perhaps that we touch a critical point in Maximus' relations with his masters, Evagrius and Denis. On the one hand, Evagrius allows that love for neighbor may not always be the same for all, but that at least we must be free from hate and rancor.[116] Further, the love for neighbor can be a hindrance to the love for God.[117] This certainly is not Maximus' doctrine who exacts an equal love and declares that the love given to God and neighbor is one and the same.[118] On the other hand, for Denis goodness, whose relation with love in Maximus we have just seen and of which apparently Evagrius does not make capital, is the name pre-eminently befitting the transcendental substance of God.[119] This enhancement of the goodness of God to parity with His simplicity as chiefly imitable in Him[120] has consequences which will be seen later in treating of deification.

God alone is simple; all creatures are in some way compound, either of matter and form as bodies, or of substance and accidents as non-corporeal things.[121] God exceeds every multiplicity, every duality, every relation even if it be only that of subject and object, of thinker and thought.[122] The divine transcendence and the divine uniqueness (μόνας) are alike implied in this doctrine of the divine simplicity. Certainly this is common doctrine and forms part of the teaching of Maximus' chief masters, Gregory Nazianzen, Evagrius, and Denis the Mystic.[123] But if it be a common doctrine it is also of capital importance in Maximus' thought. It is this which hinders any confusion of creature and creator, it is in becoming simple that the vision of God is attained.[124] This aspect of the divine simplicity is met with on every page of Maximus and of Evagrius for whom the state of prayer always requires the absence of concepts, the mind's utter simplification.

The simplicity of God leads at once to a consideration of the divine transcendence, to what is customarily termed negative or apophatic theology. God and creatures can in no way be included in the same affirmation or negation. If we assert that God is, then creatures are not; if we affirm of creatures that they exist, then God does not exist. The reason is that there is absolutely no common causal ground

which would justify including God and creatures in the
same affirmation or negation. Our concepts, not less that
of being, are totally inadequate before the transcendent
reality of God. 'For He has an existence simple, unknowable, inaccessible to all and entirely inexplicable, being
beyond both affirmation and negation.'[125] This last point
should not be overlooked: neither affirmation nor negation are adequate in God's regard. God infinitely exceeds
any relation or category whatsoever.[126] In fact our knowledge of God is at best tenuous. Our knowledge of Him
attains only the fact of His existence, in no way that which
He is, His substance.[127] In the 15th question of the
Ambigua[128] Maximus is most explicit on this point. He is
there treating of the motions of creatures towards God,
who is of course the term of all such motion. All things
receive the end of their motion 'in the infinity about God.'
And he explains the phrase: 'the infinity about God, but
not God, who indeed lies incomparably above it.' This
infinity (ἀπειρία) is not to be taken as our unique knowledge about God; it rather summarizes the things about
God which we may know. These are His eternity, limit-
lessness, goodness, wisdom, and power that creates, provides for, and preserves beings.[129]

The distinctions or powers just indicated are those taken
later from Denis the Mystic as the foundation of the
Palamite theology, understood however in this special
sense, that is, as 'uncreated energies ineffably distinct from
the divine nature' which remains completely unknowable
in its essence, but completely revealed in its energies.[130]
This doctrine presents itself as the development of the
patristic tradition, especially, of course, of Denis and also
of Maximus. It is worth noting therefore how Maximus
designates the things knowable about God. They are

θεωρήματα. 'The Divine,' he says, 'is knowable in the contemplations concerning It, unknowable in the things of
Its essence.'[131] The intention of this terminology is clear—
it is to safeguard the distinction between Creator and
creature.

We have here a problem of the relations of the finite
with the infinite, of our participation in the divine
nature,[132] a problem of mystical theology which is not
solved by the block rejection of, or the failure to understand, those distinctions and tendencies in Byzantine
writers which were developed later into the Palamite
theology.[133] This problem cannot be entered into here;
I would only note that the elements and phrases of
Maximus' distinctions are already to be found in Gregory
of Nazianzus, whom Maximus quotes in this connection
in the last chapter of the first Century on Charity.[134]

The divine infinity occurs not only in connection with
our capacity for knowing God and for union with Him,
as we have just seen, but similarly in connection with our
desire for Him. The similarity, however, goes no further.
The satisfaction of our desire, the participation in God
Himself, who is our end, is extended *ad infinitum* in proportion to our desire, without satiety ever being reached.[135]
Thus, however one considers the activity of creatures, it is
God's infinity that they attain and in that infinity God,
who alone sets a limit to His own infinity.[136]

The Triune God

What we have so far said about God is common to the
three Persons; we have now to speak of what is proper,
that is, Unbegottenness, Begottenness, and Procession, or,
more simply yet, of the mystery of three in one and one

in three. Father von Balthasar gives three pages to Maximus' doctrine on the Trinity. He there says:

> In the end God remains for the Greek the ultimate unity at the top of the multiple structure of the world pyramid—since Aristotle and Philo nothing has changed in this regard. Maximus makes no exception. A thoroughly, a startlingly significant indication of this is the way the Trinity is assigned to the negative theology, while the positive is concerned only with the 'economic' God who governs the world with Providence and Judgment.[137]

For the present I would note but two things. Something *has* changed since Aristotle and Philo, the supreme unity is no longer utterly one, but triune. This is at the very heart of Maximus' thought and the kernel of the imitation of God. Nor is it surprising that the Trinity should be assigned to the negative theology, inasmuch as this distinction refers to our human efforts to know God, not to the divine self-revelation. Our knowledge then of the blessed Trinity is to be sought primarily in that revelation, in the Church, and in her sacramental-liturgical life. Von Balthasar therefore very justly remarks that the litanies of Trinitarian formulas[138] in which Maximus sometimes indulges are not dry, but full of liturgical spirit.[139] Yet his generalization remains too broad to touch Maximus' doctrine in the quick. This should be apparent from the following exposition and from the apposite paragraphs in the third chapter on man's deification.

There are five headings under which we may class the passages more explicitly referring to the blessed Trinity: (1) the assertion of the fact; (2) the reference of the Trinity to the negative theology; (3) the consideration of nature and person with regard to the Trinity and Christ; (4) the relations of the persons of the Trinity to the Incarnate Dispensation; (5) traces of the Trinity.

1. Assertion of the fact. This we have just noted occurs in a long series of formulas not unlike those of the Athanasian creed. Maximus insists on the unity of the divine substance, by reason of its essence and being excluding all thought of any sort of composition, and on the Trinity of persons by reason of the mode of their existence without the least sort of confusion or alienation of one person from the other.[140] The supreme mystery is unity in trinity, whose imitation in the soul is the summit of God-likeness, the similitude which perfects the image.[141]

2. The reference to negative theology. It should be patent to all that the mystery of the Trinity as such is known only through Revelation.[141a] It therefore properly falls outside the scope of positive and negative theology, which consists in the motion of the human reason towards God from creatures by means of affirmative and negative predication, neither of which is adequate for the purpose in view—a knowledge of the transcendent deity, in the mode of His existence.

Maximus affirms that positive theology gives a basis for our faith.[142] But with regard to the Trinity he expresses himself differently. In the first *Ambiguum* he considers one of Gregory's texts in which he speaks of unity passing beyond the dyad to the triad. 'There is here,' he says, 'no αἰτιολογία (explanation from causes), but the exposition of a pious opinion about the Trinity.'[143] The motion in the Godhead from unity to trinity is apparent only, due not to God, but to us who understand first that something is, then its mode of existence.[144] And he concludes: 'The motion of the Godhead effected through manifestation (ἔκφανσις) constitutes a knowledge, for those able to

receive it, about Its being and the mode of Its existence.'[145]
The basis then of our knowledge of the Trinity is a
revelation. The mystery we may not only accept, but
also exercise our intelligence upon it in an effort of
understanding. That Maximus himself could and did
make such efforts will be evident from the following
sections.

Nonetheless, to emphasize the divine transcendence,
Maximus can in a subsequent *Ambiguum* remand the
mystery of the Trinity to the negative theology. The
passage in question is a direct citation of Denis: 'And
therefore the transcendent deity, celebrated at once both
as Unity and as Trinity, is knowable neither as Unity nor
Trinity neither to us nor to any other. . . .'[146] The context
has nothing to do with Revelation.

3. Nature and Person in the Trinity and in Christ. The
distinction of nature and person coincides with that of the
common and proper. It is a two-edged weapon in the
Monophysite controversies; assured as regards the divine
nature and persons, it applies equally but inversely to the
two natures and divine person in Christ. For the most
part, however, the distinction appears in Maximus in a
particular form as a distinction between the λόγος of the
nature and the τρόπος—mode—of its existence.[147]

As we shall see more fully later, it is not simply the
nature of a thing that is immutable, but its λόγος. This
λόγος φύσεως is practically what we are accustomed to
term the metaphysical essence of a thing whose change in
the slightest detail involves the whole in corruption. These
λόγοι do not exist in the nude, but each has its certain
mode of existence (τρόπος ὑπάρξεως).[148] Whatever pertains to the λόγος of a certain nature pertains equally and
inalienably to all who partake of that nature; it is the

common. The mode, however, pertains to the person and always refers to the concrete reality; it is the proper. In man, because the human mode of existence is common to all as contrasted with the divine mode of human existence in Christ, Maximus will speak of the mode of use or of motion (τρόπος χρήσεως, κινήσεως).

The distinction is very sharp for Maximus, nor ever far absent from his mind. The abstract character of the λόγος φύσεως is clear. This leads to conceiving οὐσία similarly in an abstract manner as second substance, whereas in the earlier Trinitarian doctrine it had always signified a concrete reality, first substance. This shift of sense makes the defense of the divine unity more difficult.[149]

On the other hand, the mode of existence, the modes of use and motion are always concrete realities, pertaining to the person. In the Godhead the properties which determine the three divine modes of existence are: Unbegottenness, Begottenness, Procession.[150]

4. The relations of the persons of the Trinity to the Incarnate Dispensation. The whole Trinity co-operated in the mystery of the Incarnation, each Person being wholly in the other, yet only the Son and Word took flesh. The Father approved, the Holy Spirit co-operated, the Son effected His own Incarnation.[151] In this manner the effective causality of the Incarnation and of our salvation that flows from it is reserved to the substance of the Godhead, yet the personal activity of the divine Persons is not obscured. And in fact our salvation is often enough put in relation with the diverse Persons, as is clear in the matter of our sonship by adoption,[152] or as when life and sanctification are especially referred to the Holy Spirit as His personal prerogative.[153] This preference for noting the personal relations in regard to our salvation is cognate

with the manner of conceiving the divine processions prevalent among the Byzantines.

Maximus, however, finds no difficulty in defending the Latin *Filioque*. The Latins do not acknowledge a double cause (αἰτία) by the said phrase, but indicate thereby the 'through Him' and identity of substance.[154]

Elsewhere the same doctrine is expressed in a context which draws together the illuminating role of the Holy Spirit and His Procession. Christ in His humanity is head of the Church, as God He possesses the Spirit whom He imparts to the Church as its head.

> The Holy Spirit, then—*says Maximus*—as He is by nature and in substance God the Father's, so also He is by nature and in substance the Son's as ineffably proceeding out of the Father substantially through the Son in the latter's being begotten—this Holy Spirit bestows on the candlestick, that is on the Church, His own operation as it were lamps.[155]

The reason why Maximus inserted in this context this concise exposition of the divine processions is his effort to tie up the work of our salvation with the Persons of the Trinity, particularly with the Son and the Spirit. So is explained the *co-operation* of the Holy Spirit in the Incarnation.

5. Traces of the Trinity. In a passage cited by von Balthasar,[156] Maximus affirms that the Godhead has left no trace, however insignificant, for an understanding of Itself, especially how It is one and three. After what we have just said of the reference of the Trinity to negative theology, this further passage is no surprise. Again there is no question of Revelation. Hence the denial of a trace for comprehension, the disallowance of any idea of the mystery left to any creature, would wrongly be understood as a denial of any traces discoverable when the fact

of Revelation is taken into consideration. Maximus' practice is here more instructive than isolated affirmations in the spirit of the negative theology.

The thirteenth question of Thalassius asks about the famous verse of St. Paul on *the invisible things of God* being knowable through the visible creation; and not only that, but also *His eternal power and divinity*.[157] The first explanation tentatively identifies the invisible things of God with the essences of things; His power with providence that preserves all in existence; His divinity with His deifying operation.[158]

The second explanation tentatively identifies the *invisible things of God* with *His eternal power and divinity*. Maximus then reasons as follows:[159]

> As from creatures we believe of the really existent God that He is, so from their essential distinction into species we are taught of His essential and inborn Wisdom that it is objectively existent and conserves creatures. And again, from the essentially and specifically distinct motion of creatures we learn of His essential and inborn Life that it is objectively existent and brings creatures to their fulfilment. From a wise consideration of creation we perceive the idea concerning the Holy Trinity, I mean the Father, Son, and Holy Spirit. For the Word of God is eternal as consubstantial power and the Holy Spirit eternal divinity.[160]

However imperfectly, there cannot be the slightest doubt that Maximus here indicates an adumbration of the Trinity in creation. The Scriptural question is but an occasion for him to develop his thought. The triad to be descried in creation is the cause and its properties, power and divinity, which announce, he says, the Father, Son, and Holy Spirit.[161]

In one of the *Ambigua*[162] Maximus gives us an even more explicit explanation of the possibility of proceeding from

creatures to some adumbration of the Trinity. This is all
the more valuable as in this Difficulty he undertakes to
give a summary exposition of the five ways of 'natural
consideration.' The five considerations are: substance,
motion, difference, composition (κρᾶσις), and position
(θέσις). Of these the latter two refer rather to ethics; thus
the first three, referring to ontology, concern us more
directly. Through these three aspects in things God is
known to man as maker, provident, and judge. Now
Maximus has immediately to explain very clearly what he
means and does not mean by provident and judge (discerner); for Origen and Evagrius had used these same
terms in the context of their heretical speculations on the
origin of the world. First of all, one can attain only to a
knowledge of God's existence, not at all of what He is in
Himself. The motion is ontological, by which creatures
are seen in their respective inalienable identities, whence
we understand Him who preserves each of them inviolate
according to its proper λόγος. The motion meant is that
of the power and operation essentially consequent on the
λόγος of each creature. By difference, the discerner is
manifest who distributes wisely to every creature the
natural powers that suit it.

Therefore in these ontological considerations the moral
sense of providence and judgment does not enter at all,
that is, providence as leading men to right action and
judgment as distributing punishment. It was Origen's
error—Maximus does not say so, but clearly he knew it to
be so—to use the moral sense of these terms in an ontological context, so that judgment decreed the crassness of
each spirit's body in proportion to its sin, while providence, through many worlds, would bring back all to the
original spiritual state and unity.[163]

So far there is no reference to the Trinity. But when the ethical considerations are joined to the ontological—position, implying firmness in virtue, to motion and providence; composition, implying virtuous life, to difference and judgment—then, declares Maximus, we may perceive the cause by the caused: that it is, that it is wise, that it is alive; by which perception one goes beyond the simple knowledge of God's existence to perceive also its mode—Father, Son, and Holy Spirit.[164]

We are here in presence, in each of the examples just given, of triadic arrangements; their sources we may identify and so control the extent of Maximus' manipulation. The triads are the Origenist-Evagrian:

maker	provider	discerner
δημιουργός	προνοητής	κριτής

and the Dionysian:

being (goodness)   wisdom   life (power).

Of the first the Origenist element is manifest; however a passage of Evagrius is its immediate antecedent. In the *Selecta in Psalmos*, 138.16, Evagrius[165] says that God is known as demiurge, wise, provident, and judge. He then assigns reasons. Notice, Maximus has reduced a fourfold division to a triad and expressly corrects the false explanations given by Evagrius for provider and judge.

Of the second triad the source may be found in Denis the Mystic. In the *Divine Names*, 5.2 and 3,[166] there recur repeatedly *goodness, being, life, wisdom*. Sometimes goodness is omitted so that a triad is already present. In fact we may also indicate Denis' source. Proclus in Propositions 101 and 102 of his *Elements of Theology*[167] propounds the triad: *being, life, mind*. The order is fixed according to the extent of predication. This is the ground of Denis' objection in 5.3. The dependence therefore is manifest. Denis, while changing *mind* to *wisdom*, has added a fourth term, *goodness*, which is his chief name for God. Maximus returns to a triadic arrangement, but places *wisdom* in second place as representing the Son; life is for the Spirit the *life-giver*.

In these two instances it is clear that Maximus not only uses his sources with discretion, but adapts them to his own thought—an express Trinitarian thought, not a mere Proclean triadism. In each case the Evagrian triad remains a thing of 'natural consideration' whence the spiritual man may ascend to some perception of the Trinity in Dionysian terms.[168]

The foregoing traces of the Trinity are drawn from the external world and can be attached to the famous verse of St. Paul to the Romans that the invisible things of God are perceived through the works of creation. But there is within us an image of the Trinity, our mind and word and spirit, which should be conformed to the archetype, to the great Mind and Word and Spirit.[169]

Maximus is here using an image of the Trinity first occurring, so it seems, with Gregory Nazianzen and precisely as a living image.[170] The relation of Νοῦς to Λόγος as illustrative of Father and Son was employed by Origen in a passage that Maximus borrowed for his theological centuries.[171]

But in this triad what can be the function of the spirit, coming necessarily in the third place, while St. Paul places it above the νοῦς: *if I pray in a tongue, my spirit prays, but my understanding (νοῦς) is unfruitful?*[172] Gregory leaves no doubt as to the sense he attaches to this triad; he says: 'to know the one and the same nature of the Godhead, characterized by lack of origin and birth and procession,

as by our mind and word and spirit.'[173] The spirit then is
the breath, the breathing out (of the word conceived by
the mind) and thus falls naturally into third place in this
triad. Maximus in fact enlarges on the master's teaching
as to the role of the Spirit. As the soul equally pervades
the whole body giving its various members life, so God
operates among men, making them members of God.[174]
Such functions of spirit are among those related by
Verbeke. Spirit is considered as a 'bond of union, whether
it be between soul and body, or between man and
divinity.'[175]

In a passage already cited from the tenth *Ambiguum*
Maximus describes the summit of the spiritual life not only
as union with the blessed Trinity but as 'the unity understood in the Holy Trinity.' This unity is made up of three
elements: a perfect simplicity, realizing as much as may be
the substantial simplicity of God; goodness, by the habitual
possession of the virtues in imitation of the divine goodness; the putting off of divisive idiosyncrasies, by the grace
of the unitive God.[176] One could easily indicate the relations of this triad with the single persons of the Trinity;
Maximus however finds a statement of the triad sufficient.

In another place Maximus undertakes to explain these
words of Gregory: 'At the start the monad was moved to
a dyad and stood fast at a triad.'[177] Clearly some explanation is needed, for God is before all immovable. The reply
is wholly and consciously based on Denis. First of all,
Maximus establishes that God as uncaused is completely
immobile; then, that as principle and end of created things
He moves them. But further, as cause of all that exists God
in some way receives the predication of the things He has
caused, and thereby is said to be moved.[178] This is but a
preliminary explanation. He continues with a free citation

of Denis.[179] God is *eros* and charity and at the same time
object of *eros* and charity; as the first He is moved, as the
second He moves. This being moved is for Denis the
ecstasy of goodness and love by which God places being
and goodness outside Himself.[180] But they are placed
outside Himself only that they may be brought back to
Himself; all of which He Himself operates. Maximus is
more precise and restricts this natural overflowing of the
divine goodness. The Divine, he says,

> is moved inasmuch as He implants an immanent relation of
> eros and charity in those capable of receiving it; and moves
> as naturally attractive of the desire of those moved towards
> Him.[181]

Now then as regards Gregory's remark he explains the
matter thus:

> The blessed Trinity is moved in the mind, whether angelic or
> human that is receptive of it, in that by means of It and in It it
> (the mind) makes enquiries about It; and to speak more clearly,
> It teaches it immediately at its first movement the aspect of
> oneness, lest division be attributed to the first cause; but then
> leads the mind on to perceive the ineffable divine fecundity of
> this oneness, lest it should ever be forced to suppose the Good
> bereft of the consubstantial, objective Word and Wisdom or
> sanctifying Power; lest the divine be conceived as composed of
> these as of accidents and not be believed always to be these
> existent things. The Godhead therefore is said to be moved as
> cause of the enquiry as to the mode of its existence.[182]

The overflowing of the primal goodness, the divine
fecundity, is satisfied then within the Trinity Itself, in contrast to Denis' doctrine where this fecundity is seen
primarily in creation. Yet even so the term Maximus uses
for the Holy Spirit (sanctifying power) implies a necessary

reference to creatures. Whom else would this power sanctify?

This is a speculative explanation of the movement to Trinity; Maximus adds an historical one. The Scriptures only gradually manifest the mystery of the Trinity, beginning with the Father and going on to the Son and ending with the Holy Spirit—one substance and Godhead, one power and operation, worshipful in three Persons.[183]

This question of movement to Trinity was a persistent difficulty. Maximus deals with it again in the first of the later *Ambigua*. The answer is quite the same, but stripped of explanations. The first that we know of God is that He is; there follows knowledge of the mode of His existence, namely in three Persons.[184] Thus for Maximus the ultimate mystery of Christianity and of mystical theology is simply 'the unity understood in trinity.'

> The Trinity is truly triad completed by no divisive number . . ., but the substantial existence of three-personed monad. For the Trinity is truly monad, because so it is; and the monad truly triad, because so it objectively exists—one Godhead that is being as monad and objectively exists as triad.[185]

Whatever may be the difference of Trinitarian doctrine between Maximus and the Cappadocians, the sum and summit of their teaching is the same. Dr. Prestige condenses their teaching thus: 'God is one object *in* Himself and three objects *to* Himself. Further than that illuminating paradox it is difficult to see that human thought can go. It secures both the unity and the trinity.'[186]

To close our study of Maximus' doctrine of the Trinity with the citation of these hard, arid formulas would give a false impression of the whole. This mystery is first of all a fact which we grasp by our participation in the life of the

Church and only then conceptually explain as much and as best we may. It is to this participation in the Triune life that Maximus refers in his comment on the *Our Father* as recited in the Liturgy :

> The all-holy and venerable invocation of the great and blessed God and Father is symbol of our adoption as sons freely to be given through the grace of the Holy Spirit, an objective and existent reality. By reason of this the saints, every human peculiarity overcome and covered over, will be called and will be sons of God—all those who already in this time through virtues adorn themselves brilliantly with the divine splendor of goodness.[187]

Here is expressed the blessed Trinity and the Christian life in its present struggle and future consummation when we shall stand in the perfection of our sonship in Christ before the Father.

b. Man

Theology and anthropology are two quite distinct objects of study, yet one cannot be understood without the other. This is especially true of St. Maximus, who tends always to consider everything, especially man, in the light of the first Cause and the last End. Thus it is that after our description of Maximus' doctrine of the one God in three Persons we have now to consider his doctrine on the constitution of the world and of man; then the concrete situation of mankind ensuant upon his creation and fall. Here will be manifest some of the enrichments of Christology and anthropology due to Maximus and the Monophysite and Monothelite controversies. The last section will then draw upon the first two in explaining Maximus' doctrine of deification.

GOD AND THE WORLD

Before describing the constitution of the world, it will be good to make quite plain the insuperable difference that exists between the world or any of its beings and the Creator of all. Though the distinction of negative and affirmative theology is based on this difference, it is seldom that Maximus comes to speak explicitly of the creation of the world from nothing. Yet when he does so, it is with perfect clarity and force.

God in His utter simplicity and transcendence is alone; nothing whatsoever can be conceived as eternally co-existing with Him. The very thought, that of eternal coexistents one should be the maker of the other, is absurd. No, God, who ever is, made time and eternity[188] and all that is in them, bringing things into being from nothing, not imperfectly and in parts, but altogether and completely. In Him they are conserved and to Him they return, each as to its proper term.[189]

Note that he says that things are brought into being altogether and completely. The reason for this is that God creates things according to their λόγοι that pre-exist in Him from all eternity. Nothing in God is adventitious, nothing contrary to His intent. Things are in their substance forewilled, preconceived, foreknown, and brought to being each at its appropriate time. These λόγοι as complete in God cannot suffer any increase or diminution on their realization in the created order; therefore whatever comes into existence, whether a simple or a composite nature,[190] does so as a whole, neither part, in the latter case, existing before the other.[191]

The dominion and pre-eminence of God is transcendent not only as regards the bringing of things into existence, but also as to their activity. When it is objected that one cannot speak of rest in connection with God inasmuch as there is no precedent motion, Maximus replies: 'Creature and creator are not the same.' And then:

> One ought not to say of any creature that it acts with absolute independence, lest we introduce the senseless notion of an un-caused something apart from God; but, that it is naturally energized to do what as energized its nature is capable of doing.[192]

THE CONSTITUTION OF THE WORLD AND OF MAN

Maximus developed his doctrine of the constitution of the world and of man in conscious opposition to the here-tical Origenist doctrine. This doctrine supposed that the created spirits had originally formed but one thing with God in whom they had their abode and resting place. After this primitive rest and unity the spirits were scattered diversely, occasioning the formation of the material world, in which world some of the spirits were bound to bodies in punishment for former sins. Such is the myth as it was current in Maximus' own time. He presents it at the outset of the 7th Difficulty as a Hellenization of a passage of Gregory of Nazianzus.[193]

This myth acquired a summary expression in the triad: becoming, fixity, motion (γένεσις, στάσις, κίνησις). Maximus did not object to the terms of the triad, but to their order. The uniquely possible order is becoming, motion, fixity. In the Origenist view motion followed fixity, resulting from a certain satiety with the good; thus not only sin, but the visible world was explained. Yet motion so understood is properly inconceivable because interminable. Motion can only be understood in relation to an end. For motion is a 'natural power tending to its proper end. And this motion is either a passion, that is, a change from one state to another, the end being the impassible, or effective operation, whose end is the perfect-in-itself (τὸ αὐτοτελές).'[194] The *impassible*, the *perfect-in-itself* are none other than God Himself. Thus God Himself is the end of all creaturely motion; in Him is the perfection of creatures; in Him they find their fixity through the activity of their natural powers.[195]

It is at once obvious that the Maximian triad—becoming, motion, fixity—in no way reduces the extent of the Origenist, that largeness of cosmic view. The Maximian goes from creation to the final consummation; it provides the framework for the whole of his anthropology. It will be useful then to consider more closely two points concerning this triad: how is the result of this becoming to be conceived; and, what is the type of motion proper to the rational creature?

The resultant of becoming is, of course, the creature. Though, very emphatically, God alone is immovable,[196] yet Maximus can qualify the creature's becoming also as immovable.[197] In what sense? It is here that one must put in relation with the triad of becoming this other: substance, power, operation (οὐσία, δύναμις, ἐνέργεια).[198] For in the passage just now referred to it is implied that motion is the power of becoming since fixity is the end of the dynamic operation. It would, indeed, be over-simple, too mechanical, merely to superimpose one triad upon the other. The thought seems rather to emphasize that the term of the becoming is οὐσία (together with its natural power and operation), an οὐσία which, as produced according to its divinely foreknown λόγος, is utterly immutable. Thus it is that Maximus can say that God alone is immobile and then speak of an immobile becoming. In fact these three—οὐσία, natural power, operation—flow from one another in the order named, remaining nonetheless immanent in one another.[199] For the privation of things that are commonly and generically predicated of a substance make it cease to be what it is by nature, would alter its λόγος.[200]

The subject then of motion as a substance, a nature essentially immutable, and the motion itself, essentially teleological not in relation to a created end[201] but to God Himself in His unattainable majesty and mystery, make up the chief elements of Maximus' theory or rather philosophy of motion, by which he rejects the Origenist errors and retains the characteristically Alexandrine and Neoplatonist tendency to, and drive toward, God.

This motion has its ultimate base in the very nature of man, in his natural desire for the enjoyment of God. Of this more will be said when we consider the concrete situation of man ensuant on the Fall. This motion, however, inasmuch as it is not merely an impulse and drive of nature but a rational act and activity, is properly a human, a gnomic act directed to man's well-being with regard to the end. This motion then is of the same sort as man's nature, free and intellectual; if, however, intellectual, then with love for the object of understanding; but if this be loved, then the subject is outside itself (ἔκστασις) until it attains and is wholly informed by the object of its love and is conformed as an image or seal to its archetype. In fact this is no destruction of the free will, Maximus is careful to remark, but rather its solid, unalterable affirmation, that is, its 'gnomic emigration' (ἐκχώρησις γνωμική).[202] We seem without any doubt to be moving here in a Dionysian atmosphere, the ecstasis of the soul toward the good and the lovable. Yet it is interesting to note that the term of this motion is expressed by an Evagrian phrase: 'when the *ultimate desirable* appears and is participated.'[203]

If here it is only the term that is Evagrian, we have in the 10th Difficulty a long description of the three motions of the soul which introduce us into the eminently Evagrian 'natural considerations.' Once more the disposition is triadic; the general motions are those of mind, reason, and sense. The whole is presented as being carried out under the influence of grace. The motion of the mind is simple, ineffable, receiving no knowledge of God whatsoever from creatures and, no longer operating in its connatural fashion, effects a commingling with God through the Spirit.[204] The motion of reason is natural, causal, scientific, penetrating to the reasons (the λόγοι) of things, which, united, it refers to the mind.[205] The motion of sense is composite, drawing from sensible and visible things, ennobled by reason, and represents to reason the λόγοι of these things.[205] In a word, for the spiritual man neither sense nor reason operates on its own account but only as contributing to and under the influence of the higher power. The mind, on the other hand, employs sense and reason, but also operates absolutely. This operation is the summit of prayer.

The term then of becoming is substance which has its powers and operations—of the mind, of the reason, of sense. These are moved and move towards the end, which is God. Maximus is not at all interested in the specific and proper objects of these powers, but only how they may all be made to subserve the attainment of God.

Such in its main lines is Maximus' correction of Origen's triad and his refutation of the Origenist myth. There is however implied in this myth another error which

Maximus combatted at even greater length—the pre-existence of souls. Such a doctrine, of course, serves no purpose once the phantasy of a primitive fixity of spiritual beings is rejected and refuted. Yet it is perhaps with more vehemence, certainly with greater frequency, that Maximus opposes this supposition.

Such an error was the more easily admitted in that Christian writers before Maximus' time had on the whole tended to follow the Platonic doctrine of the soul as a complete substance. This they did with the best and quite necessary intention of defending the soul's immortality and incorruptibility. In fact Maximus' more recent predecessor, Leontius of Byzantium, expressly affirms that the parts of man, body and soul, are perfect (in the sense of: not incomplete) and that this must be maintained if the incorporeality and immortality of the soul is to be saved.[206]

THE COMPOSITE NATURE OF MAN

Maximus classes man with composite natures. Now composite natures are characterized first by the fact that the parts have nothing whatsoever to do with their being joined (this in contradistinction to the synthetic person of Christ); secondly, that the parts are joined simultaneously; thirdly, that a complete whole is formed, which in its turn is conducive to the splendor of the universe.

The first point is forcibly expressed in a letter to John the Chamberlain:

The soul, without use of will, holds the body fast and is held by it; without choice it gives it life by the very fact of being in it; and by nature receives motions of pain and grief on account of its innate susceptibility for them.[207]

The thing that binds the parts together is no special power inherent in either of them, but rather the creative act by which they were brought into being.[208] This implies that composite natures are brought into being according to their respective λόγοι pre-existent in God. The ultimate reason therefore of the simultaneity of parts in composite natures and these natures' character as a complete whole is the pre-existent λόγοι of each several nature.

The necessary simultaneity of parts in composite natures is rather a negative fact, preventing the affirmation either of the pre-existence of the soul or its post-existence[209] with regard to the body; it says nothing however of the relation in which these two parts of the whole stand with regard to one another. In fact for Maximus the parts are not merely simultaneous in their coming to be, but at that moment enter into an essential relation with one another so that a *complete species* is formed. Now here the fundamental point, which Maximus does not attempt to prove but simply accepts, is that man forms a complete species; so much so that even death does not dissolve it.[210] The reason why the body and soul cannot be admitted to be complete substances is that on being joined one or the other would have to give over its proper identity, as body or soul, in order that the composite might truly become a complete species.[211]

Here then we finally have a doctrine on the structure of the human being which assures either part of the composite a sure place. It is true that Maximus does not always seem to have kept this position in mind, at least not always to have been aware of its implications. Thus he is able to follow Leontius of Byzantium in comparing the union of the two natures in Christ to the union of the body and soul in the human hypostasis.[212]

Maximus therefore marks a signal advance in Christian metaphysical anthropology. He has really explained the essential unity of the human composite, without however recurring to the Aristotelian hylomorphic definition, which in the then common estimation was still too deeply stained with materialism for Christian use. And if he has made an advance, it is only in part that this is due to his philosophical acumen, that is, for the technical expression and defense of his doctrine. The doctrine itself and the firmness with which he held to it comes from his concentration on the mystery of Christ. The Son of God from the first instant of His being conceived in the womb of the Virgin was perfect man; therefore all the elements of a perfect man were there at the moment of conception, nothing existing beforehand nor being added afterwards.[213]

Von Balthasar's statements therefore in his *Cosmic Liturgy* need to be read with some added precision. He there[214] writes:

> The ineradicable distrust of an independent, objective nature, composite of body and soul, anterior to all grace, the distrust of the radical analogy of being, was necessarily a constant temptation to the Fathers, in the wake of Origen, to look for the *truth* of the creature in its immanence with God, . . . and on the other hand to put its actual reality in connection, either overtly or covertly, with the Fall.

This it seems is that intuition (*Weltgefühl*) which, according to von Balthasar, Maximus and with him the Byzantine middle ages have taken over almost intact from the Origenist myth. Now I would note that there are in this sentence of von Balthasar three questions which must be carefully distinguished: the question of the metaphysical structure of man; the question of his concrete, historical condition; the question of his finality. We have just seen Maximus' doctrine of the λόγος of man; we shall have to explain shortly his doctrine of the natural desire for God, which was diverted in the very first movement of the first man to sensible things—this is the explanation of the historical condition; the unique end of man is God, the enjoyment of God as He is. Maximus does not confuse these questions, but precisely corrects Origen by developing his theory of γένεσις, κίνησις, στάσις, in which the λόγος of man and nature's concrete, historical tendency to the end have their due place. It would seem therefore that it is legitimate, even necessary, to seek the *truth* of man (it is von Balthasar who underlines in the original text) in his supernatural finality and to understand his actual condition in relation to the Fall, provided only—and this is of utmost importance—that this end and this condition are not metaphysicized.[215]

In refuting the doctrine of pre-existence of souls Maximus succeeded in establishing a far saner metaphysical doctrine of the unity of the human composite; in connection with the Origenist doctrine of experience of evil as necessary to liberty Maximus again develops a clearer doctrine of freedom, which it will now be enough to indicate.

Correlative to Origen's hypothesis of the pre-existence of souls is that of reaching the good through experience of evil or that freedom necessarily consists in the possibility of choosing good or evil.[216] Such an hypothesis brings with it a whole false concept of the nature not merely of human liberty but of man. Therefore its refutation to be successful must be built upon a just concept of man and his liberty. This Maximus has done not only in refuting the Origenists but in defending the perfect humanity of Christ.

For Christ in His humanity was perfectly free and yet incapable of deflecting from the good. Freedom therefore cannot consist in the possibility of choice between good and evil.

FREEDOM

Maximus' doctrine of freedom has its roots in motion. Bodies are by their nature immobile, in so far as they lack an internal principle of movement.[217] Movement derives from the soul; in movement and operation the life of creatures is made manifest.[218] Now there are three kinds of life, vegetative, sensitive, and intellectual, each with its distinctive movements, that is, of nutrition, growth, and generation for the plant, of impulse for the animal, of self-determination (αὐτεξούσιος κίνησις) for the rational being. This self-determinative power is, without any question, to be identified with the will.[219] It forms an essential element, is the image of God which man is.[220]

In defining this self-determination Maximus twice cites freely the definition given by Diadochus of Photice. 'Self-determination is a willing of the rational soul, tending without let to whatever it wants.'[221] Elsewhere it is variously expressed. For instance: 'legitimate dominion over the things we may do,' 'unhampered dominion of the use of the things subject to us,' 'unenslaved appetite of the things subject to us,'[222] 'naturally inherent self-moved and masterless power,'[223] or again, 'self-commanding will.'[224] The essential then of free will seems sufficiently clear: the instrinsic self-determination of the rational creature. This self-determination, however, is not absolute but essentially relative, as image to the archetype.

God alone is perfectly immobile (ἀκίνητον) not only because as incorporeal and omnipresent there can be no

question whatsoever of spatial motion, but, more funda-
mentally still, because He alone is absolutely free, so that
He only may be called *self-movement, self-power* (αὐτοκίνησις,
αὐτοδύναμις). Every creature in relation to God is said
to be moved, not in contradistinction to God's activity,
but because in being created they received their essence
from Him who is the cause sustaining the universe.[225] If
then the rational creature is essentially free, self-determinative, he is so by analogy. We are said to be and are
existent, living, good, and the like, not just as God is said
to be and is existent, living, good, and the like, but as
effects of a cause. We are the participants, God the participated. The predication of existence, life, and the rest
belongs to both not as said synonymously of identical
substances, but equivocally, as it were, by a sharing in the
name, while the things themselves remain infinitely distant
one from the other.[226]

Self-determination pertains to the image, is relative. In
what then does it fall off from the archetype? This self-
determination is a movement, is therefore a movement in
regard to an end. In God this self-determination is not
merely self-moved (that can be said of every living
creature), but self-movement, because He is Himself His
end. His self-movement therefore is utterly immobile,
inflexible, immutable; the creature's self-determination,
however, is mobile, flexible, mutable. Between the divine
and human mode of self-determination Maximus makes a
perfectly clear distinction which turns precisely upon its
immutability. He says:

> The will of the human element in our Savior though it was
> natural, yet was not merely natural as with us, no more than
> was the human itself, because supremely deified among us by
> the union; to it impeccability properly belongs. But ours is

manifestly merely human and in no way impeccable, because of its deviation to this side or that. This is not to say that the nature is altered but that the movement has deviated; or, to speak more truthfully, that the nature has changed its mode. This is manifest from the fact that the nature does many things irrationally, yet its substance from its inherent rationality never passes over into something irrational.[227]

Self-determination, liberty, is natural to the creature and remains whole and intact even there where there is no possibility of choice as in the Lord, all of whose acts while being perfectly free, because of the inherently natural quality of self-determination, are wholly determined, moved by the divine Person in whom the human nature exists and whose the human acts are. But where there is not this divine fixity in the good, there the created self-determination has its created mode and cannot be other than flexible, as left to itself. This flexibility then of the human will as it exists in us is due to our creaturely condition—more precisely, is due to the fact that creatures cannot be their own end, cannot be self-movement.[228] The perfection then of self-determination is to imitate the divine fixity and immutability. In so imitating it the image is elevated to the likeness.[229]

We have just seen that the self-determination which is characteristic of every intellectual creature is anterior to the mode of its existence. It may be therefore and is preserved alike in mutable, sinful man and in the unalterable, sinless and impeccable Christ. In other words, it is something primarily of the nature in question which consequently is exercised according to the conditions of the person in whom the nature attains its act and existence. In Christ the person is divine, hence the nature and will are wholly divinized, not as to their nature which remain ever human, but as to the mode of their existence. This is the mystery of Christ, for the penetration of which it will be helpful to see more precisely what is meant by the human mode of the will.

To do this we can probably do no better than follow Maximus' use of the word γνώμη. A single-word version of it is impossible; its root, γνο-, indicates knowledge, its actual use gives a certain predominance to the will, without however excluding the sense implied in the root. A perhaps tolerable circumlocution is 'a set or tendency of the mind.' I shall use then in what follows the Greek word itself as alone capable of preserving the continuity that exists between its various uses.[230]

The first occurrence of γνώμη is in the first of Maximus' works, Ep 6 on the soul. At once there appears one fundamental distinction, concerning which Maximus never hesitates—γνώμη is not of those things that directly affect the nature and substance of things, but rather the motion consequent upon that nature. Here γνώμη receives as an explanatory alternative, διάθεσις, disposition.[231]

Further in this same letter there is a discussion of mutability (τροπή) in explanation of the rise of error and sin. Mutability is characteristic not of the substance, but of the motion; hence this mutability is not to be referred to the 'everlasting motion toward the fair or divine.' This latter is a 'natural operation' and therefore never ceases. Mutability consequently is 'weakness,' a 'falling away,' a 'motion contrary to nature.'[232]

In writing of love to John the Chamberlain, all dissension between God and man is referred to the devil as to its author by guile and to γνώμη as to its seat. Similarly all inequality, for by nature men are all equal, is attributed to γνώμη.[233]

In the Centuries on Charity I have noted two uses. The term occurs in the plural and is then practically synonymous with opinion (δόξα) and certainly implies diversity and disagreement.[234] Yet it may likewise bear a laudative sense.[235] By far more significant is the declaration of Char 4.90: 'God alone is good by nature, only the imitator of God is good through conformity of will' (γνώμη). In this sentence the whole of the spiritual life is placed in the imitation of God and the means for doing it are likewise indicated, conformity of our γνώμη with God's.

The commentary on the *Pater Noster* makes only more plain the ordinarily divisive and sinful character of γνώμη.[236] Yet the sense of the word is still large enough and the Christological debate still calm enough that a few paragraphs above γνώμη may be attributed to Our Lord with the sole proviso that in Him it was entirely without passion and in no way at odds with nature.[237]

In the earlier *Ambigua* γνώμη comes up several times. Two points are especially noteworthy. First, being and eternal being are in the sole gift of God; He is simply the Beginning and the End; well-being and the motion from the Beginning to the End is His gracious gift and at the same time the result of our γνώμη.[238] But more than this the perfect imitation of God, that is in His fixity in the good, is to be attained only through a surpassing of γνώμη, a complete handing-over of our self-determination to God; and this is not its destruction but its perfect fulfilment according to the capacity of its nature.[239]

The *Questions for Thalassius* only confirm points already noted.[240]

In the series of definitions which form TP 14, it is said that a relational union reduces different γνῶμαι to one will.[241] This is in perfect harmony with Maximus' use of

the terms in his earlier writings; but it was written before
one will had become a point of Christological dispute.
When such a use of terms is transported to Christology,
one might assert one will in Christ, denying that divisive
γνῶμαι have any place in Him; or, when the orthodox
position is maintained, one only will being denied of
Christ, every effort must be made to avoid any sort of
opposition of the volitive faculties.

The first indication of the effective operation of this logic
is in one of the early dyothelite documents where the
difference of created and uncreated, of visible and invisible
in Christ are said to be due to the properties of the natures,
not (and this in the line of argument is unexpected)
to contrariness of γνῶμαι.[242]

It was not all at once that Maximus came to deny γνώμη
to Christ. In the tome to Marinus the Deacon, which I
have reason to date about 642, he denies explicitly that
there is any opposition in Christ, not even of γνώμη and of
the things that pertain to it; for in Christ it concords with
the λόγος of nature.[243]

The intimate connection, however, of γνώμη with mutability, with sin, with rebellion against nature, brings
about finally its denial to Christ, in whom there is no
mutability, no sin, no rebellion, but only perfect concord
of nature with its divinely complete exemplar and immediate motion of the human by the divine. This is stated by
Maximus in an important tract shortly after 643. He does
so, however, not as giving his own opinion, but that of a
certain monk whose definition of will he had previously
cited.[244]

There remain the two great documents of Maximus'
Christological work, the Dispute with Pyrrhus and the
great tome to Marinus. It is hard to decide which of them

was written first. For our question it matters little as the doctrine of either is quite homogeneous with that of the other.[245]

At this stage of controversy what is γνώμη? It is 'a certain willing (θέλησις) by which one adheres by habit to a good or to what is reckoned as such.'[246] Or else it is 'an innate appetite of things subject to us, whence election comes, or the disposition for appetitive deliberation on things subject to us.'[247]

Now γνώμη is placed in a series of acts which proceed from our rational and volitive nature through wishing, enquiring, consideration, deliberation, judgment (here γνώμη fits in), election, and impetus to use.[248] For 'γνώμη is related to election (προαίρεσις) as habit to act.'[249] This being so, γνώμη implies in its subject ignorance of the thing sought, uncertainty as to the result of the thing chosen, an acceptance of contraries with judgment of them.[250] It is therefore the greatest blasphemy to attribute γνώμη to Christ.

When Pyrrhus had come to this admission in the course of the dispute, Maximus felt it at once necessary to mitigate the impact of the condemnation, lest denial of γνώμη to Christ be read back in all the texts of the Fathers (and his own too doubtless) where the word occurs.[251] In fact, according to Maximus, γνώμη or more especially its derivative γνωμικόν has quite a history, not entirely orthodox. For the union in Christ taught by Nestorius is a union of will by γνώμη, so that the unity of willing in Christ may be called—so Nestorius—a *gnomic will*.[252] It was, however, the *Ecthesis* and its patronizing of the one will in Christ that brought these elements into focus.[253]

We have seen the evidence. The summary will run thus. There are in every intellectual creature two powers, rational and volitive; in man as he now is these attain their end (use) through a series of acts which, as a whole, may be termed *gnomic*, though γνώμη in its restricted sense is as a habit preparatory to election. Inasmuch as most of these acts imply ignorance, indecision, mutability (the correlative of sin), they are excluded from Christ, under the name of γνώμη, as incompatible with the hypostatic union. Expressed in another way, these acts are of the person or hypostasis,[254] not therefore directly of the nature. They have no place in the divine Person of the God-Man; but even in simple man, heaven being attained, election and the other middle acts will no longer have a place. All ignorance and uncertainty being done away, there will be only the effective appetite delighting in its goal, God, infinitely extending beyond it. All will be alike in the natural law of willing; one willing of all will be manifest;[255] but the mode and degree of willing will differ.[256]

If now for a moment we return to the concept of self-determination, both it and γνώμη will be considerably clarified for us. Self-determination is something of the nature and, as such, not of the person. In Christ it received a divine corroboration and fixity, and in doing so suffered no detriment or diminution whatsoever. The reason is that the human will of Christ on the personal level is exercised by the divine Person, the Son of the Father. Man, on the other hand, preserves it essentially whole and intact, though it is merely human and operating through a human person. Immutability does not pertain to its λόγος. In the first movement of Adam it determined itself on itself, as only God can do, instead of determining itself on God and partaking of His immutability. Thus the primordial fault of man is self-love (φιλαυτία), whose commonest manifestation is an attachment to things of the world and of sense; yet without an essential impairment of that tendency towards the desire of the true end—God.

I have here deliberately anticipated on the following section, that I might have the opportunity of underlining the coherence of Maximus' work—Christological and ascetical, late and early. Note how the full exposition of γνώμη is from the Christological works, but in fact gives the theoretical basis for the ascetical doctrines expounded earlier. Of the Christological heresies Monothelitism at least is a transposition to the hypostatic union of the explanation given for the union of the faithful in Christ. Thus the saints and angels have but one will with God, a relational union, a *gnomic* will. Apply this to Christ and you have Monothelitism. This shows, if no more, how intimately related were dogmatic and ascetical theology at that time, an intimacy of relation working ultimately to the advantage of both.

MAN—ADAM

Maximus speaks several times of the first man, of Adam. This was inevitable for one to whom all is in Christ. For Adam is the type of the Christ. What Adam brought upon man by his act, all that Christ took away by His. The antithesis is fully Pauline; it is scarcely less Maximian. The whole of the 61st question to Thalassius is devoted to a symmetrical development of this antithesis, beginning with the Fall and continuing through baptism to the attainment of the end, deification in Sonship.[257]

Our purpose will be well served then if we follow Maximus' own exposition, elucidating and supplementing it where necessary from similar passages of his other works.[258]

Man as he issued from the hands of God was not bound to the motions of pleasure and pain in his sense faculties, but was rather endowed with a power for ineffable spiritual enjoyment of God. This power, Maximus expressly states it, is 'the natural desire of the mind for God.'[259] This is the fundamental motion of the creature towards God, his end; and it is the mainspring of all human life.

Had Adam remained as God made him, he would never have been subject to corruption and death; nor would he have initiated the chain of carnal generation that weighs so upon mankind; but would have enjoyed the life prepared for him.[260] And with him the whole of creation would have remained in peaceful subjection.[261]

But this was not to be. 'On his coming to be,'[262] man gave himself up to sense and through sense to sense objects, so that his very first movement resulted in pleasure outside the scope of his nature,[263] short of the scope of his nature.[264] This defective operation was a complete absorption of the intellectual power in sense and in sense knowledge whence derived the fatal tendency to the passions, in a word, a bestializing of man's rational nature.[265] Immediately upon this miscarriage of 'the natural desire of the mind for God,' that is, of his capacity for a divine pleasure, towards sense pleasure, God joined to this sense pleasure pain, so that from then on man was subject to these contrary motions.[266] From desire of the one and fear of the other all the passions were to spring.[267] The full extent of these consequences will have to be described below as the antithesis of the work of grace and charity; for the present the precise character of this first act must be further determined and some of its implications examined.

Adam the first man chose the tree of knowledge rather than the tree of life. His first act, done with knowledge of the divine command, makes of him a disobedient transgressor of the divine law. Of this there can be no question. Maximus explains his various interpretations of the 'tree of disobedience' in his prologue to Thalassius with the remark that ignorance of God, the first effect of this disobedience, resulted in a divinization of the creature, a self-love, a self-worship.[268]

From the exposition of self-determination already given,[269] it should be self-evident that this first act of Adam, involving his whole self and the whole of human kind after him, cannot be other than a full exercise of this most divine of intellectual faculties—an exercise in a creature who as creature must determine himself on the uniquely possible end of his nature, God alone, but who, using his inalienable prerogative, determined himself upon himself and became thereby enslaved to sense, to the search for pleasure and the flight from pain—in a word, to self-love.

The texts we have so far considered raise three suspicions about Maximus' doctrine. He says that God did not concreate, with man's nature, sense pleasure and pain.[270] Are we then to conclude that man's sense faculties are posterior additions to his nature? The conclusion would be both hasty and false. We have already seen Maximus' doctrine on the λόγος of man.[271] But he speaks more plainly of the body as instrument of the intellectual soul, as receiving life from the soul.[272] But that the soul, conversely, received from the body necessarily the sense-impressions of pleasure and pain, is not clearly stated. In the first question Maximus speaks bluntly:

5

> The passions themselves were not primarily concreated with the nature of man, as then they would enter the definition of nature. I declare, however, following the great Gregory of Nyssa, that because of the fall from perfection they were brought in, pertaining to the irrational part of nature. . . .[273]

And the result of the Fall, he goes on to say, was that man lost the divine image and took on the likeness of brutes. Passion is here used in a dominantly concrete sense, so that the passions as disordered are more in view; yet not completely. For he says in this same question that their morality depends on their use, if they be reduced to obedience to Christ. Elsewhere and before these *Questions* he has made perfectly clear the distinction between passion as a natural motion and as a moral defect. But one must wait till the year 642, in a passage already cited, for an unambiguous statement that the sense of pain, at least, is simply a consequence of the human composite: 'The soul . . . by nature receives motions of pain and grief on account of its innate susceptibility for them.'[274]

Yet Maximus must always have supposed such innate susceptibility, if man was to receive pain, labor, and death in punishment for his sin.[275]

Another suspicion is that the soul for Maximus, despite his doctrine of incomplete substances and a whole species (which alone is man), is not only subjectively independent of the body in its intellectual operations but also in this life to some degree objectively independent. A sentence of the prologue gives body to this suspicion:

> The transgressor . . . having joined fast the whole of his intellectual power with the whole of his sensitivity, acquired for himself that composite, destructive knowledge, active in the passion of the senses. . . . Inasmuch as man was anxious for knowledge of visible things by sensation alone, so far he bound on himself ignorance of God.[276]

The implication seems to be that all sense knowledge whatsoever is a result of the Fall and not inherent in man's
composite nature.

Now in one respect there can be no doubt that Maximus
asserted for the soul the ability to reason and to think *for
itself and by itself*, as the soul cannot be said to be for the
sake of the body. But it also reasons, thinks, and knows
with the body.[277] And after death the soul, will continue
to reason, to think, and to know, for these are its natural
powers, active so long as the soul has being.

There can then be no doubt that Maximus does teach a
knowledge of creation derived from the senses; but was
this a result only of the Fall? It may be; but again it may
be that this composite knowledge is compound not precisely with the senses as such, but with them as the seat of
the disordered passions. Further on in the same prologue
he speaks of

> self-love, of which there is, as it were, a mixed knowledge, the
> experience of pleasure and pain, on account of which all the
> slime of evils was brought into man's life.[278]

Can one take this 'mixed knowledge' as an equivalent of
the 'composite knowledge' mentioned in the first citation?

And the third suspicion. How is it that if there had been
no sin there would have been no carnal procreation, no
succession from corruption to corruption, that is, from
birth to death, pleasure ever uncausedly preceding? Does
not this imply that the first pair were something less than
man and woman, not having, or not having the use of,
their sex faculties; or that, in any case, the joining of man
to woman is always something sinful?

In our question to Thalassius, the universal corruptibility
of nature, when pain and death had been added to the first

uncaused sense pleasure, is emphasized. The bestializing of man's nature is rather a result of the first act, not the act itself. But our answer is clear in the doctrine of Gregory of Nyssa, cited by Maximus at this point. For the Cappadocian there was a double creation, first of man as image of God, which is in the intellectual part, and then the biological life as a consequence of sin, by which man has the likeness of the irrational beast.[279]

That this doctrine implies no scorn of marriage as evil, no Manichaeism, is quite evident from Maximus' refutation of those who would postpone the infusion of the rational soul into the body till some time after conception, because of the impure pleasure at conception. Such a position, he says, means that marriage is evil, that the law of generation is evil, that consequently the author of both these things must be reckoned the author of evil. The statement of such consequences is their refutation. Then, giving other reasons for the soul and body being joined at conception, chief of which is this same simultaneity in Our Lord's conception in the Virgin, he adds that

> nature after the transgression drew upon itself carnal conception and birth with corruption, losing thus the divine and spiritual increase, but not the λόγος φύσεως by which the rational soul and body come into being together.[280]

Maximus therefore feels nothing incongruent between Gregory's doctrine of a double creation and his own of man's essentially and simultaneously composite nature.

How did Gregory come to such a doctrine? He clearly argues to the conditions in Paradise from the future state in heaven, of which Our Lord says: *At the resurrection they will neither marry nor be given in marriage, but are as angels of God in heaven.*[281] Such also was for Maximus the state from which man fell, though it were in the very instant of his creation. It was then Adam through his disobedience and immersion in sense pleasure who gave reality to the 'law of voluptuous generation' and of 'death in condemnation of nature.'[282] The act of generation is not said to be sinful; it may be well used, marriage is good; yet the condition of mankind which dictates its use is part of the primeval curse.[283]

Let us now pick up again our account of man's fall and present condition. From man's first motion, perverted from God to sense, followed the enslavement to pleasure, with its correlative flight from pain and hardship, added in punishment by a provident God, ending in death, lest such a perverted order should continue indefinitely.[284]

The first result of the perversion is negative, aversion from and, consequently, ignorance of God; the second is positive, conversion to sense and experience of material delight with the ensuant self-love that drives us to pleasure and away from pain and hardship. From these spring all evils. The first and greatest is division from God; there follows division of our nature whether internally in the struggle of passions within a man or externally (socially) in the fragmentation of the race in warring groups.[285] There follows likewise the whole throng of vices, due either to pursuit of pleasure, avoidance of pain and hardship, or to some mixture of these causes.[286]

The remedy for this situation, man's salvation, is on two levels, which in the individual compenetrate, the work of Christ and asceticism.

As in nature, that is in Man, in Adam[287] the first pleasure was uncaused, save by the wilful perversion of man's Godward desire, so the consequent hardships were fully caused in punishment and ultimately death fully justified in condemnation of the sinful nature; so in the new Adam—in

Christ, there having preceded His birth no carnal pleasure (as the conception was virginal), the hardships were fully unjustified and the death most wicked. And here the wonder of this counterpoint—the hardships and death that had been in condemnation of nature are now converted into condemnation of sin and liberation of nature. The disobedience of the first man had ended in the condemnation of nature; the obedience of Christ, the second Adam, in undergoing the punishment of the first, freed that nature, restored it, deified it.[288]

This is realized generally for nature at the time of the great mystery of the Man-becoming;[289] and actually for individuals at the time of baptism, when each receives the grace of sonship. This new generation in the Spirit enables them in the observance of the commandments through much suffering and finally death, to condemn sin.[290]

Here we have clearly expressed the ultimate theological basis of Christian asceticism, although this asceticism is not here fully expressed. Much will be said of self-mastery (ἐγκράτεια). The quest for this may be expressed in a wealth of moral analysis and terminology of Stoic origin. Yet it is part of the condemnation of sin in the large sense; for this condemnation is not merely negative but implies finally restoration to the paradisiacal state and deification. For Pyrrhus, therefore, Maximus will explain asceticism and its consequent hardships as the separation from the soul of the deceit effected by immersion in sense, so that the virtues stand out in their natural character.[291]

c. DEIFICATION

We have just remarked (at n. 286 f.) that the remedy for man's fallen condition is on two levels—the work of

Christ and asceticism; and that moreover the two levels compenetrate in the individual. Now this compenetration takes place not in the isolation of the individuals but in the community of the Church, in the sacraments from whence the eternal, supernatural worth and power of the ascetical struggle is drawn.

All these then are the medium in which and the means by which the end is attained. This end is objectively God, subjectively our salvation or deification in Christ. Our procedure therefore in this section will be first to elucidate the meaning of deification, then to speak briefly of the sacramental medium and means, and finally to expound in a brief synthesis Maximus' ascetical and mystical doctrine, in such a manner that it will form an immediate introduction to the following translations.

Deification is the ultimate fulfilling of human nature's capacity for God. The λόγος of our nature remains intact; its powers are renovated, in the Incarnation, that it may attain this end; so then deification is wholly a gift of God and is not attainable by nature's nude powers. In actual historical fact deification and salvation are the same.[292]

To illustrate this statement I shall cite a few passages, warning the reader that all must be understood in the light of the doctrine on God and man already expounded.

By reason of our salvation He takes delight in these (our good works), and alone standing in need of nothing, He will grant us whatsoever He truthfully promised us. These are *what eye hath not seen. . . .*[293] For unto this He made us, that we might become partakers of the divine nature[294] and sharers of His eternity, and that we appear like to Him according to the deification of grace, on account of which there exists and abides the system of created things, and the creation from nothing of non-existent things.[295]

According to this text the last end of the whole created order is man's deification, which is here at once placed in connection with salvation and based on St. Peter's celebrated text.

In practically every instance where mention is made of deification there also it is qualified as being by grace, or by some other limiting phrase. Once Maximus had to excuse a loose statement he had made of there being one operation of the saints and God in heaven. It is God's working alone, he replies, that deifies. In fact, a deifying power is not implanted in our nature, and consequently there can be no exercise of it.[296] Yet, and this is important for the ascetical life, our salvation and deification lie within the possibility of our own renewed power. This renewal is of course God's own pure gift, yet it makes possible our own participation in the work of Redemption. Indeed if deification is rather in the powers and qualities of man (for it cannot alter his nature), then these divinized powers and qualities must have also their proper divinized function.[297]

Again and again deification is represented as the result of the Incarnation. It is then often expressed with an antistrophic arrangement: to the condescension of God in His Man-becoming responds the imitation of man in God-becoming, by the grace and power of the God-man.[298]

Inasmuch as the likeness given in deification necessarily excludes any mutation in the λόγος of man's nature, it remains that he become God by possessive imitation of the divine qualities. Thus immortality is granted to the body and immutability to the soul;[299] or it is a question of the divine simplicity.[300] But the fullest effect of this deification is in love, whereby as Christ loved us still being His enemies and died for us, so we not only care for spiritually but are ready to die willingly for one another.[301]

If one seeks for the agent of this transformation, it is immediately the Holy Spirit who seizes upon man in his will and brings him to suffering divine things by grace, whereas God is these things by nature.[302]

It is only occasionally that mention is thus made of the Spirit in regard to deification; but this relative infrequency does not adequately represent the place of the Spirit in Maximus' thought. We have already cited a passage about the Church[303] in which it is declared that all the activity of the Godhead is finally bestowed in the Church through the Holy Spirit.

AGENTS OF DEIFICATION

The Church

There is also another series of passages which attribute all life in the Church to the Spirit. As the soul is entirely present in the whole body and in each part, giving it life and unity, so likewise the Spirit of God.[304] This doctrine is consciously developed in the Pauline context of the Epistle to the Ephesians; and refers not merely to a spiritual doctrine but to the concrete reality of ecclesiastical life, as is clear from his letter of exhortation to some apostate nuns to return to the 'living, whole, and spotless body of the holy Catholic and Apostolic Church.'[305]

Now this Church Maximus nowhere defines; he describes it though with a certain ampleness when he comes to explain the text: *Behold a candlestick all of gold, and its lamp upon the top of it. . . .*[306] The candlestick of pure gold is the Church.[307] This Church is adorned with virtues, not stained with passions, free of impure spirits, unchanged as to faith and morals under the impact of heresies and persecutions; and above all keeps whole and intact the mystery in faith of knowledge of God.

Another powerful description of the Church, this time as imitator of God, is found in the *Mystagogia*.[308] Here God is looked upon as cause, beginning, and end of all, to whom therefore all are seen to be related in unity. The Church by giving the one faith and name to all sorts and conditions of men, differing in age, sex, tongue, capacities, and so on, brings them all to unity as a body worthy of the head which is Christ. The supreme work of God and of His Church is unity.

And the basis of this unity is faith. Right faith is of supreme value for Maximus. By exact profession of the faith is a man sanctified.[309] The unity of faith is more important than cultural unity.[310] This faith is given in baptism and should be accepted with good will, lest it afterward be rejected.[311]

It is not faith alone whose function it is to bring peace among men and some order. Rulers have their part in keeping the divisive and destructive tendencies of fallen man in check.[312] But these functions are clearly to be distinguished. In doctrinal questions 'it belongs to the bishops to enquire and define the saving dogmas of the Catholic Church.' In this the emperor has no part. 'He does not stand at the altar, nor after the consecration of the bread raise it and say *the Holy to the holy*. Nor does he baptize or consecrate the myrrh. . . .'[313] Thus on the ecclesiastical side all is clear. But to the objection that Scripture makes Melchizedek king *and* priest, Maximus replies that Melchizedek is a type of one thing only and cannot therefore have two diverse fulfilments, one sacerdotal, one regal. The question of the relation of Christ's royalty and priesthood in the Church is left unanswered.

If now we turn our attention to authority in the Church, whether to teach or to rule, we find Maximus again most explicit in the Process. When urged once more to accept the *Type* for peace' sake, he cries out:

> I cannot grieve God by keeping silent what He ordered to be spoken and confessed. For if, according to the divine Apostle, it is *He Himself who has set in the Church, first apostles, secondly prophets, thirdly doctors,*[314] it is clear that He has spoken through them. By all of Holy Scripture, by the Old and the New Testament, by the holy doctors and synods we are taught. . . .[315]

This passage is doubly interesting. It gives us an unmistakable seventh-century interpretation of a disputed text[316] that identifies the doctors of St. Paul with the bishops. It further joins the synods to the bishops, thus giving them a share in the same authority.

If then the doctors are the bishops and they owe their authority in the Church to their divine institution, this authority is exercised in certain preferred ways, such as are indicated in the following passage.

> The natural essences of united objects the God-minded doctors of the Church in no way denied, but concordantly with the evangelists and the apostles and prophets they declared Our Lord and God Jesus Christ in both His natures volitive and operative of our salvation. PYRRHUS: Can this be shown from the Scriptures of the Old and New Testament? MAXIMUS: Of course, for the Fathers did not draw from their own resources but learned this from the Scriptures and charitably taught us. For it is not they who speak but the grace of the Spirit who entirely permeated them.[317]

Here then the *Fathers* are the *doctors*, are the *bishops*. I do not pretend that either term is exclusively applied to bishops; in a context, however, of tradition and authoritative teaching it would remain the ordinary sense. Now in this passage the authority of the Fathers is based on their

Spirit-assisted understanding of Scripture. Authority in the Church therefore has a threefold basis: the divine institution of bishops; Holy Scripture; the bishops' Spirit-assisted interpretation thereof.

How was this ordinarily exercised? In synods, at least for the more serious affairs. But what synods are binding and true? The question was necessarily put, because Sergius and Pyrrhus had held several synods in favor of their heretical doctrine. Of synods Maximus notes that not all dogma is expressed in synodical decrees.[318] Further-more, practice shows that imperial convocation is not required; many Arian synods were so summoned and many orthodox synods were not so summoned. No, the ecclesiastical canon accepts those synods known for their *right doctrine*.[319] This surely is a rather indecisive criterion. But the ecclesiastical canon knows of another means. The emperor and the patriarch with his synod should refer the case (in this instance rejection of the *Type* and absolution) in writing to Rome. Maximus, a simple monk, can do nothing, especially as the Roman anathema of the *Type* has intervened.[320]

Concerning the Roman See but two documents deal directly, TP 12 and 11. The former, as we have already noted, urges Pyrrhus' submission to Rome and the Roman doctrine.[321] The reason for this he also makes plain: satisfaction to the Roman See suffices for the whole Church:

> The Apostolic See . . . from the very Incarnate Word of God and from all the holy synods of all the churches throughout the world in their sacred canons and definitions has received and possesses, in and for every thing, dominion, authority, and power to bind and to loose. With it the Word, set at the head of heavenly powers, binds and looses in heaven.[322]

Words could scarcely be clearer. This supreme power of absolution is of Dominical institution, sanctioned by all the councils.

The other document, written after the Lateran Council, witnesses to the same doctrine. From the Roman Church all receive the holy dogmas of the Fathers, as the six synods (the Lateran must here be included) declared them. From the beginning the other churches had their basis in the Roman Church against which the gates of hell should not prevail. She holds the keys of right faith and confession in Christ.[323]

Here there is no question—the authority is primarily and properly doctrinal. In the first document it may have seemed to pertain rather to discipline—an absolution from condemnation and excommunication, but here it is said that the Roman Church holds 'the keys of the orthodox faith and confession in Him.'[324]

These last remarks on the Church's hierarchy may seem far removed from our theme of salvation and deification. Yet if we are saved by right faith, it is clearly pertinent to know who holds the keys of the orthodox faith and confession in Christ.

The Sacraments

Of the Church I have first spoken because she is the milieu in which salvation is apprehended; the means by which we apprehend are the sacraments, of which the first and fundamental is baptism.[325]

Already I have had occasion to note that the whole of salvation which Christ effected in the Incarnate dispensation was individually laid hold of in baptism.[326] It is therefore essential to anyone who would be saved, yet the mere rite performed with faith is not sufficient. It is the first mode of birth which grants adoption potentially only. The second mode is actual and effects in addition to faith the likeness of the Father, inasmuch as the election and γνώμη of the individual are formed anew like God. The Holy Spirit is the artificer of this reformation that is effected in man's γνώμη.[327] In fact it is through our human powers and habits being renewed in the Incarnation and by their good use that we are able to realize to the full the effects of the new birth given at baptism.[328]

Baptism then is a new, a second birth, not according to the law of corruption established by Adam's sin and presiding at our first birth, but a birth in the Spirit that renders us sinless,[329] restores a provisional incorruptibility,[330] that is only preserved by the keeping of the commandments. A fuller view of baptism is that which sees the power of Christ's hardships and death to condemn sin conveyed to the baptized so that their hardships, sufferings, and even death condemn sin also, not merely their personal sin, but those of mankind.[331]

Most of these elements are contained in a chapter from the *Theological and Oeconomic Centuries*:

> We, who have put on the first incorruptibility with ritual baptism in Christ through the Spirit, let us await the last (which will be) with Him in the Spirit, having preserved the first unspotted through progress in good works and death voluntarily accepted. . . .[332]

After baptism one might expect some word on penance. The material however is far too scanty, so far as I have found it, to provide a satisfactory account of this sacrament.[333]

While baptism frees from original sin, penance frees from post-baptismal sin.[334] But there remains a variable use of the word: does penance (μετάνοια) remit the guilt only, or also in its fulness wipe out the consequences of sin, so that the fruit of penance may be said to be the calm of detachment (ἀπάθεια)? So then, how may we understand the forgiveness of post-baptismal sin in the text just referred to? As due to the sacrament or as due to the spirit of penance?

Of the Eucharist only have special studies appeared.[335] Of these the first is quite superficial; the second is a refutation of the first and, though it adduces more texts, is not a complete study of Maximus' Eucharistic doctrine.[336]

There are two difficulties that beset any such study. Maximus has nowhere left us a complete exposition of the Eucharist. Even in the *Mystagogia* he has deliberately passed over some things lest his inadequacy should reflect on the work of the divine Denis;[337] among these things are all those that occur between the *Sanctus* and the *Our Father*. Another difficulty is the luxuriousness of allegorical interpretation which passes with utmost ease through the various modes by which the soul is nourished. The Word of God is the connatural food of the soul; that the soul is fed is, for Maximus, paramount whether this be by the Scripture, which is the word of God, whether by contemplation, whether by the Sacrament, whether by compagination in the body of Christ—it matters only that the soul is fed.[338]

Clearly there is a 'priesthood of the gospel' after the 'order of Melchizedek,'[339] which was instituted by Christ to take His place visibly on earth and to make present His mysteries for those capable of perceiving them.[340] The purpose of this priesthood is to be deified and to deify.[341] It therefore involves leadership in the whole of Christian life and is above all else an imitation of its author.[342] This priesthood is here understood with an amplitude and an exigence not always met with among ourselves.

In the sacrifices of the Old Law the flesh was eaten, the blood was poured out at the foot of the altar.

> However, Christ being come high priest of the good things to come, He sacrifices Himself an ineffable sacrifice and in addition to His flesh gives His blood to those who have the senses of their soul exercised by perfection, for distinguishing good and evil.[343]

Such a combination of Pauline texts[344] forms a distinctly soteriological and eucharistic context, though the strictly eucharistic aspect, that is, the reception of the Body and the Blood in the Sacrament, is entirely passed over, or rather presupposed in the deeper interest for the *res sacramenti*. For the flesh is straightway explained as virtue and good works; the blood as knowledge of the λόγοι of things.

Of the reception of the Sacrament he speaks directly in the *Mystagogia*. It comes at the end of the whole service and by the participation in the Sacrament the recipients are made over in its likeness, so that they may be called really gods by grace, because of the divine presence of God, who leaves nothing unfilled by His presence.

The conformation to the *Logos* thus achieved, the deification is neither identical for all men nor uniform. It is more fully given to those who have done greater works, according to exaltedness of mind.[345] It is furthermore adapted to the 'harmony of the divine body.'[346] This indication permits also an ecclesiological understanding of the eucharistic and nourishment texts.

Though these texts be few, though they be difficult for us, of another mentality, to savor and to understand, yet they are enough to permit us to say: the Eucharist is at the heart of the Christian life. Maximus supposes it so; he, a simple monk, never had occasion to catechize, but rather to exhort to go on to gathering the fruits of this tree of life which is given us by the Word of God.[347]

Asceticism and its Technique

We come now to describe what may be called the *technique*[348] of the ascetic and mystical life in St. Maximus. One must in no way think that this forms a separate entity[349] in Maximus' thought; it is integral with the Christian life in its ecclesiastical and sacramental aspects, with which we have just dealt. They are all aspects of one and the same life. In this integral view he is but following his predecessors—Gregory of Nyssa,[350] his beloved Denis, and is typical of the whole subsequent Byzantine tradition.

The reason for the relative distinctness of the ascetical work is that it is precisely a work which each man can and must do for himself, a work cut to each man's measure. Maximus will himself even say that salvation is in our own will. For it is the work of *gnomic* reform, of a perfect realization of the capacities of our nature.[351]

Again, from the human side the principal motive force of the whole struggle is the desire for God. This, as we have seen, is identified with the will of man and is fully natural. It is at the same time a teleological impulse of an intellectual nature for its end, an impulse which cannot be eradicated and, because a tendency of an intellectual creature, realized in the mode proper to this creature's self-determinative character. But how can this *natural* and this *self-determinative* be reconciled—the one implying necessity, the other freedom? So far as I understand Maximus, this question (which he nowhere raises) would

6

have been for him no insoluble difficulty. His answer is to be found in the distinction of λόγος and τρόπος, which is coincident with that of nature and person. The will is free first in the nature; its freedom is exercised only by the person according to the concrete, actual conditions of its existence; the nature of man is essentially self-determinative, this power of self-determination may be realized in a strictly divine mode (the Incarnation) or in a variety of human modes—in Adam, before the law, under the law, in the light of Revelation, and in all the diversity of circumstances in which men may find themselves. It happens therefore that this fundamental desire which is by rights a desire for God is perverted to the creature; it may take a right direction but be misinformed and extrinsically deformed; it may reach full blossom in the Church. Or those who are of the Church may again pervert it by preferring the creature. But always the freedom remains as also the distinction of what we now term the natural and supernatural order, since, in fact, the explicitation of this desire follows immediately not the metaphysical structure of man, but each man's concrete historical condition as a living person. If it be explicitated in the right sense, really for God, it tends towards God in His fulness; but if without Revelation, towards Him in His fulness, remaining, however, for such an individual, the material object only; it tends towards God in proportion to the powers of its nature, which unless renewed by Christ by His Incarnation, necessarily remains totally inadequate to attaining the divine, because merely human.

This fundamental orientation of the individual to God is the primordial exercise of the creature's power of self-determination, of his free will. It is that of which some modern theologians are again speaking in regard to

another question, namely the final determination of the
damned in hell and, contrariwise, of the saved in God.[352]
Yet if a man has not now to die, but to live, this fundamental determination must be made now as best it may
and deployed consequently in all the contingencies of life,
so that the human γνώμη may be in all things deiform.

Another question immediately arises. This desire is the
mainspring for the ascetic and mystic life. It places therefore Maximus' doctrine under the patronage of ἔρως; the
charity which crowns and satisfies it is therefore necessarily
tainted.

Without adding an excursus to a digression in criticism
of Nygren's work,[353] it will be necessary to remark that
this desire is natural and even inevitable in an intellectual
creature (though still capable of perversion). Ἀγάπη then
cannot eradicate it, nor can it be opposed to it in its natural
reality; yet in its actual expression in fallen man this desire
puts on all the forms of self-love, which is directly contrary
to ἀγάπη. The divine gift then of ἀγάπη to the creature
enables him so to be fixed in the faith already here on earth
and in the good, that, partaking of the divine fixity and
firmness, he can in that measure imitate the divine love
which loved us while yet sinners and sends His rain on the
just and the unjust—the divine love, whose condition is
precisely that fixity of fulness and non-indigence, of which
man partakes by faith.

But if this desire be the mainspring of the ascetical and
mystical life, it is utterly impotent to overcome its own
perversion into self-love. Therefore all turns upon the
Incarnation and the struggle of Christ with the devil who
strained every nerve to induce Him to fail in love for God
or neighbor. This is the theme developed in the first part
of the *Ascetic Life*. This is the model for all ascetic struggle,

as is not only indicated there, but reaffirmed in the *Centuries*.[354]

Now in Christ the combat was necessarily extrinsic; for mere men it is largely intrinsic, a war of passions and virtues. The devil always remains active; but he has an entrance within us, through our body or through our love for it.[355]

This struggle gives rise to a technique of opposition, elaborated first for the control of the passions and the right use of the natural powers—the practical aspect; and also for the attainment of understanding and knowledge—the theoretical, the contemplative aspect. These are two aspects of one life which should never be separated, nor, if separated, can they attain the goal. The theoretical has an absolute need of the practical; it may however be left in a relatively inchoative state as in the *Ascetic Life*. In any case God and deification remain the unique goal.

The practical aspect of this life is analyzed according to the psychological structure of man. Maximus in this drew chiefly from Evagrius.[356] The basic distinctions may be expressed in the following table:

$$\text{mind} = \text{the reasonable (part of the soul)}$$
$$\text{soul} = \left\{ \begin{array}{l} \text{the concupiscible} \\ \text{the irascible} \end{array} \right\} \text{the passible}$$
$$\text{body}$$

There are here two triads. Neither of them is reckoned a metaphysical distinction by Maximus, whatever may be the judgment on its use by other authors.[357] The combination of these parts will vary. Thus the reasonable, concupiscible, irascible will be reckoned as parts of the soul,[358] or the mind will be distinguished from the passible part, or more frequently the passible part will be considered alone.[359] It is properly in the control of this latter part that asceticism and the practical life consist; the direction of the reasonable part or the mind is the work of natural contemplation and prayer.

The whole of the moral life is in the tension between the two elements of the passible and in their control. Whether one speaks of the concupiscible and the irascible, of desire and anger, of pleasure and pain, the antithesis is always the same and the various virtues and vices are ranged under one or the other.[360] The mother of all the vices is self-love, which is the perversion of desire and therefore pertains to the concupiscible part of the soul. Pain, we have seen, is secondary to the miscarriage of the primordial desire. It is necessary to note the subordination of these two parts of the soul. In their generation desire comes first and always supplies anger with its matter; but anger is the more firmly rooted, and dislodged with greater difficulty. It is therefore over it that the victory is the greatest.

So far the doctrine is common to Evagrius and Maximus.[361] But whereas Evagrius sees the evil of anger in the harm done to knowledge, Maximus finds it predominantly in the transgression of the commandment of love.[362] It is thus that the place held in Evagrius by meekness[363] as the great antidote for anger is assumed by love in Maximus' thought. Maximus, however, does not exclude meekness from this role, especially in his commentary on the Our Father.[364]

Anger then and the irascible are the more redoubtable foes in the ascetic struggle; they nourish themselves on desire and concupiscence of all sorts—for food, for money, for the pleasures of the flesh. Against all these is the other

master virtue of the practical way—self-mastery or continence (ἐγκράτεια). This virtue has a larger sense than is
conveyed by its ordinary English equivalent, continence.
It restrains every kind of desire and permits the individual
only what is necessary and useful.[365] The fruit of this
restraint is detachment (ἀπάθεια), which is the calm of
ordered faculties now responding only to those things
that are good and worthwhile.[366]

Parallel with this struggle for self-mastery and charity is
a struggle with demons. This is foreshadowed in Maximus
in the *Ascetic Life* where the whole struggle of Our Lord,
proposed for our imitation, is a struggle with demons,
either directly or through his agents, the Sadducees and
Pharisees. But in fact demons play a much less prominent
part in Maximus than in Evagrius. The reason is that
Evagrius lived in the Egyptian desert, that was reckoned
as the proper habitation of devils.[367] Maximus never even
came to Egypt. With the Lord the demons could work
only from the outside; with fallen man they have an
entrance through his desires. The ascetic, however, by
his very way of life has cut off the occasion of sinning
with most things. It remains that his great danger
and temptation is first and principally in thoughts
(λογισμοί). Now thoughts are of two sorts: they are
either simple and unadulterated, or composite and joined
with the passions.[368] And often, especially in Evagrius,
it seems to make little difference whether the temptation
is attributed to a thought or to the corresponding
demon.[369]

Again, as there is a certain hierarchy among the passions,
so among the demons. The demon of anger is by far the
most difficult to fight off. This is the demon who strove
throughout Our Lord's ministry to make Him sin against

fraternal charity. It is against hate and anger that the commandment of love works.[370]

The ascetical struggle therefore is comprised in the acquisition of self-mastery or continence and love.[371] This supposes throughout a severe renunciation that in all things God may be preferred to the creature. The fruit is that calm of detachment which permits the mind to devote itself to a God-directed contemplation of creatures and to pure prayer.

Prayer and Contemplation

The necessity of methodical exposition has forced me to treat first of the practical aspect and now of the contemplative aspect of the Christian life; in fact, they are aspects of one Christian life and only with disaster are they separated.

But having made this statement, I feel that I must at once modify it. There are actually two elements which are here comprehended under the contemplative aspect— 'natural contemplation (or: consideration) of things' and prayer. The first is a technical procedure for rising from the simplest sense impressions to the λόγοι of things and thence to the supreme Λόγος who in Himself comprehends all others. I have already had occasion to write of these above, where I spoke of the Trinity and of motion.[372] This procedure supposes no small philosophical culture and, doubtless, a perseverence in following it out, possible only to a few monks. Laymen may have had the culture, but scarcely the necessary leisure and retirement; not all monks had the philosophical training of an Evagrius or a Maximus.

Πρᾶξις should always be joined with some θεωρία, that is, with prayer. 'Natural contemplation' of course must always be joined with πρᾶξις; yet it may be omitted. This view suggests itself because in the *Ascetical Life* there is no mention at all of 'natural contemplation'; but there is of prayer, in which the mind stripped of every image is joined to God and does not fail to ask what is fitting.[373] Similarly Ep 2 on charity, addressed to a man of the world, though it reckons charity as the first good beyond which one cannot go, effecting union with God and man and opening the door to the vision of the blessed Trinity,[374] makes no mention of 'natural contemplation.'

This practical disappearance of 'natural contemplation' in the highest stages of prayer is confirmed by Char 2.6, where two supreme states of pure prayer are distinguished, one for the practical, one for the contemplative. The first is characterized by the uninterrupted making of prayers in the presence of God; the other by seizure by the divine light and love, apart from all perception of things. Consequent on this rapture the mind is moved constantly about the properties of God and receives clear impressions of Him.[375]

Now if we look once again at those places where 'natural contemplation' and pure prayer are described side by side or as the second and third members of a triad, where therefore their interrelation should be most manifest, we find a distinct break of continuity. This is true of the description of the three motions of the soul according to sense, reason, and mind. The mind in its own proper motion receives no knowledge of God from any created thing, it is fully separated from any motion in regard to things.[376] It is true that the 'reasons of things are referred to and unified in the mind,' but this is quite another function, however necessary, however useful, and cannot be confused with its activity toward God.

In the 25th question for Thalassius, Maximus explains the phrase of St. Paul, *the head of every man is Christ*,[377] interpreting it of the practical mind, of the mind given to 'natural contemplation' in the Spirit, and of the mind of mystical theology. Has Maximus confused his teaching in Char 2.6, as Pegon there supposes? The conclusion is hasty. For here as elsewhere the 'natural contemplation' is turned towards things and their essences, λόγοι, reducing them ever to the first Λόγος Christ, while mystical theology implies that one deprive oneself of oneself and things.[378] For the mind, stripped of every idea and knowledge, can look upon the very Word of God only without eyes.[379]

It is in this context that are to be understood the numerous references to the mind in God, that is, in the highest state of prayer, being *stripped*, shapeless, formless, uniform, deiform. These are but so many ways of saying our images and concepts have no place in the highest prayer.[380] It is another way of saying that the attribute of God which, when imitated, makes us most like Him, is His simplicity.[381] This imitation can naturally imply for Maximus no immutation of the λόγος of man's composite nature, no etherialization.[382]

Here a delicate and difficult question cannot be avoided. Is this supreme state of prayer conceived by Maximus in the Evagrian mode or the Dionysian? Is, in other words, the mind stripped of all images, concepts, and created things that in itself it may regard the perfect image of God and so see God,[383] or must it go outside not only all created things but also itself that it may attain thus to the ray of the divine darkness?[384] Hausherr[385] has dealt with the problem. And while he has made unmistakably clear the antithetic nature of these two concepts, he has not considered Maximus' writings other than the *Centuries on*

Charity and has assumed with Viller not only the textual borrowing but also that Maximus borrowed likewise the Evagrian doctrine. Hence his conclusion that the Dionysian element is merely superimposed.

Note that in the very chapter (Char 3.99) which occasioned the discussion occur the words *providence* and *judgment*, eminently Evagrian but, as I have already pointed out,[386] understood by Maximus in a different sense. Hausherr (355) remarks that Evagrius even where he is citing other authors *en passant* may very well be expressing his own thought. This possibility cannot be denied to Maximus.

In relation to the Evagrian doctrine it must be remembered that Maximus refutes the Origenist errors and has a very definite doctrine on the λόγος of man as composite of body and soul.

Our evidence comes from the *Ambigua* and the *Questions for Thalassius*.[387] In Amb 10 the unknowable motion about God does not derive from knowledge of any creature, because the divine exceeds, so that the mind ceases from its natural activity. But then:

> Some say that God and man are examples (παραδείγματα) one of the other; and that for man God becomes man out of kindness, insofar as for God man, enabled by charity, has deified himself; and that man is rapt by God to the unknown [387a] insofar as he has manifested God, invisible by nature, through his virtues.

Whoever may be the man whom Maximus here quotes, the whole passage (with its strange inverted allusion to the Incarnation) cannot be a patron for the Dionysian *ecstasis*; but it can neither be taken as a full affirmation of Evagrian doctrine. The emphasis falls on charity and virtues.

In Thal 63 wisdom, the gift and activity of the Holy Spirit, is granted those who are worthy of deification, which leads them without intermediary to the cause of things. They are characterized by the properties of divine goodness. Thus from God they know themselves and from themselves God. Thus they were brought to the infinitely infinite summit of all, through speechless and ineffable silence and ignorance. Here again note that these wise men are known by the *properties of divine goodness*. But if through their virtues holy men manifest God, is it not by this manifestation also that from themselves they know God?

These are the clearest passages in an Evagrian sense. They suggest a moderate acceptance of the Evagrian position in this point, with a shift of emphasis towards charity. After seeing what role Maximus attributes to charity, I shall return again to the question of Evagrian *introspection* and Dionysian *ecstasis*.

Charity

The true heart of Maximus' doctrine is love. The lodestone of all his thought, I noted at the outset, was the mystery of the Incarnation. This is for him the mystery of love.[388] In the two treatises of which the English version is here published, love is deliberately chosen as the main theme—in the *Ascetic Life* illustrated by Our Lord's life and passion, in the *Centuries* inculcated directly by many aphorisms and indirectly by the very number of the Centuries. They number four and this was doubtless chosen as being the number of the gospels in which the commandment and example of love are contained. In charity the whole of Christian life is summarized and contained.

A special consideration of charity is further forced upon us for other reasons. In it Maximus is most clearly distinguished from his master Evagrius; the import of this divergence must be assessed.

The doctrine on charity I shall recapitulate under ten heads.

1. Charity is first of all the preference of God to all creatures, even one's own body. This is the absolute requirement and goes directly contrary to the primordial sin, self-love. Of the commandment of love it is the first part exacting love for God. In the definition of charity given in Char 1.1 it is the *knowledge of God* that must be preferred. This is typically Evagrian, but it is not the last word on charity.[389]

2. We have already seen that love (of neighbor) is opposed in a special way to anger.[390] This is part of Maximus' greater emphasis on fraternal charity, in which he manifests a greater sensitiveness to the communal and social life of the Church.

3. Charity and the calm of detachment (ἀπάθεια)[391] again and again stand in the same relation to knowledge and the mystical life. They are the finished product of the practical life[392] which, as a continuing possession, permit the fulness of contemplation. They both are natural to God and for us are acquired by the exercise of choice and intention (γνώμη).[393]

4. But if *charity* can be used synonymously with the *calm of detachment*, they are not in the full extension of their meanings synonymous. This is quite manifest when we find Maximus putting love not only after *calm* but after knowledge.[394] The full sense of this will be clear later.

5. Now charity is not merely the supreme virtue, the summary of the commandments, it is further an abiding

condition and state without which any knowledge or
other term of the Christian life would be impossible. Thus
Maximus speaks of the charitable state, to which a region
of hate is opposed.[395]

6. In this state of charity all are loved equally and indeed
it is but one and the same love which we extend to God
and man.[396] This is a distinct change from the Evagrian
doctrine, for whom the most that is possible is to be without hate or rancor towards any, to maintain the calm of
detachment in their regard.[397] Now Maximus not once
but many times insists on love for one's neighbor and six
times in the *Centuries* exacts an equal love, and precisely
as an imitation of the divine love which is the same for
all without distinction and without special attachments.[398]
This must be particularly noted: though the calm of
detachment is necessary for such love, it is only love itself
which can go out to men in imitation of the divine love.
This equality of love is based on the divine will 'to save
all men and bring them to a knowledge of the truth,'[399]
but does not exclude a diverse modality of love for the
good, who are loved for their virtues, and for the bad, to
whom compassion is shown in their estrangement.[400]

7. Charity, especially fraternal charity, is opposed to
self-love. As it was self-love that originally destroyed the
unity of man and the harmony of his powers, so it is
charity, made possible to us in Christ, which restores that
unity and harmony.[401] Charity, having such a role, cannot
be something inferior; it is supreme, it imitates God, it
makes like God, so that a man will lay down his life for
another.[402]

8. In a word, charity unites with God and deifies. This
is often repeated in various ways. Essentially it ties in with
the Incarnation. The Word out of love became man,

fully and perfectly, with the intent that in proportion as
He had become man out of love, so man might become
God, as much as his nature would permit.[403]

9. It is necessary to know a little more precisely what
this divinization implies. There are passages which speak
of knowledge (ἐπίγνωσις) as the ultimate goal, after the
phrase of St. Paul.[404] This certainly is not to be forgotten;
but more useful for us is the statement of Char 2.52 that
the man of prayer has practically all the divine properties,
elsewhere, qualities.[405] This enables us to ask what are the
properties or qualities of God which most of all effect this
deification. One can reply with a list of virtues and
qualities, as Maximus does in the chapter just cited. But if
we look for those source qualities from which the others
derive, we can name perhaps but two, goodness and simplicity. Of these I have already spoken.[406] It remains now
to see how their imitation and participation by man effects
his deification.

It is easy enough to see how the divine simplicity exacts
of the ascetic and gnostic a progressive purgation in his
prayer of every sense image and concept, so that the mind
itself becomes in this way simple as its archetype. And this
process, accomplished in the uppermost reaches of prayer,
is a withdrawal *within* oneself. It is in the line of the
Evagrian mysticism. Maximus speaks of the divine simplicity alike in the *Centuries*[407] as elsewhere,[408] and very
explicitly in connection with our deification in the
Questions for Thalassius.[409]

Let us not suppose for a moment that the notion of the
divine simplicity is peculiar to Evagrius or to the Alexandrians. Clearly it is a cardinal doctrine also for Denis.
The point is that diverse materials were at hand in the
building lot of mystical theology. Evagrius built chiefly

with simplicity; Denis rather with goodness and love; Maximus entering the same lot, with the same materials at hand and the examples of his predecessors, endeavored to use in the construction of his arch not one but both.

The emphasis on the good as the principal attribute of God Maximus doubtless took over from Denis.[410] Now the divine good is the end of every created motion, in which only the creature may attain an immutable firmness.[411] It is the going out of the free will, the self-determinative power, to God, this '*gnomic* emigration' which achieves for us the final unshakable union with God in Christ through the grace of the Spirit according to the words of St. Paul: *I live, now not I, but Christ liveth in me.*[412]

It is true, the climax of this passage refers to the future state of the blessed, as Maximus himself says in a later explanation,[413] where there will be but one operation of God and the saints. Yet this does not permit us to overlook that the tenor of the whole passage is that of an *ecstasis*. Is one therefore directly to conclude that this is Dionysian doctrine pure and simple? Let us not be hasty. Clearly we are here dealing with *ecstasis*. Earlier in this same passage Maximus had said: 'If (the rational creature) loves, then surely it suffers *ecstasis* towards the intelligible object as lovable.'[414] Then, having introduced the idea of subjection to God and hence the exercise of self-determination, Maximus speaks of this deifying '*gnomic* emigration' which brings the image to the archetype and so, among other things, it 'enjoys the *ecstasis* from the things that naturally are and are understood of itself, because of the grace of the Spirit.'[415]

What does *ecstasis* here mean? Or rather, outside of what things is the image reckoned as standing? It would seem outside its natural powers and their exercise; for deification, of which this *ecstasis* is here a consequent, is always the work of the divine power and operation, and manifest in the assumption of the divine properties—virtues even now, and eventually stability and immortality.[416] Further, the sense of the whole passage is to refute the Origenist doctrine of the *henad*.[417] It is this that explains the emphasis on deification and the infelicitous phrase about one operation between God and the saints.

If then this use of *ecstasis* is due to the Dionysian influence, it is not here used in the full Dionysian sense of an irrational, supra-rational estrangement of the mind in the divine darkness. The over-all sense is that of an outgoing of the volitive power, which effects the final gnomic harmony and unity in love.

We see now that Maximus has modified or at least muted both the Evagrian and the Dionysian concept of the mystical life. Are these two as really incompatible as Hausherr suggests? Von Balthasar proposes to consider the two doctrines as extreme examples of a mysticism of immanence and of transcendence. 'Why cannot they both be reconciled in the one analogy of being?'[418] In this case the antithesis which Hausherr has so clearly made manifest is not to be understood on the metaphysical level, except insofar as Evagrius or Denis are exclusive extremists, but, for the truth involved in their positions, as a difference of mystical technique. Maximus has perhaps himself indicated the solution when he affirms[419] that God is above every relation of subject and object, of thinker and thought. Immanence and transcendence fall easily into such a dyadic polarization. God is Himself therefore above them.

10. It remains now only to summarize what is most characteristic in Maximus—his doctrine of love. And how

can one better do this than by turning to the epistle (2) to John the Chamberlain? Love is the fulfilment of faith and hope, it embraces the ultimate in desire and puts a term to that motion; it restores man to unity within himself and with other men, because of the harmony already established with God.[420] Than love there is nothing higher to be sought. The love given God and man is one and the same, due to God and joining men. The activity and proof of perfect love for God is love for our neighbor. Love is the way of Truth which is the Word, that places us in the calm of detachment before the Father; it is the door[421] by which he who enters makes his entrance into the holy of holies and is made worthy to see the holy and royal Trinity; it is the true vine. The whole of the Law and the prophets and the Gospel is directed towards it; by it God is honored above the creature and all men are equally honored.[422]

In all this it is to be noted that love knows no limits; or rather its limits are those of God. It repairs nature; it is expressed in the Johannine figures of the way, the door, and the vine—figures which of their very nature surpass the limits of a mere ascetical and mystical interest. Charity for Maximus is as catholic as the Church.

The Maximian Synthesis

Yet, however much one may exalt charity, it is not alone as the ultimate in Christian perfection. It is a door, it is a way as well as a vine and a state. It leads to truth. So far as I know, Maximus never asserted the relative superiority of one to the other; that belongs to a controversy of a later time. He does, however, very definitely co-ordinate them and insist on their mutual necessity. If he does give at times a preference to charity and the practical, his ultimate

7

reason is doubtless the fact of the mystery of love, the Incarnation.

Let us see how he does co-ordinate them. Two passages will suffice.

In the *Mystagogia* he speaks of the soul alone as image and type of the Church. The soul's intellectual power is distinguished into the theoretical and the practical, to which correspond the mind and reason, the term of whose activity is the truth and the good, which are God.[423] It is useless to follow all the subtleties of the five pairs which he builds up and the comparison of this decade with others. The essential is simple and clear: the whole of the ascetic and spiritual life are unified in their one object, though they may tend toward it under different aspects. This will be the ultimate basis why, apart from the example of the Incarnation, one must always insist on having both theory and practice.

This same thought appears more concretely in the preface of one of his later works. Maximus summarizes briefly Marinus' struggle for God and then concludes:

> So then life has become for you (Marinus) interpreter of reason; and reason has become the substance of life, the two thus describing the man verily new in Christ, who is a well-made copy of God the creator, bearing His image and likeness, which here must be understood as truth and goodness, which are respectively the goal for theory and practice.[424]

Here a further note is added. The image is referred to the truth, the likeness to the good. Why? Because the image is the rational soul itself; the likeness was lost and is restored only by the gnomic activity, returning the image to the divine likeness.[425] I do not wish to imply that the image, the rational part, suffered not at all; in fact ignorance is its primary defect[426] from which all the others flow. Yet, in this phrase Maximus perhaps best of all indicates what is most proper to his thought: the insistence on *gnome* and on love.

⁊   ⁊   ⁊

III. SPECIAL INTRODUCTION

THE ASCETIC LIFE (LA): The text used is simply that of F. Combefis, as reproduced in MG 90.912–56. It presents no difficulties. There are the following translations: in German by M. Garbas, *Des heiligen Maximus Confessor . . . Liber Asceticus* (Breslau 1925), and by F. Murawski, *Führer zu Gott* (Mainz 1926), a group of Byzantine ascetical writings among which is found the LA; in Italian by R. Cantarella, *S. Massimo Confessore La Mistagogia ed altri scritti* (Florence 1931) 30–99, with Greek text. Cantarella gives a list of corrections to the Migne reprint, cf. 277–79; the only correction of any importance I have noted in n. 140. There is no previous translation into English.

The form is the familiar one of question and answer (cf. *The Earlier Ambigua* 5); with this difference, that the interested parties are presented in person, that is, a young novice and an old monk. It remains a dialogue of sorts for the first part (1–26); the second part consists, however, of successive monologues—the first and longest on compunction (27–39), the second an exhortation to hope and trust in God's mercy (40–45).

The development is simple and springs directly from the nature of Christian life, particularly as the monk seeks to achieve it. It is above all the quest of salvation, that is, the Lord's purpose is His Incarnation. It is by making this purpose our own and by fulfilling the commandments that we shall be saved, deified.

69321

The commandments are summarized in the two-fold commandment of love for God and neighbor. This Our Lord spent His whole life and death in observing. For us 'love for one another makes firm the love for God which is the fulfilling of every commandment of God' (7). This purpose of the Lord is twice explained and illustrated, by the Lord's own life and by that of the apostles, as exemplars. In this strife the chief opponent is always the devil and those he deceives. The devil's tactics are always the same—to induce men to prefer creatures to God and so, in seeking them, to hate their fellow men. The Christian's tactic is the opposite: renunciation of creatures that God may be preferred above all, and love of neighbor. The purpose and foundation of the ascetic life is thus described with sufficient detail and illuminating repetition in the first 16 sections. The intimate connection of this life with that of Christ is evident, as also the close connection of this treatise with the *Questions to Thalassius* (see Introd. 64). The purpose made clear, the principal means of attaining it are then indicated in more particular (17–26). Three virtues are essential: love, self-mastery, prayer. Love tames anger; self-mastery, desire; prayer joins the mind to God. This is but a brief indication of spiritual doctrine for the more advanced, such as will be developed in the following *Centuries*. But note the strongly Christological and soteriological context in which it places the *Centuries*. We shall return to this point as occasion serves.

The second part (27–45) is likewise divided into two sections. At the end of 26 Maximus (that is, the old man) bemoans the fact that we no longer keep the way of our fathers. The brother then abruptly asks why he has no compunction. The response forms the first monologue (27–39). The reason is lack of fear of God, faith without works (34). Finally, the brother, at the end of a long prayer, declares himself touched. The old man then turns to encouragement and exhortation to fraternal charity (40–45).

The dismal picture painted in this section may seem excessive. Surely the times in which Maximus lived were enough to give matter for penance. I have tried to read allusions to these events between the lines, but with no result. The real answer for this great emphasis on compunction is to be found in the keen appreciation of the value of salvation, in the sense of solidarity not alone with Christ and the saints, but also with the sinful mass of mankind. In the face of such a contrast what soul is not touched? See on this question the exquisite essay of Hausherr, *Penthos* (Rome 1944), esp. 188; also Maximus Ps 59–861C; Thal 10–288 ff. (on the fear of God and love); Ep 4,5,24–416B, 421D, 612A.

The Four Centuries on Charity (Char): The text again is basically that of Combefis, as printed in MG 90.960–1080. Yet through the courtesy of Mr. Aldo Ceresa-Gastaldo, who is preparing a critical edition and new Italian version of Char, I have been able to note a few variants from the *Palatinus graecus* 49, a manuscript of the late 9th century. There exists the recent French version of Pegon, indicated in the bibliography. Pegon naturally owes much to Viller's article (see Introd. n. 356), but comes to a maturer judgment on the homogeneity and originality of Maximus' doctrine (see his introduction 57 ff.). Only two other versions are known to me: that contained in the Russian *Philocalia* (cf. LA n. 49) and that made by the monk Cerbanus and dedicated to the archimandrite David of Pannonhalma. This David was abbot in the latter two decades of the first half of the 12th century. The MSS in which this version is contained were noted by de Ghellinck: *Le mouvement théologique du xiie siècle* (2 ed., Paris (1948) 398 nn. 4,5). The text itself was published in 1944 at Budapest by A. B. Terebessy: *Translatio latina s. Maximi Confessoris De Caritate s. xii^o in Hungaria confecta*; cf. *Rev. d'hist. ecclés.* 42 (1948) 384. This last version is of interest as an example of the twelfth-century revival of Greek thought in the west. The form is that of the gnomic or sententious literature, first fixed in centuries by Evagrius. Both the number 100 and the number of the centuries are significant; the first as a perfect number, referring directly to the One, God; the other, in our case 4, as representing the four Gospels, whose commandment is that of love. This latter point Maximus himself notes in his preface. He also gives the reason for the sententious form: concision, facilitating the work of memory, that the monk may have a store of pithy sayings on which he may ruminate and develop at leisure (cf. the request of the brother in LA 6). An abuse of the form, namely a willed or perverse obscurity, he likewise recognizes; and, though denying this abuse in his own case, he has to allow that not all his chapters are easy to understand. See Hausherr, 'Centuries,' in *Dict. de Spiritualité* 2 (1938) 416–18.

As to the nature of the notes offered below, my aim will be to mark critical divergences from Evagrius as well as similarities and identities, that Maximus may appear in his own character; and to add such other notes as may be necessary for the understanding of the text. For this a reference to the Introd. may often suffice. It will not be my aim to write an historical commentary on the chapters. The effect would be only to distract the reader from Maximus' thought, to the hundreds of rivulets from which he drew.

THE ASCETIC LIFE

(by question and answer)

A BROTHER   THE OLD MAN

A brother asked an old man and said: 'Please, Father, tell me: What was the purpose of the Lord's becoming man?'

The old man answered and said: 'I am surprised, brother, that you ask me about this, since you hear the symbol of faith every day. Still, I will tell you: the purpose of the Lord's becoming man was our salvation.'[1]

Then the brother said: 'How do you mean, Father?'

The old man replied:[2] 'Listen: man, made by God in the beginning and placed in Paradise, transgressed the commandment and was made subject to corruption and death. Then, though governed from generation to generation by the various ways of God's Providence, yet he continued to make progress in evil and was led on, by his various fleshly passions, to despair of life. For this reason the only-begotten Son of God, Word of God the Father from all ages, the source of life and immortality, *enlightened us who sit in darkness and in the shadow of death.*[3] Taking flesh by the Holy Spirit and the holy Virgin, He showed us a godlike way of life; He gave us holy commandments and promised the kingdom of heaven to those who lived according to them, threatening with eternal punishment those that transgressed them. Suffering His saving Passion and rising from the dead, He bestowed upon us the hope of resurrection and of eternal life. From the condemnation of ancestral sin He absolved by obedience; by death He destroyed the power of death,[4] so that *as in Adam all die, so in Him all shall be made alive*.[5] Then, ascended into heaven and seated on the right of the Father, He sent the Holy Spirit as a pledge of life, and as enlightenment and sanctification for our souls, and as a help to those who struggle to keep His commandments for their salvation. This, in brief, is the purpose of the Lord's becoming man.'

2. Then the brother said: 'What are the commandments[6] I ought to do, Father, to be saved by them? I would like to hear in just a few words.'

The old man answered: 'The Lord Himself said to the Apostles after the Resurrection: *Go, teach ye all nations, baptizing them in the name of the Father, and of the Son, and of the Holy Spirit, teaching them to observe all things, whatsoever I have commanded you*.[7] So then one must keep whatever He has commanded, every man that is baptized in the name of the life-giving and deifying Trinity. It is for this reason that the Lord joined to right faith the keeping of all the commandments: He knew that one, apart from the others, was not able to save man. Therefore David, who also had right faith, spoke to God: *I was set right towards all Thy commandments; I have hated all wicked ways*.[8] For against every wicked way were the commandments given us by the Lord, and if one of them is omitted, it will surely bring in the contrary way of wickedness.'

3. Then the brother said: 'And who, Father, can do all the commandments? There are so many.'

The old man said: 'He who imitates[9] the Lord and follows in His footsteps.'

The brother said: 'Who can imitate the Lord? Though He became man, the Lord was God. But I am a man, a sinner, enslaved to a thousand passions. How then can I imitate the Lord?'

And the old man answered: 'None of those enslaved to material things can imitate the Lord. But those who can say: *Behold, we have left all and followed Thee*[10]—these receive power both to imitate Him and to do well in all His commandments.'

Then the brother: 'What sort of power?'

The old man answered: 'Listen to Him speak: *Behold, I have given you power to tread upon serpents and scorpions, and upon all the power of the enemy; and nothing shall hurt you.*[11]

4. Now Paul, who had received this same power and dominion, said: *Be ye imitators of me as I also am of Christ.*[12] And again: *There is now no condemnation to them that are in Christ Jesus, who walk not according to the flesh but according to the spirit.*[13] Again: *And they that are Christ's have crucified their flesh with its passions and desires.*[14] And again: *The world is crucified to me and I to the world.*[15]

5. About this dominion and help David said in prophecy: *He that dwelleth in the aid of the most High, shall abide under the protection of the God of heaven. He shall say to the Lord: Thou art my protector, and my refuge; my God, in Him will I hope.*[16] And a little further on: *Thou shalt walk upon the asp and the basilisk and thou shalt trample under foot the lion and the dragon; for He hath given His angels charge over thee, to keep thee in all thy ways.*[17] But those given to lust and loving material things—listen to what they hear from Him: *He that loveth father or mother more than me is not worthy of me.*[18] And a little further on: *And he that taketh not up his cross and followeth me, is not worthy of me.*[19] Again: *Every one that doth not renounce all that he possesseth, cannot be my disciple.*[20] Therefore he who wants to be His disciple and to be found worthy of Him, and to receive

power from Him against the spirits of wickedness, will separate himself from every fleshly attachment and strip himself of every worldly passion. And thus he contends with the invisible enemies in behalf of His command-ments, just as the Lord Himself set an example for us in being tried both in the desert by their chief and, returned to civilization, by the demoniacs.'[21]

6. Then the brother said: 'But the Lord's commands are many, Father, and who can keep them all in mind, so as to strive for all of them? And especially myself, who have such a poor memory? I would like to hear a brief explana-tion, that I may retain it and be saved by it.'

The old man replied: 'Though they are many, brother, yet they are all summed up in one word: *Thou shalt love the Lord thy God with thy whole strength, and with thy whole mind, and thy neighbor as thyself.*[22] And he who strives to keep this word succeeds with all the commandments together. And no one that does not separate himself as was said before, from passion for worldly things, can love genuinely either God or his neighbor. Indeed at the same time to attend to the material and to love God, simply cannot be. This is what the Lord says: *No man can serve two masters;*[23] and: *No man can serve God and mammon.*[24] For so far as our mind clings to the things of the world, it is their slave and scornfully transgresses God's commandment.'

7. Then the brother said: 'What things do you mean, Father?'

The old man replied: 'Food, money, possessions, acclaim, relatives and the rest.'

'But, Father,' said the brother, 'did not God make these things? And has He not given them to men for their use? How is it that He commands us not to cling to them?'[25]

The old man replied: 'It is clear that God made them and

has given them to men for their use. Yes, everything that has been made by God is good and fair, so that we who use them may be pleasing to God. Yet, we, in our weakness and material-mindedness, preferred material and worldly things above the commandment of love; and clinging to them we fight with men, though love for every man must be preferred above all visible things, even the body. This is the sign of our love for God, as the Lord Himself shows in the Gospels: *He that loves me*, He says, *will keep my commandments.*[26] And what this commandment is, which if we keep we love Him, hear Him tell: *This is my commandment, that you love one another.*[27] Do you see that this love for one another makes firm the love for God, which is the fulfilling of every commandment of God?[28] This then is the reason why He commands every one that is really desirous of being His disciple not to cling to these things, rather to renounce[29] all his possessions.'

8. Again, the brother said: 'Since you said, Father, that we must prefer love for every man above all visible things, even the body, how can I love the man that hates and repulses me? Suppose he is envious and aims abuse at me, lays snares and tries to trick me, how can I love Him? This seems impossible to me, Father, of its very nature, as the suffering of grief[30] naturally forces one to repulse him that causes it.'

Then the old man gave his answer: 'With creeping things indeed and beasts that are motivated by instinct, it really is impossible that they should not ward off, as much as they can, whatever molests them. But for those that are created after the image of God and are motivated by reason, that are thought worthy of knowledge of God and receive their law from Him, it is possible not to repulse those that cause grief and to love those that hate them.

Hence when the Lord says: *Love your enemies; do good to them that hate you*, and what follows,[31] He does not command the impossible, but clearly what is possible; for He would not otherwise rebuke the transgressor. The Lord Himself makes it clear and has shown it to us by His very works; and so too all His disciples, who strove till death for love of their neighbor and prayed fervently for those that killed them. But since we are lovers of material things and of pleasure, preferring them above the commandment, we are then not able to love them that hate us; rather we often, because of these things, repulse them that love us, being worse disposed than beasts and creeping things.[32] And that is why, not being able to follow in the steps of God, we are likewise unable to know His purpose, so that we might receive strength.'

9. Then the brother said: 'Look, Father, I left everything—relatives, property, luxury, and the world's good opinion; in this life I have no possessions but my body; still I am not able to love a brother that hates and repulses me, even if I force myself actually not to return evil for evil. Tell me then what ought I to do so as to love him from my heart, or in fact anyone that troubles me or contrives against me in any way at all?'

The old man replied: 'It is impossible for a man to love his tormentor, even though he think that he has renounced worldly things, unless he truly know the purpose of the Lord; but if by the Lord's gift he is enabled to know it and lives by it zealously, then he can love from his heart him that hates and troubles him, as did the Apostles, too, after they had known it.'

10. And the brother said: 'And what the Lord's purpose was, I beg to know, Father.'

The old man said: 'If you want to know the Lord's

purpose, listen intelligently. Our Lord Jesus Christ, being God by nature and, because of His kindness, deigning also to become man, was born of a woman and made under the law,[33] as the divine Apostle says, that by observing the commandment as man He might overturn the ancient curse on Adam. Now the Lord knew that the whole law and the prophets depend on the two commandments of the law—*Thou shalt love the Lord thy God with thy whole heart, and thy neighbor as thyself.*[34] He therefore was eager to observe them, in human fashion, from beginning to end.

But when the devil, who deceived man from the beginning and thereby had power of death, had seen Him receive at baptism the Father's testimony and, as man, the Holy Spirit from heaven, consubstantial to Himself, and also when he saw that He had come into the desert to be tempted by himself: then he mustered all his battle force against Him, thinking that in some way he might make even Him prefer the substance of this world to love for God. Now then, as the devil knew that there are three things by which every thing human is moved—I mean food, money, and reputation, and it is by these too that he leads men down to the depths of destruction—with these same three he tempted Him in the desert. But Our Lord, coming off victor over them, ordered the devil to get behind Him.

11. Such then is the mark of love for God. Now the devil was, by his promises, unable to persuade Him to transgress this commandment. So making use of the wicked Jews and his own machinations, he strove to persuade Him, on returning to society, to transgress the commandment of love for neighbor. For this reason while the Lord was teaching the ways of life, and actually demonstrating the heavenly manner of life, and preaching the

resurrection from the dead, and promising believers eternal life and the kingdom of heaven, but threatening unbelievers with eternal punishment, and, in confirmation of what He said, making a display of extraordinary divine signs and inviting the crowds to faith, that vindictive wretch stirred up the wicked Pharisees and Scribes to their various plots against Him in order to bring Him to hate the schemers. He thought that He would not be able to bear up under their plots; and so he would be attaining his purpose by making Him a transgressor of the commandment of love for neighbor.

12. But the Lord, since He was God, knew his intimate designs; nor did He hate the Pharisees that were thus egged on [35]—how could He, being good by nature? On the contrary, out of His love for them He fought back against the Instigator: He admonished, rebuked, reproached, berated, ceaselessly did good to those who were egged on, who, though able to resist, yet through sloth had willingly borne with the Instigator. Blasphemed, He was long-suffering; suffering, He patiently endured; He showed them every act of love. Thus against the Instigator He fought back by His loving-kindness towards those egged on—O paradoxical war! Instead of hate He sets forth love, by goodness He casts out the father of evil. It was for this reason that He endured such evils from them; rather, to speak more truly, on their account He, as man, contended until death on behalf of the commandment of love. And, after securing complete victory over the devil, He crowned Himself with the Resurrection for our sake. Thus the new Adam renewed the old. It is what the divine Apostle says: *Let this mind be in you, which was also in Christ Jesus,* [36] and what follows.

13. This then was the Lord's purpose, that as man He

obey the Father until death, for our sake, keeping the commandment of love; that against the devil He fight back, in being subject to attack from him by means of those whom he egged on, the Scribes and Pharisees. Thus by being conquered deliberately, He conquered him who hoped to conquer and snatched the world from his dominion. In this way Christ *was crucified through weakness.*[37] Through this weakness He killed death and *destroyed him who had the empire of death.*[38] In this way also Paul was weak as to himself, yet *boasted in his infirmities that the power of Christ might dwell in him.*[39]

14. Realizing what sort of victory this was, Paul wrote to the Ephesians, saying: *Your wrestling is not against flesh and blood, but against principalities, against powers,*[40] and what follows. He said to take the breastplate of justice and the helmet of hope and the shield of faith and the sword of the Spirit that they might be able to extinguish all the fiery darts of the wicked one, all they that carry on war against invisible enemies.[41] By deeds he showed the manner of wrestling, saying: *I therefore so run, not as at an uncertainty; I so fight, not as one beating the air; but I chastise my body and bring it into subjection, lest perhaps, when I have preached to others, I myself should become a castaway.*[42] And again: *Even unto this hour we both hunger and thirst, and are naked, and are buffeted.*[43] And again: . . . *in labor and painfulness, in much watchings, in hunger and thirst, in fastings often, in cold and nakedness, besides those things which are without.*[44]

15. Now in this wrestling he wrestled against the demons that excite pleasures in the flesh, driving them out through the weakness of his own body. But against those who war to stir up hatred, who therefore rouse the more negligent against the pious, that under the thrust of such temptation they may hate them and transgress against the

commandment of love—against such he once again by deeds indicated to us the manner of victory, saying: *We are reviled, and we bless; we are persecuted, and we suffer it; we are blasphemed, and we entreat; we are made as the refuse of this world, the offscouring of all even until now.*[45] And therefore the demons suggested reviling, blaspheming, persecuting that they might incite him to hatred of the reviler, the blasphemer, the persecutor, their purpose being the transgression of the commandment of love. But as the Apostle was not in ignorance of their schemes, he blessed the revilers and suffered the persecutors and entreated the blasphemers both to keep away from the demons that did these things and to draw near to the good God. With this kind of wrestling he defended himself against these machinations of the demons, ever conquering evil with good[46] in imitation of the Savior. So, too, he and the rest of the Apostles set the whole world apart from the demons and brought it near to God; by giving way, they conquered those who thought to conquer. Now, brother, if you too hold this purpose, you too can love those that hate you; but otherwise, it is in no way feasible.'

16. Then the brother said: 'Of a truth, Father, things are just that way, and no other. And that is why the Lord, when blasphemed and struck and suffering the other things that He suffered from the Jews, endured, yet with sympathy for them as ignorant and deceived. Therefore also He said upon the cross: *Father, forgive them, since they know not what they do.*[47] Over the devil's and his rulers' trickery and deceit He triumphed on the cross; contended against them for the commandment of love, even, as you said, until death; and granted us His victory over them. He loosed the power of death and bestowed upon the entire world His Resurrection unto life. But pray for me,

Father, that I may have strength to know perfectly the Lord's and His Apostles' purpose, and that I may be sober-minded in time of temptations and be aware of the schemes of the devil and his demons.'

17. The old man answered: 'If you always are attentive to what has been said above, you can have that awareness, but provided you understand that as you are tempted, so also your brother is tempted; that you pardon the tempted and, by refusing to respond to his trick, withstand the Tempter, who wants to bring you to a hatred of the tempted. That is what God's brother, James, says in the Catholic epistles: *Be subject to God, but resist the devil, and he will fly from you.* [48] If then, as has been said, you attend soberly and uninterruptedly to the foregoing, you can know the Lord's and His Apostles' purpose: to love men and to have sympathy for them when they fall, but by love to war constantly against the wicked demons. But if we are soft, careless, slothful and confuse our mind with carnal pleasures, we war not against the demons but against ourselves and our brothers; rather, by such things we serve the demons and for their sake fight men.'

18. Then the brother said: 'So it is, Father. For out of my carelessness the demons always take occasion against me. I entreat you, then, Father: tell me how I ought to lay hold on soberness.' [49]

The old man answered: 'Complete lack of concern for earthly things and continuous meditation on the divine Scriptures brings the soul to fear of God; and fear of God brings soberness. Then the soul begins to see the demons warring against it through its own thoughts [50] and begins to fight back. Of these David said: *And my eye hath looked down upon my enemies.* [51] As to this wrestling, the Prince of the Apostles, Peter, also said, rousing up the disciples: *Be*

8

sober and watch, because your adversary the devil, as a roaring lion, goeth about seeking whom he may devour; whom resist ye, strong in faith.[52] And the Lord: *Watch ye, and pray that ye enter not into temptation.*[53] And Ecclesiastes says: *If the spirit of him that hath power ascend upon thee, leave not thy place.*[54] Now virtue is the place where the mind should be, as also knowledge and fear of God. The admirable Apostle, who contended very soberly and nobly, said: *For though we walk in the flesh, we do not war according to the flesh. For the weapons of our warfare are not carnal, but mighty to God unto the pulling down of fortifications, destroying counsels and every height that exalteth itself against the knowledge of God, and bringing into captivity every understanding unto the obedience of Christ; and having in readiness to avenge all disobedience.*[55] If, therefore, you both imitate the saints and assiduously devote yourself to God, you will be sober-minded.'

19. And the brother said: 'And what should one do, Father, in order to be able to devote oneself continously to God?'

The old man answered: 'It is impossible for a mind[56] to devote itself perfectly to God, except it should possess these three virtues:[57] love, self-mastery, and prayer. Love tames anger; self-mastery[58] quenches concupiscence; prayer withdraws the mind from all thoughts and presents it, stripped, to God Himself. These are the three virtues that comprise all the virtues; without these the mind cannot devote itself to God.'

20. Then the brother said: 'I entreat you, Father: teach me how love tames anger.'

The old man answered: 'For a fact, it belongs to it to be merciful and to do good to one's neighbor, to be long-suffering in his regard, to endure what he inflicts, as we have often said. By these means, then, love tames the anger of him who has got hold of it.'

The brother said: 'Its works are no slight things. Blessed indeed he who can lay hold on it. But I, I am far from it. Still I entreat you, Father: tell me, what is long-suffering?'

21. Then the old man answered: 'Perseverance in adversity, endurance of evils, to abide to the end of temptation, not to let one's anger out by chance, not to speak a word in folly, not to suspect or to think anything that does not become a God-fearing man, as Scripture says: *A long-suffering man shall bear for a time, and afterwards joy shall be restored to him. He will hide his words for a time, and the lips of many shall declare his understanding.*[59]

22. These then are the marks of long-suffering. Yes, and to reckon oneself the cause of temptation, also belongs properly to long-suffering. Perhaps that is the way things are. In fact, many of the things that befall us, befall us for our training, either to do away with past sins or to correct present neglect or to check future sinful deeds. He then, who reckons that temptation has come upon him for one of these reasons, is not vexed at its attack, especially as he is conscious of his sin. Nor does he censure him through whom the temptation came; for whether through him or through another, he surely has to drain the chalice of the divine judgments. Rather, he looks to God and gives thanks to Him that pardons; he censures himself and heartily accepts the chastisement, as did David with Semei,[60] and as Job with his wife.[61] The foolish man often asks God to be merciful; when the mercy comes, he does not accept it, as it did not come, in fact, as he willed, but as the Physician of souls thought fitting. And so he gives no heed and is thrown into confusion: now he is angered

at men, now he blasphemes God; indeed he only shows his want of sense and receives nothing but the rod.'

23. Then the brother said: 'Well said, Father; yet I entreat you—tell me this also: how does self-mastery quench concupiscence?'

The old man answered: 'In fact, it keeps away everything that fulfills no need but causes pleasure. It permits one to share in nothing but what is necessary for living, to pursue not the pleasant but the beneficial, to measure food and drink by need, to allow the body no excess of humors, to conserve merely the life of the body and to preserve it undisturbed from tendency to intercourse. In such a way then continence quenches concupiscence. But pleasure and surfeit of food and drink heat the stomach, inflame the appetite to shameful desires and drive the whole animal to illicit union. Then are the eyes shameless, the hand unchecked, the tongue a speaker of charm, and the ear a recipient of foolish reports; the mind a scorner of God, the soul, in intention, a worker of adultery and provoking the body to illicit actions.'

24. Then the brother said: 'Yes, indeed, Father, things are that way. But I entreat you to teach also about prayer, how it withdraws the mind from all thoughts.'

And the old man answered: 'Thoughts are directed to things. Now, of things some are sense-perceptible, some mental.[62] The mind, then, tarrying with these things, carries about with itself thoughts of them; but the grace of prayer[63] joins the mind to God, and joining to God withdraws it from every thought. Then the mind, associating only with Him, becomes God-like. And being such, it asks of Him what is proper and at no time fails of its petition. Therefore the Apostle commands to *pray without ceasing*,[64] that, unremittingly joining our mind to

God, we may little by little break off our passionate clinging to material things.'

25. Then the brother said: 'And how can the mind pray
without ceasing? For in psalmody and readings, in mini-
strations and chance meetings we distract it with many
thoughts and sights.'

The old man answered: 'Divine Scripture commands
nothing impossible, since the Apostle himself both sang
psalms and read and ministered and prayed without
ceasing. For unceasing prayer is to keep the mind in great
reverence and attached to God by desire, and to cling
always to hope in Him, to be of good courage in Him in
all things, alike in our activity and in what befalls us. It
was in such a disposition that the Apostle said: *Who shall
separate us from the love of Christ? Shall tribulation? or
distress?* and so on; then: *For I am sure that neither death, nor
life, nor angels.* [65] Again: *In all things we suffer tribulation, and
are not distressed; we are straitened, and are not destitute; we
suffer persecution, but are not forsaken; we are cast down, but
we perish not: always bearing about in our body the mortifica-
tion of the Lord Jesus, that the life also of Jesus may be made
manifest in our mortal flesh.* [66]

26. With such dispositions then the Apostle prayed
without ceasing. For in every activity, as we said, and in
all that befell him he clung to hope in God. For this
reason all the saints always rejoiced in their tribulations,
in order to come to the habit of divine love. For this
reason too the Apostle said: *Gladly therefore will I glory in
my infirmities, that the power of Christ may dwell in me.*
Then, further on: *When I am weak, then am I powerful.* [67]
But woe to us wretches, because we have abandoned the
way of the holy fathers, and for that reason we are
destitute of every spiritual work!'

27. Then the brother said: 'Father, why do I have no compunction?'⁶⁸

And the old man answered: 'Because there is no fear of God before our eyes, because we have become the resting place of all evils, and, for that reason, we scorn as a mere thought the dreadful punishment of God. For who does not feel compunction at hearing Moses speaking about sinners in God's person: *A fire is kindled in my wrath, it shall burn to the lowest hell. It shall devour the earth and her increase; it shall burn the foundations of the mountains. I will heap evils upon them, and will spend my arrows upon them?*⁶⁹ And again: *I shall whet my sword as the lightning, and my hand shall take hold on judgment, and I will render vengeance to my enemies, and repay them that hate me?*⁷⁰ And at hearing Isaias crying out: *Who will tell you: Fire burns? who will tell you the everlasting place?*⁷¹ *Walk in the light of your fire and in the flames which you have kindled?*⁷² And again: *They shall go out and see the carcasses of the men that have transgressed against me. For their worm shall not die, and their fire shall not be quenched; and they shall be a sight to all flesh?*⁷³ And at hearing Jeremias saying: *Give ye glory to the Lord your God, before it grow dark and before your feet stumble upon the dark mountains?*⁷⁴ And again: *Hear, O foolish and heartless people. They have eyes and see not, they have ears and hear not. Will not you then fear me, saith the Lord; and will you not become reverent before my face? I have set the sand a bound for the sea, an everlasting ordinance, and it will not pass over?*⁷⁵ And again: *Thy apostasy shall chastise thee, and thy wickedness shall rebuke thee. Know thou, and see that it is a bitter thing for thee that thou hast left me, saith the Lord. I planted thee a fruitful vineyard, entirely genuine; how art thou turned into bitterness, O alien vineyard?*⁷⁶ And again: *I sat not with the assembly of jesters, but I was in fear of the* *presence of Thy hand: I sat alone, because I was filled with bitterness?*[77]

And who does not shudder at hearing Ezechiel saying: *I will pour out my wrath upon thee, and I will accomplish my anger in thee: and I will judge thee in thy ways, and I will lay upon thee all thy abominations; and my eye shall not spare, neither will I show mercy: and then thou shalt know that I am the Lord?*[78]

And who does not feel compunction at hearing Daniel explicitly describe the fearful day of judgment,[79] in such words as these: *I, Daniel, beheld till thrones were placed and the Ancient of days sat: His garment was white as snow, and the hair of His head like clean wool, His throne like flames of fire, the wheels of it like a burning fire. A stream of fire flowed, issuing forth from before Him. Thousands of thousands ministered to Him, and ten thousand times ten thousand stood before Him. The judgment sat, and the books were opened* (that is, each man's deeds)?[80] And again: *I beheld in a vision of the night, and lo, one like the Son of Man was coming with the clouds of heaven, and He came up even to the Ancient of days: and He was presented before Him. And there was given Him sovereignty and honor and royal might. And all peoples, tribes, and tongues shall serve Him. And His power is an everlasting power; His kingdom an everlasting kingdom. My spirit shuddered, yes, I, Daniel, in my condition; and the visions of my head troubled me?*[81]

28. Who is not frightened, hearing David say: *God hath spoken once, these two things have I heard, that power belongeth to God, and mercy to Thee, O Lord; for Thou wilt render to every man according to his works?*[82] Again, when Ecclesiastes says: *The end of the discourse—hear its sum: fear God, and keep His commandments, for this is the entire man, for God will bring to judgment every deed, whether good or bad, for what was neglected therein?*[83]

29. Who does not tremble at hearing things of the same sort from the Apostle, who says: *For we must all stand before the judgment seat of Christ, that every one of us may receive reward for things done through his body, whether good or evil?*[84]

Who then will not mourn at our unbelief and at our blindness of soul? For, though we hear all these things, we do not repent and weep bitterly at our own great carelessness and sloth. Jeremias foresaw this and said: *Cursed be he that doth the work of the Lord carelessly.*[85] For if we had consideration for the salvation of our souls, we would tremble at the Lord's word and be eager to follow out His commandments well—and indeed by them we are saved. Yet, when we heard the Lord saying: *Enter ye in at the narrow gate that leadeth to life,* we preferred *the wide and broad way that leads to destruction.*[86] Therefore we hear, when He comes from heaven to judge the living and the dead: *Get from me, you cursed, into everlasting fire, which was prepared for the devil and his angels.*[87]

30. And we hear this, not as having done ill, but as not having cared for the good and the noble nor loved our neighbor. But how shall we endure that day, being thus careless-minded, if also we do evil? Now, *Thou shalt not commit adultery, thou shalt not steal, thou shalt not kill,*[88] and the rest was said to them of old through Moses; but knowing that for a Christian's perfection the observance of these alone is not enough, the Lord said: *Amen I tell you that unless your justice abound more than that of the scribes and Pharisees, you shall not enter into the kingdom of heaven.*[89] Therefore at every turn He prescribed the sanctification of the soul, by which also the body is sanctified, and genuine love for all men. And by both these we are able to attain true love for Him. Likewise He gave Himself to us as a

model until death, and also His disciples, as has so often been said.

31. What defence then will we have on that day, we, who have such an example and are so careless? Jeremias mourned over us, who have received so great a grace and are so careless-minded—rather who are filled with every evil. He said: *Who will give water to my head and a fountain of tears to my eyes? And I will weep day and night for this people.*[90] About ourselves I also hear Moses speaking: *Jacob ate and was filled; and the beloved kicked: he grew fat and thick and gross, he forsook God who made him, and departed from God his savior.*[91] Micheas mourns and says: *Woe is me, my soul! For the pious man is perished out of the earth, and there is none upright among men: everyone afflicts his neighbor with oppression, they ready their hands to evil.*[92] And the Psalmist likewise says about us: *Save me, O Lord, for there is now no saint: truths are diminished from among the children of men,*[93] and the rest.

32. The Apostle also prophetically mourned over us and said: *There is none that doth good, there is not so much as one. Their throat is an open sepulchre, with their tongues they have dealt deceitfully. The venom of asps is under their lips, whose mouth is full of cursing and bitterness; destruction and misery in their ways, and the way of peace they have not known. There is no fear of God before their eyes.*[94] Again therefore, with a look to future things, he writes to Timothy about our present wicked course of life: *Know also this, that in the last days shall come difficult times. Men shall be lovers of themselves, covetous, haughty, proud, blasphemers, disobedient to parents, ungrateful, wicked, without affection, without peace, slanderers, incontinent, savage, with no love of the good, traitors, headlong,*[95] and the rest.

Woe therefore to us, for we have come upon the extreme

of evil. Tell me, who of us has no part in the aforesaid evils? Is not the prophecy fulfilled in us? Are we not all gluttonous? Are we not all lovers of pleasure? Are we not all mad for, and lovers of, material things? Are we not all savages? Are we not all nurturers of wrath? Are we not all bearers of malice? Are we not all traitors to every virtue? Are we not all revilers? Are we not all fond of scoffing? Are we not all hasty and rash? Do we not all hate our brothers? Are we not all puffed up? Are we not all haughty? Are we not all proud? Are we not all vainglorious? Are we not all hypocrites? Are we not all deceitful? Are we not all jealous? Are we not all unruly? Are we not all listless? Are we not all fickle? Are we not all slothful? Are we not all neglectful of the Savior's commandments? Are we not all full of evil? Instead of God's temple have we not become the temple of idols? Instead of dwellings of the Holy Spirit are we not dwellings of evil spirits? Is not our calling upon God the Father make-believe? Instead of sons of God are we not become sons of hell? We, who now bear the great name of Christ, are we not become worse than the Jews? And let no one be vexed at hearing the truth. For transgressors of the law as they were, they said: *We have one Father, even God.* But they heard from the Savior: *You are of your father the devil, and the desires of your father you will to do.*[96]

33. How then can it be that we, transgressors of the commandments as we are, will not hear the like from Him? For indeed the Apostle said that those that are led by the Spirit are sons of God: *For whosoever are led by the Spirit of God*, he says, *they are the sons of God.*[97] How then can we, led by death, be called sons of God? *For the wisdom of the flesh is death.*[98] But those led by the Spirit are manifest in the fruits of the Spirit. So then let us know the fruits

of the Spirit: *For the fruit of the Spirit,* he says, *is charity, joy, peace, patience, benignity, goodness, faith, meekness, continency.*[99] So we have these things in us? Rather, would that we had not all their opposites! How then can we be called sons of God and not rather the contrary? For what is born of a creature is like the creature that begot him. This the Lord makes plain, saying: *That which is born of the Spirit, is spirit.*[100] But we have become flesh, burning with desires contrary to the Spirit, and rightly therefore we hear from Him: *My spirit shall not remain in these men . . . because they are flesh.*[101] How then can we be called Christians, who have nothing at all of Christ in us?

34. Now perhaps someone will say: I have faith and faith in Him is enough for me for salvation. But James contradicts him, saying: *The devils also believe and tremble;*[102] and again: *Faith without works is dead in itself,*[103] as also the works without faith. In what manner then do we believe in Him? Is it that we believe Him about future things, but about transient and present things do not believe Him, and are therefore immersed in material things and live in the flesh, and battle against the Spirit? But those who truly believed Christ and, through the commandments, made Him to dwell wholly within themselves spoke in this fashion: *And I live, now not I; but Christ liveth in me. And that I live now in the flesh: I live in the faith of the Son of God, who loved me, and delivered Himself for me.*[104] For that reason while they were suffering for Him for the salvation of all,[105] as exact imitators of Him and as genuine keepers of His commandments, they said: *We are reviled, and we bless; we are persecuted, and we suffer it; we are blasphemed, and we entreat.*[106] They in fact heard Him say: *Love your enemies, do good to them that hate you. Bless them that curse you, and pray for them that treat you despitefully,*[107] and the

rest. And by their words and deeds Christ, who works in them, was made manifest.

But we, because we do the contrary of all His commandments, are therefore filled with every uncleanness. For this reason we have become, instead of a temple of God, a place of business;[108] and instead of a house of prayer, a den of thieves;[109] instead of a holy nation, a sinful nation;[110] instead of a holy seed, a wicked seed; instead of sons of God, lawless sons, because we have forsaken the commandments of the Lord and serve the evil spirits by our unclean passions, and have provoked the Holy One of Israel.[111]

35. Therefore the great Isaias mourns over us and cries out, for he wants at the same time to help us in our fall, and says: *Why should ye still be smitten, transgressing more and more? Every head in pain, and every heart in grief; from the feet to the head there is no soundness therein. No wound, no weal, no festering bruise is healed; there is no applying of a plaster, nor of oil, nor of bandages.*[112] Then, what follows? *The daughter of Sion shall be left as a covert in a vineyard, and as the hut of a garden-watcher in the cucumber patch, as a city that is besieged.*[113] The Apostle also indicated this desolation of our soul, saying: *And as they liked not to have God in their knowledge, God delivered them up to a reprobate sense, to do those things which are not convenient; being filled with all iniquity, evil, wickedness, avarice, full of envy, murder, contention, deceit, malignity, whisperers, detractors, hateful to God, contumelious, proud, haughty, inventors of evil things, disobedient to parents, foolish, dissolute, without affection, without fidelity, without mercy; who, having known the justice of God that they who do such things are worthy of death, not only do them but consent to them that do them.*[114] Therefore *God delivered them up to disgraceful passions to dishonor their*

own bodies with one another.[115] And what follows on this? *The wrath of God,* he says, *is revealed from heaven against all ungodliness and injustice of men,*[116] and the rest.

36. The Lord also declared this desolation of soul saying: *Jerusalem, Jerusalem, that killeth the prophets and stoneth them that are sent unto her, how often would I have gathered together thy children as the hen doth gather her chickens under her wings, and thou wouldst not! Behold, your house is left desolate.*[117] Again, seeing us would-be monks performing corporal services only, but despising the spiritual, and thereby puffed up, Isaias said: *Hear the word of the Lord, ye rulers of Sodom, attend to the law of God, ye people of Gomorrha. What to me is the multitude of your sacrifices? I am full of holocausts of rams; the fat of lambs, the blood of bulls and goats I do not want. For who required these things at your hands? Walk not any more in my courts. If you offer fine wheat flour, it is vain; incense is an abomination to me. Your new moons and sabbaths and great day I will not abide. My soul hateth your fast and rest from work and your festivals. You are become a surfeit to me; no longer will I endure. When you stretch forth your hands to me, I will turn away my eyes from you: and when you multiply prayer, I will not hear you.* And why is this? *For your hands,* he says, *are full of blood;*[118] for, in fact, *whosoever hateth his brother is a murderer.*[119] Therefore any ascetic life or practice that is without love is a stranger to God.

37. For this reason Isaias rebuked also our hypocrisy, saying from afar: *This people honors me with their lips, but their heart is far from me, and in vain do they reverence me,*[120] and the rest. And what Our Lord said of those unhappy Pharisees, I hear also of ourselves, who are the modern hypocrites, recipients of so much grace yet worse disposed than they. Or is it not true that *we bind heavy and insupport-*

able burdens, and lay them on men's shoulders; yet with a finger of our own we will not move them?[121] Is it not so that *we do all our works to be seen of men?*[122] Is it not so that *we love the first places at feasts, and the first chairs in the synagogues, and to be called by men, Rabbi,* Rabbi?[123] And if they are not generous in giving us these things, we fight with them till death. And is it not so that *we have taken away the key of knowledge* and *shut the kingdom of heaven against men,* ourselves neither entering nor permitting them to enter?[124] And do we not *go round about the sea and the land to make one proselyte; and when he is made, we make him the child of hell twofold more than ourselves?*[125] Or is it not so that we are *blind guides, who strain out a gnat, and swallow a camel?*[126] Is it not so that we also *make clean the outside of the cup and of the dish, but within we are full of rapine and* avarice—more precisely—*of incontinence?*[127] Is it not so that we also *tithe mint and rue and every herb; and pass over judgment and the charity of God?*[128] And is it not so that we too are *as sepulchres that appear not, outwardly indeed appearing to men just, but inwardly full of hypocrisy* and iniquity *and* every uncleanness?[129] And is it not so that we also build the tombs of the martyrs and decorate the monuments of the Apostles and are like to those that killed them?[130]

Who then will not lament over us who are of such dispositions? Who will not bewail this great captivity of ours? Therefore we, noble sons of God, are esteemed as earthen vessels. Therefore the gold is become dim; the fine silver is changed.[131] Therefore we, Nazarites of Sion who were brighter than snow, are become like Ethiopians; those that were whiter than milk are blackened more than ink. Therefore our beauty is made darker than soot.[132] We that were nourished in luxury covered ourselves with dung; our iniquity has grown greater than the iniquities of

Sodom.[133] Therefore children of the day and of light, we have become children of the night and of darkness.[134] Children of the kingdom, we have become children of hell. *Sons of the most High, we shall die like men and shall fall like one of the princes.*[135] Therefore were we *delivered into the hands of wicked enemies,* I mean wild devils, *and* to a *king unjust and most evil beyond the whole world*[136]—that is, to their prince, because we sinned and did wickedly, transgressing the commandments of the Lord our God, *treading under foot the Son of God* and *esteeming the blood of the testament unclean.*[137]

But[138] *deliver us not up forever for Thy name's sake,* Lord, *and scatter not Thy covenant. And take not away thy mercy from us*[139] for Thy pity's sake, our Father who art in heaven, and because of the compassion of Thy only-begotten Son[140] and because of the mercy of Thy Holy Spirit. *Remember not our former iniquities,* but *let Thy mercies speedily prevent us, for we are become exceeding poor. Help us, O God, our Savior. For the glory of Thy name, O Lord, deliver us; and forgive us our sins for Thy name's sake, Lord.*[141] Be mindful of our first fruits which Thy only-begotten Son took of us out of kindness and holds for us in heaven, that He may bestow on us a firm hope of salvation and that we may not, because of despair, become worse; for the sake of His precious blood, which He shed for the life of the world; for the sake of His holy Apostles and martyrs, who shed their own blood for His name; for the sake of the holy Prophets and Fathers and Patriarchs, who strove to please Thy holy name. *Despise not our supplication,* Lord, *and cast us not off to the end.*[142] *For it is* not on *our justifications* that we have relied, *but* on *Thy mercy,*[143] by which Thou dost preserve our race. We beseech and entreat Thy goodness that the mystery, which Thy only-begotten Son effected for our salvation, may not be our judgment, *nor cast us away from Thy face.* Abominate not our unworthiness, but *have mercy on us according to Thy great mercy and according to the multitude of Thy tender mercies,* take away our sins,[144] that, coming before Thy holy glory uncondemned, we may merit the protection of Thy only-begotten Son and not be reprobate, as slaves, evil in their sins. Yea, Master, almighty Lord, hear our supplication, for we know no other but Thee. We name Thy name, for Thou art *He who worketh all in all,*[145] and from Thee we all seek aid. *Look down, Lord, from heaven, and behold from the habitation of Thy holy glory. Where is Thy zeal and Thy strength? Where is the multitude of Thy mercy and of Thy tender mercies,* that Thou hast permitted our ruin? *For Thou art our Father, as Abraham knew us not and Israel had no knowledge of us; but Thou, Lord, our Father, deliver us,* because *from the beginning Thy holy name is upon us* and Thy only-begotten Son's and Thy Holy Spirit's. *Why hast Thou made us to err, O Lord, from Thy way?* Punish us not with the rod of Thy judgments. *Why hast Thou hardened our heart, that we should not fear Thee?* Hast Thou abandoned us to the self-rule of error? *Convert, O Lord, Thy servants,* for the sake of Thy holy Church, for the sake of all Thy saints of old, *that we may inherit but a little of Thy holy mountain. Our adversaries have trodden down Thy sanctuary. We are become as in the beginning, when Thou didst not rule over us, nor was Thy name called upon us.*[146]

38. *If Thou wouldst open heaven, the mountains will quake before Thee; and they will melt away as wax in the presence of fire; and fire will burn up the adversaries; and Thy name will be formidable to the adversaries. When Thou dost deeds of glory, the mountains will quake before Thee. From of old we have not heard, nor have our eyes seen a God but Thee, and*

*Thy works which Thou wilt do for them that await mercy.
These will meet with them that do justice, and they will
remember Thy ways. Behold Thou art angered and we have
sinned.*[147] Rather, we have sinned and Thou art angered.
*Therefore have we erred and are all become as one unclean; all
our justice is as the rag of a menstruous woman. And we have
fallen as leaves because of our iniquities; thus the wind will take
us away. There is none that calleth upon Thy name or remem-
bereth to take hold on Thee. And Thou hast hid Thy face from
us and delivered us over because of our sins. And now, O Lord,
Thou art our Father, and we are clay, all the work of Thy
hands. Be not exceeding angered at us and remember not our sins
forever. And now, behold, we all are Thy people. Sion, the city
of Thy sanctuary, is become a desert. Jerusalem is become a
desert. The house of our sanctuary is a curse. The glory which
our fathers blessed is burnt with fire, and all our glorious things
are fallen together. And with all these things Thou didst bear,
O Lord, and hold Thy peace and humiliate us exceedingly.*[148]

39. These things, indeed, befell Thy former people as
type and figure;[149] but now they are actually fulfilled in
us. *And we are become a reproach to our neighbors* the demons:
a scorn and derision to them that are round about us.[150] But
look down from heaven, and behold and save us for the
sake of Thy holy name. Make known to us the tricks of
our adversaries and deliver us from their devices. Turn
not Thy help away from us, for we are not sufficiently
strong to overcome opposition, but Thou art powerful to
save from every adversity. Save us, O Lord, from the
difficulties of this world according to Thy kindness, that
we may pass over the sea of life with a pure conscience and
take our stand untainted and incorrupt before Thy dreadful
judgment seat; and then may we be judged worthy of
eternal life!'

9

40. After having heard all this and being deeply struck with compunction, the brother, in tears, said to the old man: 'From what I see, Father, there is no hope of salvation left me. *For my iniquities are gone over my head.*[151] Yet, I entreat you, tell me what ought I to do?'

Then the old man answered and said: '*With men salvation is impossible; but with God all things are possible,*[152] as the Lord Himself has said. Therefore *let us come before His presence in contrition and thanksgiving; let us adore and fall down and weep before the Lord that made us, for He is our God.*[153] And let us listen to Him say by Isaias: *When you return and moan, then you will be saved.*[154] And again: *Is the hand of the Lord without power to save, or His ear heavy so as not to hear? But our sins make a division between ourselves and God; and because of our sins He has turned His face away, that He should not have mercy.*[155] Wherefore He says: *Wash yourselves, be clean; take vice away from your souls before my eyes; cease from your vices. Learn to do well: seek judgment, relieve the oppressed, judge the fatherless, and vindicate the widow. Then come and let us hold converse together, saith the Lord. And if your sins be as crimson, I will make them white as snow; and if they be as scarlet, I will make them white like wool. And if you be willing and will hearken to me, you shall eat the good things of the land, for the mouth of the Lord hath spoken it.*[156] And again through Joel: *Be converted to me with all your heart, in fasting, and in weeping, and in mourning. Rend your hearts, and not your garments. For merciful and gracious is the Lord, and ready to repent of evils.*[157] And to Ezechiel He says: *O son of man, say to the house of Israel: Thus you have spoken, saying: our errors and our iniquities are upon us, and we pine away in them. How then can we live? Say to them: As I live, saith the Lord, I desire not the death of the wicked, but that he turn from his way and live.*

Turn ye, turn ye from your way; and why will you die, O house of Israel?[158]

The third book of Kings tells the following and so shows the excess of God's kindness. When Achab was in Naboth's vineyard—which he had possessed himself of by killing him at the instance of Jezabel—he heard the words of Elias: *Thus saith the Lord: Thou hast slain, and thou hast taken possession. In this place wherein the dogs have licked the blood of Naboth, there the dogs shall lick thy blood. And dogs will devour Jezabel in the outwork of Israel.*[159] *And when Achab had heard these words, he rent his garments, and put haircloth upon his flesh, and fasted and slept in sackcloth. And the word of the Lord came to Elias, saying: Behold, Achab has felt compunction before me. I will not bring evil in his days.*[160] And David says: *I have acknowledged my iniquity, and my sin I have not concealed. I said: I confessed against myself my iniquity to the Lord, and Thou hast forgiven the impiety of my heart. For this shall every one that is holy pray to Thee in a seasonable time. And in a flood of many waters, they will not come nigh unto Him.*[161] And in the Gospel the Lord says: *Do penance, for the kingdom of heaven is at hand.*[162] When Peter inquires: *How many times a day, if my brother sins against me, shall I forgive him? Till seven times?* He who is good by nature and of incomparable kindness answers him: *I say not to thee, till seven times; but till seventy times seven.*[163] What can be the equal of this goodness? The match for this loving-kindness?

41. We, then, who have knowledge of the fear of the Lord, yes, and from the Old and New Testament alike, knowledge of His gentleness and loving-kindness: let us turn back with our whole heart. And why should we perish, brothers? Sinners, let us cleanse our hands; double-minded, let us purify our hearts; let us bewail, let us

mourn, let us weep because of our sins. Let us quit our vices; let us trust the mercies of the Lord. Let us fear His threats; let us keep His commandments. Let us love one another with our whole heart. Let us say 'Brothers' even to those who hate and abominate us, that the Lord's name be glorified and manifest in its joyfulness. Let us, who are harrassed one by the other, grant pardon one to another, since we are all warred upon by the common enemy. Let us withstand our bad thoughts, calling upon God as our ally; and let us banish from ourselves the evil and unclean spirits. Let us subject the flesh to the spirit, mortifying and enslaving it by every sort of ill-treatment.[164] *Let us cleanse ourselves from all defilement of the flesh and of the spirit.*[165] Let us rouse one another to emulation in charity and good works.[166] Let us not envy one another; nor, grown envious, become savage. Rather let us show sympathy for one another and by humility heal one another. Let us not rail nor jeer at one another; *for we are members one of another.*[167]

Let us cast from us negligence and sloth and stand manfully in strife against the spirits of wickedness. And *we have an advocate with the Father, Jesus Christ the just; and He is the propitiation for our sins.*[168] And let us beseech Him with a pure heart, with our whole soul, and He will forgive us our sins. *For the Lord is nigh to all them that call upon Him in truth.*[169] Therefore He says: *Offer to God the sacrifice of praise, and pay thy vows to the most High. And call upon me in the day of thy trouble. I will deliver thee, and thou shalt glorify me.*[170] And so again Isaias: *Loose every band of wickedness, undo the knots of forced contracts, dismiss the broken with pardon, and tear up every wicked paper. Break thy bread to the hungry and bring the poor without shelter into thy house. When thou shalt see one naked, cover him, and despise not the fellows of thy seed. Then shall thy light break forth as the morning, and thy remedies shall speedily arise, and thy justice shall go before thy face, and the glory of the Lord shall surround thee.* And what follows? *Then shalt thou call, and the Lord shall hear; whilst thou art yet speaking, He shall say, Here I am. Then shall thy light rise up in the darkness, and thy darkness shall be as the noonday. And God will be with thee continually and thou shalt be filled as thy soul desires.*[171] You see how in loosing every band of wickedness from our hearts and in undoing every knot of contracts forced for grudges, and in hastening to do good for our neighbor with our whole soul—you see how we are illumined with the light of knowledge, and freed from the disgrace of passions, and filled with every virtue; and are illumined by God's glory and freed from every ignorance;[172] and praying for things after Christ's mind, we are heard and shall have God with us continually and are filled with godly desire.

42. Let us then love one another and be loved by God; let us be patient with one another and He will be patient with our sins. Let us not render evil for evil,[173] and we shall not receive our due for our sins. For we find the forgiveness of our trespasses in the forgiving of our brothers; and the mercy of God is hidden in mercifulness to our neighbor. Therefore the Lord said: *Forgive, and you shall be forgiven.*[174] And: *If you will forgive men their offences, your heavenly Father will forgive you also your offences.*[175] And again: *Blessed are the merciful, for they shall obtain mercy.*[176] And: *With what measure you mete, it shall be measured to you again.*[177] See, the Lord bestowed on us the method of salvation and has given us eternal power to become sons of God.[178] So finally then our salvation is in our will's grasp.[179]

43. Therefore let us give ourselves entirely to the Lord, that we may receive Him again entire. Let us become gods through Him, for on that account He became man, who is by nature God and Master. Let us obey Him and He will without trouble vindicate us against our enemies. *If my people had heard me,* He says, *if Israel had walked in my ways, I should soon have humbled their enemies, and laid my hand on them that troubled them.*[180]

Let us place all our hope in Him alone. And let us cast all our care on Him alone, He will deliver us from every trouble, and all our life He will support us.[181] Let us love every man sincerely, but put our hope in none; because insofar as the Lord keeps us, all friends also respect us and no enemy can do anything to us. But when the Lord deserts us, then every friend deserts too and every enemy grows strong against us. Even more, he that relies on himself will fall a mighty fall, while he that fears the Lord will be exalted. Therefore David said: *For I will not trust in my bow, neither shall my sword save me. For Thou hast saved us from them that afflict us, and hast put them to shame that hate us.*[182]

44. Let us not suffer thoughts that belittle our sins, that conjecture that already they have their forgiveness. For against these the Lord safeguarded us, saying: *Beware of false prophets, who will come to you in sheep's clothing, but inwardly they are ravening wolves.*[183] For so long as our mind is beset by sin, we have not attained forgiveness; for we have not yet produced fruit worthy of penance. Fruit of penance is the soul's detachment;[184] detachment, the wiping out of sin. And we do not yet have perfect detachment when we are sometimes beset by passions, sometimes not. We have not therefore perfectly attained forgiveness of sins. For we were freed by holy baptism from ancestral

sin;[185] but from the sin we had the effrontery to commit after baptism we are freed by penance.

45. Let us then truly do penance, so that, freed from passions, we may attain forgiveness of sins. Let us despise transient things that we may not, while we fight with men on their account, transgress the commandment to love and fall from God's love. *Let us walk in the spirit, and we shall not fulfil the lust of the flesh.*[186] Let us watch and be sober; let us at last cast off the sleep of sloth. Let us emulate the holy athletes of the Savior. Let us imitate their combats, *forgetting the things that are behind, and stretching forth to those that are before.*[187] Let us imitate their tireless course, their flaming eagerness, their perseverance in continence, their holiness in chastity, their nobility in patience, their endurance in long-suffering, their pity in compassion, their imperturbed meekness, their warmth in zeal, their unfeignedness in love, their sublimity in lowliness, their plainness in poverty, their manliness, their kindness, their clemency. Let us not be overturned by pleasures, let us not be softened by thoughts, let us not stain our conscience. *Let us follow peace with all men, and holiness, without which no man shall see the Lord.*[188]

And in addition, brothers,[189] let us flee the world and the world's ruler.[190] Let us leave the flesh and carnal things. Let us run on to heaven; there let us have our citizen rights. Let us imitate the divine Apostle. Let us lay hold on the author of life, let us rejoice in the fountain of life. With the angels let us make chorus, with the archangels let us hymn our Lord Jesus Christ; to whom be glory and power together with the Father and the Holy Spirit, now and ever, and for endless ages. Amen.'

THE FOUR CENTURIES ON CHARITY

PROLOGUE

See, in addition to the discussion on the *Ascetic Life*, I have sent this one on charity to Your Reverence, Father Elpidius, arranged in four sets of a hundred according to the number of the Gospels. While it does not perhaps come up to your expectation, still it does not fall short of my ability. Your Holiness should be aware that these are not the work of my own thought; rather I went through the writings of the holy Fathers and selected whatever might turn the mind to my subject. I have recapitulated many things in a few lines that they may be seen at a glance, for ease in memorizing. These I send to Your Sanctity with the request that you read them with kindly forbearance and hunt only profit in them, overlooking the homeliness of the style, and pray for our limited ability that is barren of any spiritual profit.

I urge you not to take what I have written as a troublesome puzzle: I have merely fulfilled a command. I say this, because today we are many who get involved in words; whereas those who give or receive instruction by deeds as well, are few indeed. Rather, do give your best attention to each chapter. Nor will they all, as I think, be readily understood by everybody; on the contrary, for a great number of them will require much scrutiny, even though they seem to be simply expressed. Perhaps something useful for the soul will come out of them; but this will wholly come from God's grace to him who reads with a simple mind, with the fear of God, and with charity. But for him who takes up this or any other work whatsoever, not for the sake of spiritual profit but of ferreting out phrases serving to revile the author, while setting up his own conceited self as wiser, there will never come any profit of any sort.

THE FIRST CENTURY

1. Charity is a good disposition of the soul, according to which one prefers no creature to the knowledge of God. It is impossible to attain a lasting possession of this charity if one has any attachment to earthly things.[1]

2. Charity springs from the calm of detachment, detachment from hope in God, hope from patience and long-suffering; and these from all-embracing self-mastery; self-mastery from fear of God, fear of God from faith in the Lord.[2]

3. He that has faith in the Lord fears punishment; he that fears punishment masters his passions; he that masters his passions endures hardships with patience; he that endures hardships with patience will have hope in God; hope in God separates the mind from every earthly attachment; the mind[3] thus separated will have charity towards God.

4. He who loves God prefers knowledge of Him to all things made by Him; and by desire ceaselessly devotes himself to it.

5. If all things have been made by God and for God, He is nobler than all the things made by Him; he who deserts God, the incomparably nobler, and devotes himself to inferior things shows that he prefers before God the things made by Him.

6. He who has his mind fixed upon charity for God scorns all visible things and even his body[4] as something alien.

7. If the soul is nobler than the body and God incomparably nobler than the world He made, he that prefers body to soul and the world to God who made it differs in no way from idolaters.

8. He that turns his mind from charity and constant attention towards God and binds it over to some sensible thing—this is the one that prefers body to soul and created things to God their maker.

9. If the life of the mind is the illumination of knowledge; and this springs from charity towards God—beautifully is it said: Nothing is greater than divine charity.[4a]

10. When the mind by the burning love[5] of its charity for God is out of itself,[6] then it has no feeling at all for itself nor for any creatures. For, illumined by the divine and infinite light, it has no feeling for anything that is made by Him, as the eye of the senses has no perception of the stars when the sun is risen.

11. All the virtues help the mind towards the burning of divine love; more than them all, pure prayer. For by this winging its way to God, the mind gets outside all things.

12. When through charity the mind is ravished[7] by divine knowledge, and, outside of creatures, has a feeling of the divine infinity,[8] then, as divine Isaias explains, shocked into a sense of its own lowliness, it says with conviction the words of the prophet: *Woe is me, because I am struck at heart, because, being man and having unclean lips, I live in the midst of a people with unclean lips and the king the Lord of Sabaoth I have seen with my eyes.*[9]

13. He that loves God cannot help loving also every man as himself, even though the passions of those not yet purified disgust him. So then as he sees their conversion and betterment, he rejoices with a boundless and unspeakable joy.[10]

14. Impure is the impassioned soul, filled with notions of cupidity and hate.

15. Who sees a trace of hate in his own heart, for any fault soever, towards any man soever, is quite alien from charity towards God; because charity towards God in no way suffers hate towards man.

16. He that loves me, saith the Lord, will keep my commandments; and *this is my commandment that you love one another*.[11] He therefore who does not love his neighbor does not keep the commandment. Nor is he that does not keep the commandment able to love the Lord.

17. Happy the man who is able to love all men equally.[12]

18. Happy the man who is attached to no corruptible or transitory thing.

19. Happy the mind that has gone beyond all things and delights unceasingly in the divine beauty.

20. He that takes forethought for the flesh in its lusts[13] and, because of transitory things, bears grudges against his neighbor—such a man worships the creature instead of the Creator.[14]

21. He that keeps his body apart from pleasure and disease has it as a fellow helper in the service of better things.

22. He that flees all worldly desires places himself above every worldly grief.[15]

23. He that loves God most certainly also loves his neighbor. Such a man cannot keep money, but, God-like, distributes it, giving to each one in need.[16]

24. He that in imitation of God does almsdeeds knows no difference between evil and good, just and unjust, in regard to the needs of the body, but distributes equally to all according to their need, even though for his good intention he prefers the virtuous to the bad.[17]

25. God, who is by nature good and without passion, loves all alike as His handiwork; yet the virtuous He glorifies as one who for his good will is made intimate with Himself, while, because of His goodness, He shows mercy on the bad, with chastisements in this world to convert him. So also he, who by good will is good and without passion, loves all men alike—the virtuous because of his nature and good intention, the bad because of his nature and that fellow feeling which causes him to show mercy upon him as upon one without sense and wandering in darkness.

26. Not only by the distribution of money is a charitable intention made manifest; no, far rather by the distribution of the word of God[18] and physical service of others.

27. He that genuinely renounces worldly affairs and unfeignedly serves his neighbor out of charity, quickly is freed from every passion and is made partaker of divine charity and knowledge.

28. He that has made divine charity his possession has no labor in following after the Lord his God, as the divine Jeremias says;[19] rather, he bears nobly every hardship, every rebuke and insult, thinking no evil at all of anyone.

29. When you are insulted by someone or made of no account in some affair, then beware of angry thoughts lest by grief they remove you from charity and place you in the region of hate.[20]

30. Whenever you labor under insult or dishonor,

realize that you are greatly indebted; for that dishonor, in God's dispensation, drives vainglory out of you.[21]

31. As memory of fire does not warm the body, so faith without charity does not effect the illumination of knowledge in the soul.[22]

32. As the light of the sun draws the healthy eye to itself, so also the knowledge of God naturally by means of love attracts the pure mind to itself.[23]

33. The mind is pure which is removed from ignorance and is lit up by the divine light.

34. That soul is pure which is freed from passions and gladdened continually by divine charity.

35. A blameworthy passion is a movement of the soul contrary to nature.[24]

36. The calm of detachment is a peaceful condition of the soul in which it is with difficulty moved to vice.[25]

37. He that has by zeal obtained the fruits of charity is not moved from it, though he suffer thousands of ills. Of this let Stephen, Christ's disciple, and those like him, persuade you; and the Savior Himself praying to the Father for His murderers and asking forgiveness of Him as for men acting in ignorance.[26]

38. If long-suffering and kindness belong to charity,[27] the angry man and evildoer is clearly made alien to charity; but being alien to charity is being alien to God, since *God is love.*[28]

39. Do not say—so the divine Jeremias[29]—that you are the Lord's temple. Nor say: Mere faith in our Lord Jesus Christ can save me. For this is ineffective unless you also possess charity for Him through good works. As to mere believing: *the devils also believe and tremble.*[30]

40. The work of love is the intentional doing of good

to one's neighbor and long-suffering and patience; also the use of things in due measure.

41. He that loves God does not grieve, nor is he grieved at anyone because of passing things; with one grief only does he grieve and is he grieved—that saving grief with which the blessed Paul was grieved and grieved the Corinthians.[31]

42. He that loves God leads an angelic life on earth, fasting and keeping watches, singing the psalter and praying, and always thinking good of every man.[32]

43. If a man desires something he of course strives to attain it. Now of all good and desirable things the divine is incomparably good and desirable. How great then is the zeal we should show so as to attain this which is of itself good and desirable![33]

44. Do not stain your flesh with shameful actions; do not defile your soul with evil thoughts: then the peace of God will come upon you, that peace which brings charity.[34]

45. Afflict your flesh with lack of food and with vigils; give yourself unsparingly to psalmody and prayer; then holiness in chasteness will come upon you, the holiness that brings charity.[35]

46. He to whom divine knowledge is granted, and who, through charity, has attained its illumination, will never be blown about by the spirit of vainglory; but he to whom this is not yet granted is easily carried away by it. If then such a man in all that he does will look to God, as to Him for whom he does everything, he will, with His help, easily escape such a spirit.[36]

47. He that has not yet reached divine knowledge activated by charity thinks great things of his God-like doings. But he to whom it is given to attain this says

with deliberation the words which the patriarch Abraham spoke when he was granted the divine manifestation: *I am earth and ashes.*[37]

48. He that fears the Lord has ever as his companion humility, and through its suggestions is brought to divine charity and thanksgiving. For he is mindful of his former worldly ways, of his various mistakes, of the temptations that befell him from his youth; and of how the Lord delivered him from all these things and transferred him from this life of passion to a godly life. With fear then he receives even charity and ever gives thanks in deep humility to the benefactor and director of our life.[38]

49. Do not soil your mind by tolerating thoughts of concupiscence and anger; otherwise, falling from pure prayer, you will fall in with the spirit of listlessness.[39]

50. Then does the mind lose its free openness[39a] with God when it indulges in evil and filthy thoughts.

51. When the senseless man, led by his passions, is moved and stirred up by anger, he most absurdly will strive to flee from the brethren; when at another time he is heated by concupiscence, he thinks differently and hastens to meet them. The prudent man in either case does just the opposite: in time of anger, he first cuts away the causes of disturbance and then keeps from grieving the brethren; in time of concupiscence he controls every irrational impulse and association.[40]

52. In time of temptation do not leave your monastery; but nobly bear the waves of thoughts, especially those of grief and listlessness. Thus providentially proved by tribulations you will have firm hope in God. But should you leave, you will be held discredited, effeminate, unstable.

53. If you wish not to fall off from God-like charity, neither allow your brother to go to sleep with grief

against you, nor do you go to sleep grieved against him; but—Go, *be reconciled to thy brother and come, offer* to Christ with a pure conscience, in protracted prayer, *the gift* of charity.[41]

54. If he who has all the gifts of the Spirit, but not charity, is in no way benefited, as the divine Apostle has it:[42] how great zeal should we not show so as to possess it!

55. If *charity works no ill to one's neighbor,*[43] he that envies his brother, grieves at his good name, smears his reputation with jibes, or in any way maliciously plots against him—how does he do anything but render himself alien to charity and liable to eternal judgment?

56. If *charity is the fulfilling of the law,*[43] he that bears grudges against his brother, fixes pitfalls for him, and curses him and rejoices at his fall, how is he anything but a transgressor and worthy of eternal punishment?

57. If *he that slanders his brother and judges his brother slanders and judges the law*[44]—and the law of Christ is charity: how does the slanderer do anything but fall from the love of Christ and make himself the cause of his own eternal punishment?

58. Give no ear to the slanderer's talk nor let your talk run on in the fault-finder's hearing, by readily speaking and listening to things against your neighbor; otherwise you will fall from divine charity and be found a foreigner to eternal life.

59. Take no abuse offered your father nor encourage one who dishonors him, lest the Lord be angered at your deeds and destroy you from the land of the living.

60. Stop the mouth of him that slanders in your hearing, lest you sin doubly with him—both by accustoming yourself to this deadly vice and by not restraining him from babbling against his neighbor.

61. *But I say to you*, says the Lord, *love your enemies; do good to them that hate you; pray for them that abuse you.*[45] Why did He command all this? That He might free you from hate, grief, anger, grudges, and that He might grant you the greatest of all possessions, perfect charity—which cannot be had except by the man who loves all men equally in imitation of God[46] who loves all men equally and *wills* them *to be saved and to come to the knowledge of truth.*[47]

62. *But I say to you not to resist evil; but if one strike thee on thy right cheek, turn to him also the other; and if a man will contend with thee in judgment, and take away thy coat, let go thy cloak also unto him; and whosoever will force thee one mile, go with him other two.*[48] Why? That He might keep you unangered, undisturbed, ungrieved; that He might chasten him through your forbearance, and, good as He is, bring you both under the yoke of charity.

63. Of the things that we have once experienced, we carry about with us the voluptuous images. The man that conquers these voluptuous images quite scorns the things of which they are images. In fact, the fight against memories[49] is as much the more difficult than the fight against things as sinning in thought is easier than sinning in deed.

64. Of the passions some are of the body, some of the soul. Those of the body have their origin in the body; but those of the soul from things outside. Charity and self-control cut both of them back, the first those of the soul, the other those of the body.[50]

65. Of the passions it happens that some belong to the irascible, some to the concupiscible part of the soul. But both are moved by means of the senses. And they are then moved when the soul is separated from charity and self-control.

10

66. The passions of the irascible part of the soul are naturally harder to oppose than those of the concupiscible. Therefore a better remedy against them was given by the Lord, the command of charity.[51]

67. The rest of the passions lay hold of either the irascible part of the soul or the concupiscible only, or also of the rational, for instance, forgetfulness and ignorance; but listlessness, grasping all the powers of the soul, excites practically all the passions together. Therefore it is more burdensome than all the rest of the passions. Beautifully then the Lord has given remedy against it, saying: *In your patience possess your souls.*[52]

68. Never strike one of the brothers, especially not without reason, lest sometime not bearing the trial, he may go away, and you will never escape the reproof of your conscience, always bringing you grief in the time of prayer and driving your mind away from the divine familiarity.[53]

69. Have nothing to do with suspicions or people that would be the occasion of scandal for you in regard to anyone. For they that take scandal in any way from things that come to pass, intentionally or unintentionally, do not know the way of peace that leads the lovers of the knowledge of God through charity to that knowledge.

70. He does not yet have charity perfectly who is still moved by the dispositions of men, as when he loves one and hates another, for this reason or for that; or even, now loving now hating the same man for the same causes.

71. Perfect charity does not split up the one nature of men according to their various dispositions; but always looking to that nature, loves all men equally, the zealous as friends; the bad as enemies. It does them good and is patient and puts up with the things they do. It reckons no

evil at all but suffers for them, if opportunity offers, in order that it may even make them friends, if possible; if not, it does not fall away from its own intention as it always manifests the fruits of equal charity for all men. Therefore too Our Lord and God Jesus Christ, manifesting His charity for us, suffered for the whole of mankind and granted equally to all the hope of resurrection, though each individual makes himself fit either for glory or for punishment.[54]

72. He who does not scorn glory and dishonor, wealth and povery, pleasure and grief, does not yet possess perfect charity. For perfect charity does not only scorn these things, but also this passing life itself and death.

73. Listen to what those who have been granted perfect charity say: *Who shall separate us from the charity of Christ? Shall tribulation? or distress? or persecution? or famine? or nakedness? or danger? or the sword? As it is written: For Thy sake we are put to death all the day long. We are accounted as sheep for the slaughter. But in all these things we more than conquer through Him who has loved us. For I am sure that neither death, nor life, nor angels, nor principalities, nor powers, nor things present, nor things to come, nor height, nor depth, nor any other creature shall be able to separate us from the charity of God, which is in Christ Jesus Our Lord.*[55]

74. And concerning charity for our neighbor, hear again what they say: *I speak the truth in Christ, I lie not, my conscience also bearing me witness in the Holy Spirit: that I have great sadness and continual sorrow in my heart. For I would wish myself to be anathema from Christ for my brethren, who are my kinsmen according to the flesh, who are Israelites—* and the rest.[56] And similarly Moses[57] and the other saints.

75. He that does not scorn glory and pleasure, and avarice which increases them and exists because of them,

cannot cut away the occasions of anger. But he who does not cut them away cannot attain perfect charity.[58]

76. Humility and the bearing of evil free a man from every sin; the one by checking the passions of the soul, the other those of the body. That he did this, the blessed David makes clear in one of his pleas to God: *Look upon my humility and my labor; and forgive me all my sins.*[59]

77. Through the commandments the Lord makes detached those that carry them out; through the divine doctrines He bestows on them the illumination of knowledge.

78. All doctrines are concerned either with God, or with things visible and invisible, or with providence and judgment in their regard.[60]

79. Alms heal the irascible part of the soul; fasting abates the concupiscible; prayer purifies the mind and prepares for the contemplation of creation. For the powers of the soul the Lord has also granted us the commandments.[61]

80. *Learn of me*, He says, *because I am meek and humble of heart*[62]—and the rest. Meekness keeps the temper unperturbed; humility frees the mind from arrogance and vainglory.[63]

81. There is a twofold fear of God: the one takes its rise in us from threats of punishment; because of it self-control, patience, hope in God, and detachment—and from this comes charity—are engendered in us in due order. The other is joined with charity itself and constantly produces reverence in the soul, lest because of the bold freedom of charity it come to contempt for God.[64]

82. The first fear perfect charity casts out of the soul; for the soul possessing it is no longer afraid of punishment. The second fear it always has joined with it, as was said. With the first fear the following passages agree: *By the fear*

of the Lord every one declineth from evil. And: *The beginning of wisdom is fear of the Lord.*[65] With the second, the following: *The fear of the Lord is holy, enduring for ever and ever;* and: *There is no want to them that fear Him.*[66]

83. *Put to death your members which are upon earth: fornication, uncleanness, lust, evil concupiscence, and covetousness—and the rest.*[67] He names the care of the flesh *earth;* he calls actual sinning *fornication;* he characterizes consent as *uncleanness;* passionate thoughts he names *lust;* the mere acceptance of the concupiscent thought *evil concupiscence;* the source and propagator of passion he designates as *covetousness.* All these things as members of the *wisdom of the flesh*[68] the divine Apostle bids us to put to death.

84. First the memory brings a mere thought to the mind; and when this remains for a while, passion is roused; and when this is not removed, it sways the mind to consent; and when this is given, the actual sinning finally comes about. Therefore that wisest of Apostles, writing to gentile converts, bids them remove first of all the sinful action; then, backtracking, to end up with the cause. The cause is, as has already been said, that source and propagator of passion—covetousness. And I think here[69] it signifies gluttony, which is the mother and nurse of fornication. For covetousness is not only evil as regards money, but also in regard to food; just as self-control is not only virtuous as regards food, but also as regards money.[70]

85. As a sparrow that is tied by the foot tries to fly but is dragged to the earth by the cord that holds it, so the mind that does not yet possess detachment, when it flies to knowledge of heavenly things, is drawn down by its passions and dragged to earth.

86. When a mind is perfectly freed from the passions,

then it travels straight on to the contemplation of creatures, making its way to the knowledge of the Holy Trinity.

87. When the mind is pure and receives ideas of things, it is moved to a spiritual contemplation of them. But when it has become impure from sluggishness, it imagines mere ideas of other things; and getting ideas of men, it turns to bad or shameful thoughts.

88. When in the time of prayer no ideas of the world ever bother the mind, then know that you are not outside the bounds of detachment.

89. When the soul begins to feel its own good health, then it begins to look on its dreams as unperturbing, mere imaginings.

90. Just as the beauty of visible things draws the eyes of sense, so also the knowledge of invisible things draws the pure mind to itself. Invisible things—I mean the bodiless ones.[71]

91. It is a great thing not to be drawn by things; but it is greater by far to remain detached from the thought of them. Therefore with thoughts the demons put up a harder fight against us than with things.

92. He that has successfully cultivated the virtues and is enriched with knowledge, seeing things consequently clear in their nature, both does and considers everything according to right reason and is misled in no way. For from a duly reasonable or unreasonable use of things we are made either virtuous or bad.[72]

93. A sign of consummate detachment is that the ideas of things always arising in the heart, are mere thoughts, alike during the waking hours and in sleep.[73]

94. Through the doing of the commandments the mind puts off the passions; through the spiritual contemplation

of the visible creation, concupiscent thoughts of things; through knowledge of the invisible creation, the contemplation of the visible; and this latter it puts off through knowledge of the Holy Trinity.[74]

95. Just as the sun when it rises and lights up the world manifests both itself and the things lit up by it, so the Sun of justice, rising upon a pure mind, manifests itself and the essences of all the things that have been and will be brought to pass by it.[75]

96. We do not know God from His being but from the magnificence of His handiwork and His providence for creation. Through these as through mirrors we perceive His infinite goodness and wisdom and power.[76]

. 97. The pure mind is to be found either with mere ideas of human things, or in the natural contemplation of the visible creation, or in that of the invisible, or in the light of the Holy Trinity.[77]

98. When the mind is established in contemplation of the visible creation, it examines either the natural essences of things, or the essences that they signify, or else it seeks the cause itself.

99. Settled in the contemplation of the invisible, it seeks both the natural reasons of these things, the cause of their production and whatever is related to these; and also what providence and judgment there is about them.

100. Placed in God, and inflamed with desire, it seeks first of all the grounds of His being, but finds no encouragement in what is proper to Him; for that indeed is impossible and forbidden alike to every created nature. But it does receive encouragement from His attributes—I mean to say from the things that concern His eternity, infinity, and immensity; from His goodness, wisdom, and His power that makes, governs, and judges His creatures.

'And with regard to Him, this only is completely under-standable—infinity';[78] and the very fact of knowing nothing is knowledge surpassing the mind, as the theologians Gregory and Denis have said somewhere.[79]

THE SECOND CENTURY

1. The man that truly loves God certainly prays completely undistracted; and he that certainly prays completely undistracted also truly loves God. But he that has his mind fastened on some earthly thing does not pray completely undistracted; he therefore who has his mind bound to some earthly thing does not love God.[80]

2. The mind that gives its time to some sensible thing certainly experiences some attachment in its regard, as desire or grief or anger or ill will; and unless he scorns that thing, he cannot be freed from that attachment.

3. When the passions control a mind, they bind it over to material things and, moving it away from God, make it to be engrossed in the same. But when charity of God has control, it delivers the mind from the bonds and per-suades it to disregard not alone sensible things, but even our passing life.

4. The work of the commandments is to make the thoughts of things mere thoughts; and of reading[81] and contemplation, to render the mind clean of any material thing or form; and from this there comes undistracted prayer.

5. An active way[82] is not enough so perfectly to free the mind from the passions that it can pray undistracted, unless various spiritual contemplations succeed one another in it. Now the first-mentioned frees the mind only from incontinence and hate; the others take it away from for-

getfulness and ignorance. And thus it will be able to pray
as it ought.

6. There are two supreme states of pure prayer: the one,
for those of the active life; the other, for those of the contemplative. The one comes to the soul from fear of God
and a good hope; the other, from burning divine love
and maximum purification. The signs of the first kind are
these: namely, when a man gathers his mind from all the
thoughts of the world, to make his prayers, as though God
Himself were at his side (as really He is present), without
distraction and undisturbed; of the second, however, that
at the very onset of prayer the mind be rapt by the divine
and infinite light and be conscious neither of itself nor of
any other creature at all, save only of Him who through
charity effects such brightness in it. Then indeed, being
concerned with the properties of God, it receives impressions of Him, pure and limpid.[83]

7. What a man loves that he assuredly clings to and
everything that obstructs his way to it he despises, lest he
be deprived of it; and the man that loves God is concerned
for pure prayer and every passion that obstructs his way
to it he casts out of himself.

8. He that casts out self-love, the mother of the passions,
will easily with God's help put away the others, such as
anger, grief, grudges, and so on. But he that is in the power
of the first is wounded, though against his will, by the
second. Self-love is the passion of attachment for the
body.[84]

9. For these five causes men love one another, whether
it be to their praise or their blame: namely, for God's sake,
as the virtuous man loves everybody and as the man who
is not yet possessed of virtue loves the virtuous man;[85] or
for natural reasons, as parents love their children and vice

versa; or for vainglory, as the man that is extolled loves
the extoller; or for avarice, as one loves a wealthy man for
benefits received; or for love of pleasure, as the man who
cares only for his belly and things of sex. The first is
praiseworthy, the second is in between, the rest belong to
the passions.

10. If you hate some and some you neither love nor
hate, while others you love but only moderately and
others again you greatly love, learn from this inequality
that you are far from perfect charity which supposes that
you love every man equally.

11. *Decline from evil and do good.*[86] That is to say: War
on your enemy to lessen the passions; then, keep sober
lest they increase. Or: Fight to acquire virtues; and afterwards, keep sober so as to guard them. And this doubtless
is what is meant by *dressing* and *keeping.*[87]

12. Those who, with God's permission, tempt us either
rouse the desires of our soul, or stir up our temper, or
darken our reason, or fill the body with pain, or snatch
away bodily necessities.

13. The demons tempt us either by themselves or arm
against us those that have no fear of the Lord: by themselves, when we are alone apart from men, as they tempted
the Lord in the desert; by men, when we associate with
men, as they tried the Lord through the Pharisees. But we,
looking to our model—let us beat them back however
they come.[88]

14. When the mind begins to advance in love for God,
then the demon of blasphemy sets to tempting it and
suggests such thoughts as no man but only the devil, their
father, could ever find. He does this out of envy for the
God-devoted man, that in despair at having such thoughts
he no longer dare to approach God in his accustomed

prayer. But the vindictive wretch gains nothing thereby to his purpose; on the contrary, he makes us sturdier. For in this fighting back and forth we find ourselves more sincere and trustworthy in our love for God. *May his sword pierce his heart and his bows be shattered.*[89]

15. The mind, when it applies itself to visible things, knows them naturally through the senses. So neither the mind is bad, nor the natural knowledge, nor the things, nor the senses; for they are all the works of God. What then is bad? Evidently the passion which our natural ideas undergo. Indeed this need not be in our use of thoughts, if the mind keeps watch.[90]

16. Passion is a movement of the soul contrary to nature, either in irrational love, or in senseless hate of something or on account of some material thing. For example, in irrational love for food, or a woman, or money, or passing glory, or for some other material thing, or on their account; or again in senseless hate of one of the foregoing, as has been said, or on its account.[91]

17. Or again, vice[92] is the mistaken judgment of our ideas, upon which follows the misuse of things. For example, as regards women, the right judgment about intercourse is that its purpose is the begetting of children. He then who looked to the pleasure was mistaken in judgment in that he took what is not morally good to be such. Such a man therefore misuses a woman in having intercourse. The like holds good also for other things and thoughts.

18. When the demons have thrown chastity out of your mind and surround you with thoughts of fornication, then with tears say to the Master: *They have cast me forth and now they have surrounded me. My joy, deliver me from them that surround me.*[93] And you will be safe.

19. Violent is the demon of fornication and vehemently he sets upon those that contend against passion. This he does especially through their carelessness in eating and through contact with women. With the suavity of pleasure he imperceptibly steals upon a man's mind and then, through the memory, assails him in his retirement,[94] inflaming his body and presenting various forms to his mind. And so he provokes his consent to the sin. If you do not want these things to stay with you, take up fasting and hard work and vigils and fair retirement with constant prayer.

20. Those that forever seek our soul do so through bad thoughts that they may throw it into some sin of thought or deed. When therefore they find the mind unreceptive, then will they be ashamed and confounded; but when they find it given over to spiritual contemplation, then will they be turned back and utterly put to shame in short order.[95]

21. He who anoints his mind for the sacred contests and drives bad thoughts from it has the characteristics of a deacon; of a priest, however, if he illumines it with knowledge of beings and utterly destroys counterfeit knowledge; of a bishop, finally, if he perfects it with the sacred myrrh of knowledge of the worshipful and Holy Trinity.[96]

22. The demons are weakened when the passions in us are lessened through the commandments; but they perish when finally through detachment of soul the passions are utterly destroyed, as they no longer find anything by which they may settle in and war against it. This doubtless is the meaning of: *They shall be weakened and perish before Thy face.*[97]

23. Some men restrain themselves from the passions

because of human fear; some because of vainglory; others because of self-mastery; yet others are freed from the passions through the divine judgments.[98]

24. All the words of the Lord are contained in these four—commandments, doctrine, threats, promises. Because of them we endure every hardship, such as fastings, vigils, sleeping on the ground, toil and trouble in attending on our duties, affronts, dishonor, torturings, death and the like. *For the sake of the words of Thy lips*, Scripture says, *I have kept hard ways.*[99]

25. The wages of self-mastery are detachment; of faith, knowledge. Now detachment begets discernment, while knowledge love for God.[100]

26. The mind that follows well the active life advances in prudence; the contemplative life, in knowledge. To the one it belongs to bring the contender to a discernment of virtue and vice; to the other, to lead the participant to the essences of the incorporeal and corporeal creation. Then finally is it fit for the grace of theology when it has passed beyond, on the wings of charity, all the things just mentioned; and, being in God, it will examine, through the Spirit, the essential concerning Him, as much as the human mind may.[101]

27. When you are about to enter theology, seek not out the very reasons of His nature (for that the human mind, or that of any other creature, is incapable of finding); scan rather, in so far as possible, the things about Him: for instance, His eternity, His immensity and infinity, His goodness and wisdom and power that makes, governs, and judges His creatures. For among men he truly is a great theologian who searches out these reasons, be it ever so little.[102]

28. He is a man of power that has joined knowledge to

action; for by the one he makes his concupiscences wither and tames anger; with the other he gives wings to the mind and departs for God.[103]

29. When the Lord says: *I and the Father are one*, He indicates identity of substance; but when He says: *I in the Father and the Father in me*,[104] He shows the inseparableness of the persons. The Tritheists, therefore, who separate the Father from the Son, go off the deep end either way. For they either say that the Son is coeternal with the Father, but separate one from the other and so are forced to say that He was not born of Him and to go off the deep end—that there are three Gods and three origins; or else they say that He was born of Him, but separating still, they are forced to say that He is not coeternal with the Father and to subject to time Him who is master of time. For indeed it is necessary alike to preserve the 'one God,' as the great Gregory[105] says, and to confess the three persons, each in its individuality. For 'it is divided,' yet 'without division,' as he says; and 'it is joined together,' but 'with distinction.' Therefore both the division and the union are extraordinary. But what is there extraordinary, if as one man with another, so likewise the Son and the Father, is both united and separate and nothing more?

30. He who is perfect in love and has attained the summit of detachment knows no difference between 'mine and thine,' between faithful and unfaithful, between slave and freeman, or indeed between male and female. Having risen above the tyranny of the passions and looking to nature, one in all men, he considers all equally and is disposed equally towards all. For in Him there is neither Greek nor Jew, neither male nor female, neither slave nor freeman, but everything and in all things Christ.[106]

31. From the passions embedded in our soul the demons

seize opportunities of stirring up in us impassioned thoughts. Then, warring upon the mind through them, they force it on to consent to sin. When the mind is over-come, they lead on to a sin of thought; and when this is completed, they finally carry it prisoner to the deed. After that, those who have made the soul desolate through thoughts, withdraw together with them; and there remains alone in the soul the idol of sin. On it the Lord says: *When you shall see the abomination of desolation standing in the holy place—he that readeth let him understand.*[107] The mind of man is a holy place and temple of God, in which, having through impassioned thoughts rendered his soul desolate, the demons have set up the idol of sin. That these things have already come to pass in history no one, I think, will doubt who has read the works of Josephus; though some say these things will come to pass at the time of the Antichrist.[108]

32. There are three things that move us to the good: natural tendencies, the holy Powers, good choice. The natural tendencies—as, for instance, when what we wish men would do for us, we likewise do for them; or, when we see someone in sore straits, we then naturally have pity. The holy Powers—as when moved to some fine deed, we experience their good assistance and prosper. Good choice —when, for example, discerning good from evil, we choose the good.[109]

33. There are likewise three things that move us to evil: the passions, the demons, and evil choice. The passions—as when we desire a thing out of reason; for example, food out of times or without necessity, or a woman without intention of begetting children or one not permitted us; or again, when we are angered or grieved more than is fitting, as against him who does us dishonor or harm.

And the demons—as when they watch for the moment of our carelessness and then suddenly set upon us with great vehemence, rousing the passions just mentioned and their like. And evil choice—as when, knowing the good, we choose evil instead.

34. The wages for the labors of virtue are detachment and knowledge. These become our friends and advocates in the kingdom of heaven, just as the passions and ignorance are the advocates for eternal punishment. He then who seeks the former for the sake of reputation among men and not for the good in it, will hear from Scripture: *You ask and you receive not, because you ask amiss.*[110]

35. There are many things men do that are of themselves noble, and still for a certain reason they are not noble; for example, fasts and vigils, prayer and psalmody, alms and hospitality are of themselves noble deeds, but when they are done for vainglory, they are no longer so.

36. God seeks the intention of everything we do, whether we do it for Him or for some other reason.[111]

37. When you hear the Scripture saying: *Thou wilt render to every man according to his works*[112]—not for things done apart from a right intention, though they seem to be noble, will God make a return of noble things, but for things done with right intention precisely. For God's judgment looks not to the things done, but to the intention.

38. The demon of pride has a twofold wickedness: either he persuades the monk to ascribe his virtuous deeds to himself and not to God, the giver of good things and helper in right doing; or, failing in this, he suggests scorn for the brothers still imperfect. And so unknowingly the bedeviled man is persuaded to deny the help of God. For if he scorns them as men unable to do rightly, he puts himself forward as doing rightly of his own power. And

this is not possible, since the Lord says: *Without me you can do nothing.*[113] For our weakness is such, that roused to noble things, it can bring nothing to conclusion without the giver of good things.

39. He that has known the weakness of human nature has had experience of the divine power; by it such a man has done some things rightly, others he hastens so to do; but never does he scorn a single man. For he knows that as it has helped him and freed him from many passions and difficulties, so God is able to help all men when He wishes, especially those who are striving for His sake. Although in the dispositions of His judgment God does not at once deliver all from their passions, yet as a good and charitable physician in due time He heals each of those who are pressing on.

40. With the inefficaciousness of the passions pride arises, either from hidden causes or from the crafty withdrawal of the demons.

41. Practically every sin is committed for pleasure; it is taken away by the suffering of hardships and grief, whether this be voluntary or involuntary, through penitence, or some trial disposed by Providence. For *if*, Scripture says, *we would judge ourselves, we should not be judged. But whilst we are judged, we are chastised by the Lord, that we be not condemned with this world.*[114]

42. When a temptation comes upon you unexpectedly, do not accuse him through whom it came; but seek the why of it and you will find correction. Whether it was to be through one or through another, the fact is you had to drain the wormwood of God's judgments.

43. So long as you are disposed to do evil, refuse no hardships, that you may be humbled by them and throw up pride.

11

44. Some temptations bring men pleasure, some grief, some bodily pain. The Physician of souls by means of His judgments applies the remedy to each soul according to the cause of its passions.

45. The attacks of temptations in some cases are brought on to take away past sins, in other cases for sins now being committed, in yet others to cut off those that are liable to be committed. And this apart from the temptations that come upon one as a trial, as with Job.

46. The prudent man who reckons upon the medicine of divine judgments, thankfully bears the misfortunes that thereby come upon him, allowing that they have no other cause than his own sins. The imprudent man, however, ignorant of the supernal wisdom of God's providence, sins and is chastised, yet considers God or men as the cause of his evils.

47. Certain things put a stop to the movements of passion and do not allow them to go on to increase; others lessen them and make them decrease. For example, fasting, work, and vigils do not permit concupiscence to grow; while solitude and meditation, prayer, and burning love for God diminish it and bring it to nothing. Similarly for anger: for instance, long-suffering, forgetfulness of grudges, and meekness put a stop to it and do not allow it to grow; while charity, alms, kindness, and benevolence make it diminish.[115]

48. For him whose mind is continually with God, even his concupiscence is increased above measure into a divinely burning love; and the entire irascible element is changed into divine charity. For by continual participation in the divine illumination it has become wholly lightsome and, making the passible element one with itself, it has turned as was said above, to a divinely burning love

without end and unceasing charity, passing over completely from earthly things to the divine.[116]

49. Not to have envy, not to be angry, not to hold a grudge against him who offends you, is not for all that to bear the man charity. For it can be that a man, not yet loving, does not return evil for evil, because of the commandment; nevertheless he does not yet do good for evil, spontaneously. Purposely to do good to those who hate you belongs to perfect spiritual love alone.[117]

50. Because a man does not love some one, he does not for that hate him; and again—because he does not hate, he does not for that love him; rather, he can be in a midway position, that is, neither loving nor hating him. For the disposition to love is produced only in one of the five ways, mentioned in the ninth saying of the present Century: that is, the praiseworthy way, the one in between, and the blameworthy ones.

51. When you see your mind tarrying with pleasure over material things and fond of thinking of them, know that you love them rather than God; *for where thy treasure is*, says the Lord, *there will thy heart be also.*[118]

52. The mind, joined with God and abiding with Him through prayer and charity, becomes wise, good, powerful, benevolent, merciful, long-suffering; in a word, it contains in itself practically all the divine attributes. But when it leaves Him and goes over to material things, it becomes either like a domestic animal, pleasure-loving, or like a wild beast, fighting for these things with men.[119]

53. Scripture calls material things the world. Worldlings are those who let their mind tarry over them; such it severely rebukes, saying: *Love not the world, nor the things which are in the world. The concupiscence of the flesh and the*

concupiscence of the eyes and the pride of life is not of God, but of the world, and the rest.[120]

54. A monk is one who separates his mind from material things and by self-mastery, charity, psalmody, and prayer devotes himself to God.

55. The cattle-keeper is, allegorically, the practical man; for moral actions are of the nature of cattle. Therefore Jacob said: *Thy servants are keepers of cattle.* The shepherd, however, is the gnostic; for the thoughts, which are pastured by the mind in the mountains of contemplations, are of the nature of sheep. So also: *All shepherds are an abomination to the Egyptians,* that is, to the powerful adversaries.[121]

56. When the senses move the body to its own concupiscences and pleasures, the careless mind follows along and consents to its imaginings and instigations. But the virtuous mind masters itself and holds itself back from those impassioned imaginings and instigations; rather, as a philosopher,[122] it tries to improve such emotions.

57. There are virtues of the body and virtues of the soul. Those of the body include fasting, vigils, sleeping on the ground, service of others, manual work, done in order not to burden anybody or else to have something to share, and so on. The virtues of the soul are charity, long-suffering, meekness, self-mastery, prayer, and so on. If from some necessity or bodily condition, as sickness, or some such thing, it happens that we are unable to carry out such corporal virtues, we are pardoned by the Lord, who knows the reasons; but when we fail to carry out the virtues of the soul, we shall have no excuse—they submit to no necessity.

58. Charity for God persuades him who has it to scorn,

with neglect of all pleasure, every hardship and grief. Let all the saints convince you of this, they who have suffered so much for Christ.

59. Guard yourself from self-love, mother of vices, which is unreasonable affection for the body. For from it doubtless arise those first three capital, impassioned, raving thoughts—I mean gluttony, avarice, and vainglory. They have their origin in some needful demand of the body; from them the whole catalogue of vices is born. One must then, as has been said, necessarily be on guard and war against this self-love with great sobriety. When this is done away with, all its offspring are likewise done for.

60. The passion of self-love suggests to the monk that he indulge the body and take food oftener than is fitting. Under the pretense of considerate care it purposes to draw him on little by little to fall into the pit of voluptuousness; to the worldling it proposes at once to make provision for concupiscence.[123]

61. The supreme state of prayer is, they say, when the mind passes out of the flesh and the world and remains entirely untouched in prayer by matter and forms. He who keeps this state without blemish really prays without ceasing.[124]

62. As the body that dies leaves behind all the affairs of life, so the mind that dies in the summits of prayer leaves behind all thoughts of this world; for if it will not die such a death, it cannot be found with God and live.

63. Monk, let no one deceive you, as though you could be saved while in the service of pleasure and vainglory!

64. As the body, sinning through things, has for guidance and discipline the corporal virtues that it may be sober-minded: so the mind too, sinning through impassioned thoughts, has likewise for guidance and

discipline the virtues of the soul, that looking upon things with purity and detachment it may be sober-minded.

65. Just as night succeeds day, and winter summer, so pain and grief succeed vainglory and pleasure, either now or in the future.

66. No sinner will escape the judgment to come unless here below he undertake hard things or endure what is inflicted.

67. There are five reasons, they say, why God permits us to be warred upon by the demons: (1) that in the attacks and counter-attacks we come to distinguish virtue and vice; (2) that possessing virtue in such combat and struggle, we shall hold it firm and steadfast; (3) that with advance in virtue we do not become high-minded but learn to be humble; (4) that having had some experience of vice, we will hate it with a consummate hate; and (5) above all that when we become detached we forget not our own weakness nor the power of Him who has helped us.

68. As the hungry man's mind forms phantoms of bread and the thirsty man's of water, so the glutton imagines a variety of food, the voluptuary forms of women, the vain man attentions from men, the avaricious gain, the vengeful man vengeance on the offender, the envious man evil for the object of his envy—and similarly for the other passions. For the mind beset by passions receives impassioned thoughts, whether the body be waking or sleeping.

69. When concupiscence is grown strong, the mind dreams of the objects that give pleasure; when anger is strong, the mind looks on the things that cause fear. The impure demons, then, with our carelessness as fellow worker, strengthen and arouse the passions, while the holy angels, who move us to the exercise of virtue, lessen them.

70. When the concupiscible part of the soul is frequently roused, there is induced in the soul a fixed habit of pleasure. The temper continually stirred makes the mind cowardly and unmanly. They are healed, the first by a continual exercise of fasting, vigils, and prayer; the other by kindness, benevolence, charity, and mercy.

71. The demons make their attacks either with things or with the impassioned thoughts connected with them. They attack with things those that are occupied in affairs; with thoughts those that live withdrawn from affairs.[125]

72. As it is easier to sin in thought than in deed, so war with thoughts is harder than with things.

73. Things are outside the mind; thoughts about them have their place within. It is then for the mind to use them well or ill; misuse of things follows on the mistaken use of their thoughts.

74. The mind receives impassioned thoughts from three sources—from the senses, from the body's condition and temperament, from the memory. From the senses, when they, receiving impressions from the objects of the passions, move the mind to impassioned thinking; through the body's condition and temperament, that is, when this condition, altered by undisciplined living, by the activity of demons, or some disease, moves the mind to impassioned thinking, or against Providence; through memory, namely, when the memory recalls the thoughts of things that have stirred our passion, it likewise moves the mind to impassioned thinking.[126]

75. Of the things God has given us for use some are in the soul, some in the body, some are concerned with the body. In the soul there are its powers, in the body the sense organs and the other members, concerned with the body are food, possessions, and so on. The good or ill use

of these, or of their accidents, make us either virtuous or bad.[127]

76. Of these accidents in things some are in the soul, some in the body, some concerned with the body. Of those in the soul there are knowledge and ignorance, forgetfulness and memory, charity and hate, fear and courage, grief and joy, and so on; of those in the body there are pleasure and hardship, the use of the senses and its loss, health and sickness, life and death, and such like; concerned with the body there are fecundity and sterility, wealth and poverty, fame and ill repute, and so on. Now among these men reckon some as good and attractive, others as evil—though essentially none of them is evil. It is with regard to their use that they are discovered to be in a proper sense either evil or good.

77. Knowledge is naturally good and attractive, so also is health; yet their contraries have benefited more people. Knowledge does not turn out to the advantage of the bad, though it be naturally good, as was said; similarly neither health, nor riches, nor joy. For men do not use them advantageously. Their contraries therefore are helpful. So then they are not essentially evil though they seem to be so.

78. Do not misuse thoughts, lest you be forced to misuse things too. For unless a man first sin in thought, he will never sin in deed.

79. The capital vices are the image of the earthly man— folly, cowardice, intemperance, injustice. The capital virtues are the image of the heavenly man—prudence, courage, temperance, justice. Certainly then, *as we have borne the image of the earthly, let us bear also the image of the heavenly.*[128]

80. If you will to find the way that leads to life, look for it, and there you will find it, in the Way that says: *I am the*

way and the life and the truth. But let the search be diligent and painstaking, since *few there are that find it;* otherwise left out of the few, you will be found with the many.[129]

81. Because of these five a soul will cut itself off from sins—because of fear of men, or for fear of judgment, or because of the future reward, or for charity towards God, or finally because of the prompting of conscience.[130]

82. Some say that there would be no evil in creatures unless there were some other power that drew us on to it. And this is no other than carelessness about the natural activities of the mind. Wherefore those that have a care always do good things, evil things never. If then you too have the will, expel carelessness and you drive out vice, which is the mistaken use of thoughts, on which follows the misuse of things.

83. It is of the nature of our rational element to be subject to the divine Word and to rule the irrational element in us. Preserve then this order in everything and there will be no evil in creatures nor will anything be found to draw on to evil.[131]

84. Some thoughts are simple, some are compound. The simple are passionless; the compound are impassioned, composed, as it were, of passion and representation. Things being so, it is noticeable that many simple thoughts follow along with the compound when these are first moved to a sin of the mind. This is the case with money. An impassioned thought rises in someone's memory about gold; mentally he has the urge to steal and he completes the sin in his mind. There comes along with the memory of the gold a remembrance of the purse, the chest, the room, and so on. Now the memory of the gold is compound; for it is with passion. The memory of the purse, chest, and so on is simple; for the mind has no attachment

for them. And thus it is with every thought, with vain-glory, with women, and the rest. For all thoughts that follow after an impassioned thought are not themselves impassioned, as the explanation has shown. From this then we can know what are impassioned representations, what simple.

85. Some say the demons touch the private parts of the body in sleep and rouse the passion of fornication; the roused passion then suggests to the mind, by the memory, female forms. Others say the demons appear to the mind in the guise of a woman and then touching the body rouse desire, and thus imaginings arise. Still others say that the passion dominant in the approaching demon rouses the passion and thus the soul is prepared for thoughts and recalls the forms by memory. For other impassioned images it is the same; some say it happens so, some say in some other way. However, in none of these ways are the demons able to rouse any passion whatsoever in a soul whether awake or asleep, when charity and self-mastery are present.

86. Some commands of the Law it is necessary to keep both in actual fact and in spirit; some in spirit only. For example, *thou shalt not commit adultery, thou shalt not kill, thou shalt not steal*—these and the like one must observe both in fact and in spirit (the spiritual observance is three-fold). To be circumcised, to keep the Sabbath, to sacrifice the lamb and eat the unleavened bread with bitter herbs, and so on, are to be kept in spirit only.[132]

87. There are in general three moral conditions among monks. The first is not to sin in deed; the second not to permit impassioned thoughts to linger in the soul; the third is to look on with detachment when forms of women and of those who have offended us arise in the mind.

88. He is poor who has renounced all his goods and possesses nothing at all on earth save his body; and who, in severing his attachment to it, has confided himself to the care of God and pious men.

89. Some owners own with detachment; therefore, stripped of their goods they do not grieve, like the men who accepted with joy the seizure of their goods.[133] Some own with attachment; wherefore, about to be stripped, they become grief-stricken, like the rich man in the Gospel, who *went away sad*.[134] And if in fact they are stripped they grieve till death. Such a stripping then probes the state of detachment or attachment of men.

90. The demons war upon those who are at the summit of prayer to keep them from receiving mere representations of sensible things. Against gnostics they strive so that impassioned thoughts may linger in their minds; against those struggling in the active life, so as to persuade them to sin by deed; in every way, against all, these wretches strive to separate man from God.[135]

91. Those whose piety Divine Providence exercises in this life are tried by three sorts of temptation: by the gift of pleasant things, as health, beauty, many children, wealth, good repute, and so on; or by the infliction of grievous things, as the loss of children, of wealth, of good repute; or by painful afflictions of the body, as disease, torments and so on. To the first the Lord says: *If any one doth not renounce all that he possesseth, he cannot be my disciple;* to the second and third: *In your patience possess your souls.*[136]

92. The following four things are said to alter the condition and temperament of the body and give thoughts to the mind, whether they be impassioned or detached, namely: angels, demons, the weather, and style of living.

The angels, it is said, make the alteration by the use of reason; the demons, by touch; the weather, by its changes; the style of living, by the quality of food and drink, by excess and defect. Besides, there are the alterations coming from the memory, from the hearing and sight, by which the soul is directly affected with grief or with joy. The soul then being thus affected alters the temperament of the body; the temperament thus changed induces thoughts in the mind.[137]

93. Separation from God is, properly, death, and *sin the sting of death*. In consenting to it Adam at the same time became exiled from the tree of life, from Paradise and from God; of necessity bodily death followed after. He who says *I am life* is properly life. He in His death led back to life him who had been made dead.[138]

94. A man writes either to help his memory or to render a service, or both; either to harm certain people or to make a fine showing; or out of necessity.

95. Virtue of the active life is *the place of pasture*; knowledge of creatures is *the water of refreshment*.[139]

96. Human life is *the shadow of death*. If then anyone is with God and God is with him, clearly such a man can say: *for though I walk in the midst of the shadow of death, I will fear no evils, for Thou art with me*.[140]

97. A pure mind sees things rightly; a practiced speech places them in evidence; a keen hearing accepts them. But the mind that is deprived of these three does ill to the speaker.

98. He that knows the Holy Trinity, the Trinity's handiwork and Providence, he that possesses the sensitive part of his soul without attachment—this man is with God.

99. The rod is said to signify God's judgment, the staff, His Providence. He then who has received knowledge of

these things, may say: *Thy rod and Thy staff, they have comforted me.*[141]

100. When the mind is stripped of passions and illumined by contemplation of creatures, then it can be in God and pray as it ought.

THE THIRD CENTURY

1. The reasonable use of thoughts and things is productive of temperance, charity, and knowledge; the unreasonable use, of intemperance, hate, and ignorance.

2. *Thou hast prepared a table before me*, etc.[142] *Table* here signifies the virtue of the active life. This is prepared by Christ *against them that afflict us.* The *oil* anointing the mind signifies contemplation of creatures; the *chalice* of God, the very knowledge of God; His *mercy*, His Word and God. For He through His Incarnation follows us *all days* until He *apprehend* all that are to be saved, as He did in the case of Paul. The *house* signifies the kingdom wherein all the saints will be settled; the *length of days*, eternal life.

3. It is with misuse of the soul's powers that the vices come upon us—the vices of the concupiscible, the irascible, and the rational element. Misuse of the rational power is found in ignorance and folly; of the irascible and concupiscible, in hate and intemperance. Their proper use is in knowledge and prudence, in charity and temperance. If this is so, nothing created by God is evil.[143]

4. Food is not evil, but gluttony; nor is the begetting of children, but fornication; nor money, but avarice; nor glory, but vainglory. If this is so, nothing among creatures is evil except misuse which comes from the mind neglecting to cultivate itself as nature demands.

5. The blessed Denis[144] says that among the demons

evil manifests itself as unreasonable anger, senseless concupiscence, rash imagination. But unreasonableness, sense-
lessness, and rashness with rational creatures show themselves as privations of reason, sense, and circumspection.
Privations, however, follow upon habits. The demons
therefore once had prudent reason, sense, and circumspection. If this is so, neither are the demons evil by nature;
but have become evil by misuse of their natural powers.

6. Some passions are productive of licentiousness, some
of hate; some are productive of both licentiousness and
hate.

7. Excessive and delicate eating are the cause of licentiousness; avarice and vainglory, of hate for one's neighbor.
Their mother, self-love, is cause of both together.

8. Self-love is the impassioned, unreasonable affection
for one's body; to it is opposed charity and self-mastery.
To have self-love is clearly to have all the passions.

9. *No man*, says the Apostle, *ever hated his own flesh*, but
of course *mortifies it and makes it his slave*.[145] He grants it
nothing but food and clothing, and these only as they are
necessary for life. Thus then a man loves it without passion
and nourishes it as a servant of divine things and comforts
it with those things only that supply its need.

10. When a man loves someone, he certainly is eager to
do him service. If then one loves God, he certainly is eager
to do the things that please Him. But if he loves his flesh,
his eagerness is to perform what delights it.

11. Charity, temperance, contemplation, and prayer
please God; gluttony, licentiousness, and what multiplies
them, the flesh. Therefore *they who are in the flesh cannot
please God. And they that are Christ's have crucified their flesh
with the passions and concupiscences*.[146]

12. The mind, when it tends towards God, takes the

body for servant and grants it nothing more than the necessities of life; but when it tends to the flesh, it makes itself servant of the passions and always makes provision for its concupiscences.[147]

13. If you will to be master of your thoughts, attend to your passions and you will easily drive them out of your mind away from your thoughts. Thus for fornication, fast, keep vigil, labor, keep to yourself. For anger and grief, scorn repute and dishonor and material things. For grudges, pray for him that offends and you will be set free.

14. Do not measure yourself by the standard of weaker men, but strive rather to apply yourself to the commandment of love. In measuring yourself by the former you fall into the pit of presumption, in striving for the latter you advance to the heights of humility.

15. If you really keep the commandment of love for neighbor, what makes you conceive for him bitterness and grief? Is it not clearly because in your preference and contention for transitory things instead of the commandment, you make war on your brother?

16. Not so much from necessity has gold become the object of zealous pursuit among men, as that with it most of them serve their pleasures.

17. There are three reasons for love of money—love of pleasure, vainglory, and lack of faith and confidence. Lack of faith is worse than the other two.

18. The hedonist loves money because with it he lives sumptuously; the vain man, because it makes him well-known; the fainthearted, that he may hide and guard it for fear of famine, old age, sickness, or exile. He puts his trust in it rather than in God the maker of all creation, who provides even for the last and least of living things.

19. There are four kinds of money getters—the three

just mentioned and managers of finances. These latter, of course, alone get it in the right fashion: their purpose is that they may never run short in their distribution to each in his need.[148]

20. All impassioned thoughts either excite the concupiscible, or stir up the irascible, or darken the rational element of the soul. Hence it comes about that the mind is hampered in its spiritual contemplation and in the flights of its prayer. For this reason the monk, and especially the solitary, should accurately attend to his thoughts and both know and excise their causes. He should know this, for example: impassioned memories of women excite the soul's concupiscible element; their cause is want of self-control in eating and drinking and frequent, unreasonable association with these same women; hunger, thirst, vigils, and solitude cut them off. Again, impassioned memories of offenders stir the temper; their cause is love of pleasure, vainglory, and attachment to material things. For such reasons the man of passions is grieved, inasmuch as he has either lost or not attained them. These are cut off by scorn and contempt, out of love for God.[149]

21. God knows Himself, He knows too the things He has made. The holy Powers also know God, they also know the things He has made. But not as God knows Himself and the things He has made do the holy Powers know God and the things made by Him.[150]

22. God knows Himself from His own blessed essence, and the things He has made from His Wisdom[151] through which and in which He made all things. The holy Powers know God by participation, Him who is beyond participation, and things made by Him by the perception of what may be contemplated in them.

23. Created things are outside the mind; within, it

receives the contemplation of them. Not so with God, the eternal, infinite, immense, who freely bestows being, well-being, and ever-being on His creatures.[152]

24. Natures endowed with reason and understanding participate in the holy God by their very being, by their aptness for well-being (that is, for goodness and wisdom) and by the free gift of ever-being. In this way then they know God. Things made by Him they know, as we have said, by perceiving the ordered wisdom to be seen in creatures. This wisdom is simply in the mind without substance of its own.[153]

25. In bringing into being natures endowed with reason and understanding, God, out of His supreme goodness, communicated to them four of the divine attributes by which He supports, guards, and preserves beings, namely: being and ever-being, goodness and wisdom. Of these, the first two He grants to the essence; the other two, goodness and wisdom, He grants for fitness of will and judgment, in order that the creature may become by sharing, what He is by essence. Therefore he is said to be made to God's image and likeness; to the image of His being by being, of His ever-being by ever-being (though it has a beginning, yet it is without end); to the likeness of His goodness by goodness, of His wisdom by wisdom. The one is by nature, the other by grace. Every rational nature is made to the image of God, but only the good and wise to His likeness.[154]

26. All nature endowed with reason and understanding is divided into two kinds, angelic and human nature. All angelic nature is again divided into two universal sides or groups, holy or accursed—into holy Powers and impure demons. All human nature is divided into two universal sides only, the pious and the impious.[155]

27. God, as self-existence and as being Himself goodness

12

and wisdom (to speak more truly, He is above all such things), has absolutely no contrary quality. Creatures, inasmuch as all have their existence, and rational, intelligent ones their aptitude for goodness and wisdom, by participation and grace, do have contrary qualities. As contrary to existence they have not to exist, as contrary to their aptitude for goodness and wisdom they have vice and ignorance. That they exist forever or do not exist, this is in the power of the Maker; to share in His goodness and wisdom or not to share, this depends on the will and purpose of rational beings.

28. When the Greeks maintain that the substance of everything eternally coexisted with God and that they have only their qualities from Him, they assert that substance has no contrary, but that contrariety is found only in the qualities. We affirm that the divine substance alone has nothing contrary, since it is eternal and infinite and bestows eternity on all the rest. The substance of things, however, has not-being as contrary. It depends on the power of Him who in the true sense is whether the substance of things should ever be or not be; and *His gifts are without repentance*. Therefore it both ever is and will be sustained by His all-powerful might, even though, as was said, it has non-being as contrary, for it was produced from non-being into being, and whether it is or is not depends on His will.[156]

29. As evil is the privation of the good, and ignorance of knowledge; so not-being is privation of being, not of true Being (for it has no contrary), but of participated true Being. The former privations follow the will and judgment of creatures; the latter rests with the will of the Maker. And He of His goodness ever wills beings to be and always to receive His benefits.[157]

30. Of all creatures, some are rational and intelligent; they admit contraries: virtue and vice, knowledge and ignorance. Others are bodies, variously made up of contraries, that is, of earth, air, fire, water. Then there are others entirely bodiless and immaterial, though some of these are joined to bodies. Some, too, have their make-up only of matter and form.

31. All bodies by nature lack power of motion. They are moved by the soul—some by a rational, some by an irrational, some by an insensitive soul.

32. The soul has powers for nourishment and growth, for imagination and appetite, for reasoning and understanding. Plants share in the first only; irrational animals also in the second; men in the third in addition to the first two. The first two powers are perishable; the third is imperishable and immortal.[158]

33. In sharing with one another their illumination the holy Powers share also with humankind either their virtue or their knowledge. Thus, by their virtue—an imitation of the divine goodness—they benefit themselves, one another, and their inferiors, rendering them Godlike. As to their knowledge: this is either something more exalted about God (*Thou, O Lord, art most high for evermore*, says the Scripture[159]), or more profound about bodies, or more accurate about incorporeal beings, or more distinct about providence, or more manifest about judgment.

34. The mind is impure, first, in having false knowledge, then in not knowing some one of the universals (I speak of the human mind, for angelic knowledge comprehends also the singular), thirdly in having impassioned thoughts, fourthly in consenting to sin.

35. In not acting according to nature is the soul impure. Hence impassioned thoughts are begotten in the mind.

For then does the mind act according to nature, when its sensitive powers (I refer to anger and concupiscence) remain detached under the impact of things and the representations that come with them.

36. In sin of deed is the body impure.[160]

37. He that is not drawn to worldly things loves solitude. He that loves nothing human loves all men.[161] He has knowledge of God and of divine things who takes offense at no one, moved neither by faults nor suspicions.

38. It is a great thing to suffer no attachment for things; it is greater far to remain detached as regards their representations.

39. Charity and self-mastery keep the mind detached as regards things and their representations.

40. The God-loving mind does not war against things nor against their representations, but against the passions joined with these representations. Thus he does not war against the woman, nor against him who offends him, nor against their images, but against the passions that are joined with the images.

41. The monk's whole war is against the demons, that he may separate the passions from the representations. Otherwise he will not be able to look on things with detachment.[162]

42. Thing, representation, passion—all differ. A thing is, for instance, a man, woman, gold, and so on; a representation is a mere recollection of one of these things; passion is unreasonable affection or senseless hate for one of the foregoing. A monk's battle is then against passion.

43. An impassioned representation is a thought compounded of passion and representation. Let us separate the passion from the representation: the thought alone will

remain. If we but will, we make this separation by means of spiritual charity and self-mastery.

44. The virtues separate the mind from the passions; spiritual contemplations from simple representations; pure prayer then places it before God Himself.[163]

45. The virtues are ordered to the knowledge of creatures; this knowledge to the knower; the knower to Him who is known in ignorance and knows beyond all knowledge.[163a]

46. Not as though in need of something did God, who is plenitude beyond measure, bring into being His creatures, but that they might proportionately share in Him with delight and that He Himself might enjoy His works, seeing them rejoice and ever insatiably sated on Himself the inexhaustible.

47. The world has many poor in spirit, but not as they should be; many that mourn, but for bad bargains or for loss of children; many meek, but in the face of impure passions; many hungering and thirsting, but to seize others' goods and to gain unjustly. And there are many merciful, but to the body and its comforts; many clean of heart, but for vanity's sake; many peacemakers, but they subject the soul to the flesh. The world has many that suffer persecution, but undisciplined; many that are reviled, but for shameful sins. Only those are blessed who do and suffer all these things for Christ and after His example. Why? Because *theirs is the kingdom of heaven*, and *they shall see God*, and what follows. So then, not because they do and suffer such things are they blessed (for the men just mentioned do the same), but because they do and suffer them for Christ and after His example.[164]

48. In everything we do God looks to the intention, as has often been said, whether we are acting for Him or for

some other reason. When then we want to do something good, let us have, not human considerations, but God as our goal, that always looking to Him we may do all for Him; otherwise we shall undergo the toil and yet lose our reward.

49. In time of prayer cast away from the mind the empty representations of human affairs and contemplations of all creatures, lest in imagining lesser things you be deprived of Him who incomparably exceeds all beings.

50. If we genuinely love God, we cast out the passions by this very love. This is charity towards Him—to prefer Him to the world, the soul to the flesh, while scorning worldly matters to devote oneself to Him continually by means of self-mastery, charity, prayer, psalmody, and so on.

51. If we devote ourselves for a long time to God and keep watch over the sensitive part of our soul, we no longer run into the attacks of thoughts; rather, as we look more accurately into and cut off their causes, we become more clear-sighted, so that the words are fulfilled in us: *My eye also hath looked down upon my enemies: and my ear shall hear the malignant that rise up against me.*[165]

52. When you see that your mind is frequenting the representations of the world with justice and piety, know then that your body also remains pure and sinless. But when you see that your mind is giving itself to sins in thought and you do not check it, know then that your body too will not be long in falling into those sins.

53. As the body has things for its world, so the mind has representations for its world. And as the body commits fornication with a woman's body, so the mind with representation of the woman and the picturing of its own body. For the mind's eye sees the semblance of its own body joined with that of the woman. So also the mind beats off

the semblance of its offender, through the semblance of its own body. And similarly for other sins. For what the body does in deed in the world of things, that the mind does too in the world of representations.

54. There is no reason to be horrified, stupefied, astounded because God the Father judges no one and has given all judgment to the Son. The Son cries out: *Judge not that you may not be judged; condemn not that you may not be condemned.*[166] Similarly the Apostle: *Judge not before the time, until the Lord come.* And: *With what judgment thou judgest another, thou condemnest thyself.*[167] But men, in forgoing to weep for their sins, take judgment away from the Son and do themselves, as though sinless, judge and condemn each other. *At this heaven is astounded,*[168] earth is horrified, but they, in their insensitiveness, are not ashamed.

55. The man that busies himself with other people's sins or even judges his brother on a suspicion, has not yet laid the foundations of penitence nor begun to seek knowledge of his own sins (which are in fact heavier than many pounds of lead); nor does he know why it is that the man loving vanity and seeking after lies becomes heavy-hearted.[169] Therefore as a senseless man going about in the dark, he lets his own sins go and pictures those of others, whether they do exist or he only suspects them.

56. Self-love, as we have often said, is the cause of all the impassioned thoughts. By it are begotten the three capital thoughts of concupiscence—gluttony, avarice, and vainglory. By gluttony fornication of thought is begotten; by avarice, rapacity of thought; by vainglory, pride of thought. All the rest follow one or the other of these three —the thoughts of anger, grief, grudges, sloth, envy, detraction and the rest. These passions then bind the mind

to material things and hold it down on earth, lying upon it like a massive stone, whereas by nature it is lighter and more agile than fire.

57. The origin of all the passions is self-love, their end, pride. Self-love is unreasonable affection for the body. Who cuts this out, cuts out at the same time all the passions that come from it.

58. As parents bear affection to the offspring of their bodies, so also the mind is naturally attached to its own reasonings. And as to impassioned parents, their children, though they be complete objects of ridicule, appear as the handsomest and most gentle-bred of all; so with the man of no sense, his reasonings, though they be utterly wretched, appear to him as quite the most sensible. The wise man thinks differently of the products of his reasoning. When it seems certain that his products are true and worthwhile, then especially does he distrust his own judgment and makes others, wise men, the judges of his own writings and thoughts (lest he should run or have run in vain[170]) and from these he receives assurance.

59. When you overcome some one of the dishonorable passions, as gluttony, fornication, anger, or rapacity, then at once the thought of vainglory lights upon you. When you overcome this, pride follows after.

60. All the dishonorable passions that lay hold of the soul drive the thought of vainglory from it; when these are bested, they let it go free.[171]

61. Vainglory, whether removed or remaining, begets pride; removed it produces presumption; remaining, boastfulness.

62. Secret exercise[172] removes vainglory; ascribing our right actions to God removes pride.

63. He that merits knowledge of God and really enjoys

the consequent pleasure, scorns all pleasures begotten by the concupiscible element.[173]

64. He that desires earthly things desires either food or things that serve the baser passions or a reputation or money or some other thing that goes with them. Unless the mind should discover something better to which to transfer its desire, it would never be persuaded to scorn them. Now knowledge of God and divine things is incomparably their better.[174]

65. Those that scorn pleasures do so either from fear or from hope or from knowledge or also from love of God.

66. The passionless knowledge of divine things does not convince the mind altogether to scorn material things; it is like the mere thought of a sensible thing. Hence many men may be found with much knowledge who yet wallow in fleshly passions like swine in the mire.[174a] These men, purified for a little by their care and attaining knowledge but later grown careless, are to be likened to Saul. Saul merited the kingship, but conducting himself unworthily, he was cast out of it with fear-inspiring wrath.

67. As the simple thought of human things does not force the mind to scorn the divine, so neither does the simple knowledge of divine things persuade it to scorn completely human things; because the truth now exists in shadows and figures. Therefore there is need for the blessed passion of holy charity; it binds the mind to spiritual objects and persuades it to prefer the immaterial to the material, the intelligible and divine to the sensible.

68. Not everyone that cuts back his passions and makes his thoughts simple thereby turns them to divine things. He can on the contrary be drawn neither to human things nor to the divine. This happens in the case of men of the active life who have not yet merited knowledge; they put

off the passions either by fear of punishment or hope of the kingdom.

69. *We walk by faith, not by sight;*[175] our knowledge is by mirrors, in riddles. Therefore we need to spend much time with them that by length of meditation and discussion we may acquire a well-settled habit of vision.

70. If we cut off the causes of passions a little and are engrossed in spiritual contemplations, but do not always abide in them with constant effort, we easily turn again to the fleshly passions and gather no other fruit than bare knowledge with presumption. The result is the gradual obscuring of this knowledge itself and the complete turning of the mind to material things.

71. The blameworthy passion of love engrosses the mind in material things; the laudable passion of love binds it even to divine things. For usually where the mind has leisure there it expands; where it expands there it directs its desire and love, whether this be in divine and intelligible things (which are properly its own), or in the things of the flesh and the passions.

72. God established the invisible world and the one that we see; the soul, of course, and the body He made. Now if the visible world is so beautiful, of what sort then will the invisible be? And if this latter is better, how much more so God who founded them both? If then the artificer of all that is beautiful is better than all creatures, what reason has the mind for leaving what is best of all to be engrossed in the worst of all? I mean the passions of the flesh. Or is it not plain that the mind has not yet a perfect experience of Him that is best of all, the Transcendent, since from birth it associates with and is accustomed to the flesh? If therefore by prolonged practice of self-mastery over pleasure and exercise in the meditation of divine things we little by

little break it away from this relation, it then expands, advancing gradually in divine things, and comes to know its own dignity and, finally, to put all its yearning on God.

73. He who speaks of his brother's sin with detachment does so for two reasons, either to correct him or to help another. Otherwise if he speaks, to the brother or someone else, it is with reviling and ridicule. He will not escape being deserted by God, but will fall into the same or another transgression; he will be rebuked and reviled by others, he will be shamed.

74. Sinners have not all the same reason for committing the same sin in act, but several. For instance, it is one thing to sin out of habit, it is another to sin, caught unawares. Here he fully reflected neither before nor after the sin, rather he was even greatly grieved over the incident; there, quite on the contrary, the habitual sinner never ceased sinning mentally and after the deed he has the same intention.

75. The man that goes after the virtues out of vanity obviously goes after knowledge too out of vanity. Such a one clearly neither does nor says anything for edification, but always in eager pursuit of the approval of the on-lookers or hearers. This passion of his is discovered when some among these lay censure on his doings or his words and he is vastly grieved, not because he failed to edify them (that was not his purpose), but because he was himself brought to contempt.

76. The passion of avarice is discovered when a man receives with joy but gives away with sorrow. Such a one cannot fill the steward's office.[176]

77. For these reasons a man endures sufferings: for the love of God, for the hope of reward, for the fear of punishment, for fear of men, because of his nature, because

of pleasure, because of gain, because of vainglory, for necessity.

78. It is one thing to be released from thoughts, another to be freed from passions. Often indeed a man is released from thoughts of things to which he is attached when they are not present, yet the passions are hidden in the soul and are discovered when the things appear. In the presence of things therefore one must watch over the mind and know for which of them it holds attachment.

79. He is a genuine friend who in the times of his neighbor's trial bears quietly and without fuss his incidental tribulations, anguish, and misfortunes, as though they were his own.[177]

80. Do not disregard your conscience, which always counsels you of the best. It puts before you divine and angelic advice; it frees you from the hidden stains of your heart, and will make you the gift of free speech[178] with God at the time of your departure.[179]

81. If you want to become an arbiter, moderate, and no servant of the passion of presumption, seek always in things that which is hidden from your knowledge. You will find a great diversity of things that escape your notice; you will marvel at your lack of knowledge and be reduced in your own estimation. And when you come to know yourself,[180] you will understand many great and wonderful things; since in fact to think one knows does not permit one to advance in knowledge.

82. He surely wants to be healed who makes no resistance to the healing drugs. These are the pains and griefs which diverse circumstances bring on. The man who resists does not know what is going on here nor what he would gain from it when he leaves this world.

83. Vainglory and avarice are parents one of the other.

Vain men get rich; rich men grow vain, that is, as world-lings. The monk, since he is without possessions, grows all the vainer. And when he does have money, he hides it in shame as something unbecoming his habit.

84. This is proper of the monk's vainglory, that he grows vain over virtue and all that goes with it; of his pride this is proper, that he be elated over his good deeds, contemn others, and ascribe these deeds to himself and not to God. Of the worldling's vainglory and pride this is proper, that he be vain and elated over good looks, wealth, influence, and prudence.[181]

85. Accomplishments for seculars are faults for monks; accomplishments for monks are faults for seculars. For instance, accomplishments for seculars are wealth, reputa-tion, influence, fastidiousness, bodily comfort, numerous children, and the things that go with all these. And should a monk come to these, he is lost. The monk's accomplish-ments are to possess nothing, to have no reputation, to have no influence, self-mastery, suffering of evil, and all that goes with these. And should a worldling come to these against his will, he reckons it a great fault and often is in danger of hanging himself; some, in fact, have done so.

86. Foods were created for two reasons: for nourish-ment and for healing. Those taking food for other reasons, since they misuse what God has given for use, are con-demned as voluptuaries. With everything, misuse is sin.

87. Humility is continual prayer with tears and hard-ships. This constant calling upon God for help does not permit us senselessly to grow bold in our own power and wisdom nor to put ourselves before others. These are the serious diseases of the passion of pride.

88. It is one thing to fight mere thoughts that the

passions be not roused; it is another to fight impassioned
thoughts that consent may not be given. Neither way,
however, permits thoughts to linger.

89. Grief and grudges go together. When at the sight
of a brother a man's mind mirrors grief, it is clear that he
bears him a grudge. But *the ways of the resentful lead to
death*, because *every resentful man transgresses the law*.[182]

90. If you bear someone a grudge, pray for him and you
stop the rising passion: by prayer you are separating the
grief from the memory of the evil which he did you;
and so, becoming charitable and kind, you entirely
wipe out the passion from your soul. Conversely, if
another bears you a grudge, be gracious with him and
humble, deal fair with him, and you deliver him from
the passion.

91. You will allay the grief of the envious man with
great difficulty, since he reckons what he envies in you as
his misfortune; it can be allayed in no other way than by
your hiding something from him. But if this thing is
beneficial to many, yet to him a cause of grief, which side
will you take? It is then necessary to stay with the benefit
of the many and still, as much as you may, not neglect
him. Nor will you be carried away by the virulence of the
passion (as you are not assisting the passion but the
sufferer); but in humility you will esteem him more than
yourself; always, everywhere, and in every situation you
will prefer him. For your own envy, you will be able to
allay it, if you rejoice with the man you envy at what he
rejoices, and grieve at what he grieves. Thus you fulfil the
saying of the Apostle: *Rejoice with them that rejoice, weep
with them that weep*.[183]

92. Our mind stands midway between two things, each
of which is active in its own way, the one working virtue,

the other vice—in other words, between angel and demon. The mind has power and authority to follow or resist which one it wills.

93. The holy Powers exhort us to the good; natural tendencies and good choice help us. Passions and evil choice support the attacks of the demons.[184]

94. Sometimes God Himself enters the pure mind and teaches it; sometimes the holy Powers suggest good things; sometimes the nature of the things we contemplate.

95. The mind that has merited knowledge must keep its representations of things detached, its contemplations secure, its state of prayer untroubled. Still it cannot always preserve them from the surgings of the flesh, since it is befogged by the plotting of demons.

96. The same things do not grieve and anger us; for things that make us grieve abound apart from anger. For instance, one thing is broken, another is lost, so and so dies—for the like of these we grieve only; for the rest, in our unphilosophical[185] disposition, we are both grieved and angered.

97. The mind, in receiving the representations of things, is naturally patterned after each representation; in contemplating them spiritually, it is diversely conformed to each object of contemplation. When it comes to be in God,[186] it is entirely without form and without pattern. For in contemplating Him who is simple, it becomes simple and wholly transfused with light.[187]

98. That soul is perfect whose sensitive powers tend wholly towards God.

99. That mind is perfect which, through true faith, in supreme ignorance supremely knows the supremely Unknowable; and which, in gazing upon the universe of His handiwork, has received from God comprehensive

knowledge of His providence and judgment—but I speak after the manner of men.[188]

100. Time is divided in three; faith correspondingly extends to all three parts; hope to one; charity to the remaining two. Faith and hope remain to a certain point, charity for infinite ages in super-union with the super-infinite, ever increasing more. Therefore, *the greatest of all is charity*.[189]

THE FOURTH CENTURY

1. On reflecting on the divine, universal infinity—that inaccessible, much desired abyss—the mind first marvels; then it is astounded at how He has brought beings into existence from nothing. But as *of His greatness there is no end*,[190] so His prudence is unsearchable.

2. How can one not marvel contemplating that boundless abyss of goodness, too great for astonishment? How can one not be astounded reflecting on how and whence came rational and spiritual nature, and the four elements, the source of bodies, since no matter pre-existed their genesis? And what sort of power is it, the real source of motion, that brought these things into being? Yet men of Greek culture, in their ignorance, will not accept the all-powerful Goodness and Its effective wisdom and knowledge that no man can conceive.

3. God, who is eternally Creator, creates when He wills by His consubstantial Word and Spirit, because of His infinite goodness. Nor must you object: Why did He create at a certain time, since He was always good?—for I will reply: The unsearchable wisdom of the infinite essence does not fall under human knowledge.[191]

4. The Creator when He willed gave substance to and

sent forth His eternally pre-existent knowledge[192] of beings. It is in fact absurd, in the case of an omnipotent God, to doubt if He can give something substance when He wills.

5. Seek the cause for God's creation; this pertains to knowledge. Seek not the how and why He but recently[193] created; for that is not in the competence of your mind. Men may comprehend some divine things, others they may not. So it is some saint has said: 'Unbridled contemplation may even drive one off the cliffs.'[194]

6. Some say that created things eternally existed with God, which is impossible. For how can things that are limited in every way eternally coexist with the absolutely infinite? Or how are they properly creatures if they are coeternal with the Creator? But such is the theory of the Greeks who make God out as Creator not at all of the substance of things, but only of their qualities. We, who know the all-powerful God, say that He is Creator not of the qualities but of the qualified substances. And if this is so, created things do not eternally coexist with God.

7. The Divine, and divine things, is in part knowable, in part unknowable. It is knowable in the contemplations concerning It, unknowable in the things of Its essence.[195]

8. Do not look for habits and aptitudes in the simple, infinite substance of the Holy Trinity, lest you make it something composite like creatures. To have such notions about God is absurd and irreligious.

9. The infinite Substance, all-powerful Creator of things, alone is simple, of a single form, unqualified, peaceful and without factions. Every creature is composite of substance and accident and always in need of Divine Providence, as it is not free from mutability.[196]

10. The intellectual and sensitive substances receive

from God, when He brings them into being, powers receptive of beings; the intellectual substance receives thoughts, the sensitive, sensations.

11. God is participated only; creatures both participate and communicate. They participate being and well-being; they communicate well-being only, but the corporeal substance in one way, the incorporeal in another.[197]

12. The incorporeal substance communicates well-being by speech, by actions, by being an object of contemplation; corporeal substance by being object of contemplation only.

13. That rational and intellectual substances have ever-being or are not, depends on the will and counsel of Him who creates all things well; that they be good or bad by choice depends on the will of the creatures.

14. Evil is not considered in the substance of creatures, but in mistaken and irrational movements.[198]

15. The soul is moved reasonably when its concupiscible element is qualified by self-mastery, its irascible clings to charity, turning away from hate, and when the rational drives towards God by prayer and spiritual contemplation.[199]

16. When in time of temptation a brother does not put up with incidental annoyances, but cuts himself off from the charity of his spiritual brethren, he does not yet possess perfect love nor know Divine Providence in its depths.[200]

17. The purpose of Divine Providence is to unify by right faith and spiritual charity those whom vice has sundered in various ways. Indeed for this the Savior suffered—*to gather together in one the children of God that were dispersed.*[201] He then who does not sustain the irksome, bear with annoyances, endure the laborious, walks outside divine charity and the purpose of Providence.

18. *Charity is patient and kind.*[202] If then a man is faint-hearted in the troubles that befall him and consequently acts evilly towards his offenders, cutting himself off from charity towards them, does he not fall away from the purpose of Divine Providence?

19. Take care, lest the vice that separates brothers be found sometime in you and not in your brother. Hasten to be reconciled with him, lest you fall away from the commandment of love.

20. Scorn not the commandment of love, because by it you will be a son of God, transgressing it you will become a son of Gehenna.

21. The things that separate from the love of friends are these: to envy or be envied, to cause or suffer loss, to insult or be insulted, and suspicions. May you never have performed or suffered any such thing to separate you from the love of your friend.

22. A temptation was occasioned for you by a brother, the trouble and grief led you to hate? Be not overcome by hate, but overcome hate with love. You will overcome in this way: sincerely pray for him to God, accept his apology; or else, heal him yourself by an apology, reckon yourself the cause of the temptation; be patient until the cloud passes.

23. The long-suffering man awaits the end of temptation and attains the triumph of perseverance.

24. *He that is patient is rich in prudence,*[203] because he refers every happening to the end; and, while awaiting that, he endures the annoyances. *And the end is life ever-lasting,*[204] as the divine Apostle says. *Now this is eternal life: that they may know Thee, the only true God, and whom Thou hast sent Jesus Christ.*[205]

25. Do not be light-hearted at the loss of spiritual

love, because men have been left no other way of salvation.

26. Yesterday your brother was spiritual and virtuous; do not today judge him bad and wicked because of the hate that the abuse of the Evil One has induced in you. No, cast out from your soul today's hate, considering with the patience of love yesterday's good.

27. Whom yesterday you praised as noble and lauded as virtuous do not today disparage as bad and wicked, because you changed from love to hate, making the reproof of your brother the excuse of your wicked hate. On the contrary, stay by those same praises, though you still be possessed by grief, and you will easily return to saving charity.

28. In company with the other brethren do not adulterate a brother's customary due of praise because of the grief against him still hidden in your heart, by imperceptibly mixing censure in your conversation. Rather in company use only pure praise; pray sincerely for him as for yourself, and you will very soon be delivered of this destructive hate.

29. Do not say: I do not hate my brother in putting him out of mind. Listen to Moses who said: *Thou shalt not hate thy brother in thy heart, but reprove him openly, and thou wilt not incur sin through him.*[206]

30. If perhaps in temptation your brother insists on abusing you, do you not be carried away from your charitable dispositions, suffering the same wicked demon to infest your mind. And you will not be carried away if, being reviled, you bless, being tricked, you remain well-disposed. This is the philosophic way according to Christ; who will not walk it, does not enjoy His company.[207]

31. Do not take the reasons that bring grief to you and work hate towards your brothers as favorable thoughts, though they seem to be quite true. Turn from such as from deadly serpents in order to keep them from giving way to abuse and to deliver your own soul from wickedness.

32. Do not goad a brother by speaking in riddles, lest you receive the like from him in turn and you drive from both of you the disposition for charity. But go and reprove him in the freedom[208] of charity that you may remove the causes of grief and free the both of you from trouble and grief.

33. Examine your conscience with the greatest accuracy, lest because of you your brother may not be reconciled. Do not cheat it, since it knows the hidden things of your heart, accuses you at the time of your passing, and becomes an obstacle in time of prayer.

34. In the time of peace do not recall what a brother said in the time of grief, even though the offensive things were said to your face, even though they were said to another about you and you heard them afterwards, lest in suffering grudging thoughts you turn again to destructive hate of a brother.

35. A rational soul that nourishes hate for a man cannot be at peace with God, who gave the commandments. For, He says, *if you will not forgive men their offenses, neither will our Heavenly Father forgive you your offenses.*[209] And if he will not have peace—do you keep yourself from hate, praying sincerely for him and not abusing him to anyone.

36. The unspeakable peace of the holy angels is comprised in these two attitudes, in love for God, in love for one another. The same holds good for all the saints from the beginning. It was, then, very beautifully expressed by

Our Savior: *On these two commandments dependeth the whole law and the prophets.*[210]

37. Be no self-pleaser and you will not hate your brothers; be no self-lover and you will love God.

38. You who have determined to live with spiritual men, at the outset renounce your wills; in no other way will you be able to be at peace either with God or with your fellows.

39. The man capable of possessing perfect charity, who has ordered his whole life upon it, it is he who says *LORD JESUS, in the Holy Spirit.*[211] In the contrary case, the contrary happens of course.

40. Charity for God is ever fond of winging the mind for divine communion; charity for neighbor ever prepares the mind to think well of him.

41. The man who still loves empty fame or is attached to some material thing is the one who is offended at men for the sake of temporal goods, who bears them grudges or hate, who is a slave of shameful thoughts; to the God-loving soul all these things are foreign.

42. When mentally you say nothing nor do anything shameful, when you have no grudge against him that harms or abuses you, when in the time of prayer you ever keep your mind untouched with matter and forms—know then that you have come to the full measure of detachment and perfect charity.[212]

43. It is no small battle to be freed from vainglory. One is freed, however, by hidden exercise of virtue and more frequent prayer. It is a sign of deliverance no longer to bear grudges against him who abused or abuses one.[213]

44. If you would be just, give to each part in you that which is due its position. I speak of the soul and the body. To the rational part of the soul give readings, spiritual

contemplations, and prayer; to the irascible, spiritual love which is opposed to hate; to the concupiscible, temperance and self-mastery; and to the fleshly part give food and clothing, and that only which is necessary.[214]

45. The mind operates according to its nature when the passions are subject, when it contemplates the essences of things, and when it dwells with God.[215]

46. As health and sickness regard the body of an animal and light and darkness the eye; so virtue and vice regard the soul, knowledge and ignorance the mind.[216]

47. The Christian is philosopher[217] in these three things: in the commandments, in doctrine, in the faith. The commandments separate the mind from the passions; doctrine introduces it to the knowledge of creatures; faith brings it to the contemplation of the Holy Trinity.

48. Some who contend for the prize beat off only impassioned thoughts; others cut off the passions themselves. One beats off impassioned thoughts, for instance, by psalmody or prayer or elevation of mind or by some other suitable distraction. One cuts off the passions by despising the things by which one has the passions.

49. The things for which we have passions are, for example, these: women, money, gifts, and so on. And one is then able to contemn women when, after withdrawal into solitude, one properly emaciates his body with self-mastery; and money, when one decides to be quite content with a sufficiency; and reputation, when one loves the secret exercise of virtues, known to God alone; and similarly for the rest. Now the man who contemns these will never come to hate anyone.

50. He who has renounced things, as women, money, and the like, makes a monk of the outer man, but not yet of the inner. He that renounces the impassioned

representations of these same things, makes a monk of the inner man, that is, of the mind. It is easy to make a monk of the outer man, if only one wants to; but it is no little struggle to make a monk of the inner man.[218]

51. Who then in this generation is entirely freed from impassioned representations and has been held worthy of pure, immaterial prayer—the sign of the inner monk?

52. There are many passions hidden in our souls; they are then exposed when the objects appear.

53. It can be that a person is not disturbed by passions in the absence of the objects, enjoying a partial detachment; but if the objects appear, the passions immediately vex the mind.[219]

54. Do not think that you have perfect detachment when the object is not present. When it appears and you remain unmoved both as to the object itself and as to the recollection of it afterwards, know that then you have entered the confines of detachment. But even so, do not take matters lightly, because virtue, when it remains for a long time, kills the passions, but, neglected, rouses them up again.

55. He who loves Christ, certainly imitates Him as much as he can. Thus Christ never ceased to do good to men; when He was treated with ingratitude and blasphemed, He was long-suffering; when He was struck by them and put to death, He endured, imputing evil to no one at all. These three are the works of love for neighbor apart from which the man deceives himself who says he loves Christ or has reached His kingdom. For He says: *Not the one that saith to me, Lord, Lord, shall enter into the kingdom of heaven; but he that doth the will of my Father.* And this also: *He that loves me will also keep my commandments,* and the rest.[220]

56. The whole purpose of the Savior's commandments is to free the mind from incontinence and hate and to bring it to the love of Himself and of its neighbor. From these is begotten the splendor of holy knowledge, actually possessed.[221]

57. You, to whom God has granted a partial knowledge, must not be careless of love and self-mastery. For they purify the passible part of the soul and always prepare the way to knowledge for you.

58. The way to knowledge is detachment and humility, without which no one will see the Lord.[222]

59. Since *knowledge puffeth up, but charity edifieth*, yoke charity with knowledge and you will be not puffed up, but a spiritual builder, edifying yourself and all those that draw near you.[223]

60. This is the reason why charity edifies, because it neither envies nor is embittered towards the envious, nor does it show off publicly the object of envy, nor does it count itself to have apprehended,[224] and it confesses unblushingly its ignorance of the things it does not know. Thus it makes the mind free from self-assertiveness and constantly prepares it for advance in knowledge.

61. In a way it is natural that presumption and envy follow after knowledge, especially in the beginning; presumption interiorly only, envy both interiorly and exteriorly (interiorly, in the presence of those who have knowledge, exteriorly in their absence). Charity then overthrows these three: presumption, because it is not puffed up; interior envy, because it is not jealous; exterior envy, because it is patient and kind. It is necessary then that the man who has knowledge also take along charity that he may preserve his mind from every sort of wound.

62. He who has been granted the grace of knowledge

and yet has grief, grudges, or hate for someone, is like to the man who scratches his eyes with thorns and brambles. Therefore knowledge necessarily stands in need of charity.

63. Do not give your entire time to the flesh, but set it exercises according to its capacity; and turn your entire mind within. *For bodily exercise is profitable to little; but godliness is profitable to all things*, and so on.[225]

64. He who unceasingly concerns himself with the inner life is sober, long-suffering, kind, and humble. But this is not all, he also contemplates, attains theology, and prays, which is what the Apostle says: *Walk in the Spirit*, and so on.[226]

65. He who does not know how to walk the spiritual way is not concerned over impassioned representations, but gives his entire time to the flesh. Either he is gluttonous and licentious, is full of grief, anger, and grudges and so darkens his mind; or else he indulges immoderately in ascetic exercises and roils the understanding.

66. Scripture takes away nothing that God has given us for use, but chastises immoderation and corrects unreasonableness. Thus it does not forbid one to eat, beget children, to have money and administer it properly; but it does forbid one to be gluttonous, to fornicate, and so on. Nor does it even forbid one to think of these things (they were made to be thought of), but to think of them with passion.[227]

67. Some of the God-pleasing things we do are done in obedience to commandments, some not by commandment, but as it were, by free-will offering. Such as these are done by commandment, loving God and neighbor, loving enemies, refraining from adultery, murder, and the rest. When we transgress these, we are condemned. By free-will offering, however, there are virginity, celibacy,

poverty, solitude, and so on. These are of the nature of gifts, so that, if out of weakness we have been unable to perform some of the commandments, we may propitiate our good Master by gifts.[228]

68. He who honors celibacy or virginity must necessarily have his loins girt about and his lamp burning.[229] He girds his loins with self-mastery; he supplies his lamp with prayer, contemplation, and spiritual charity.

69. Some of the brethren suppose they have no part in the graces of the Holy Spirit.[230] Because of their negligent practice of the commandments they do not know that the genuine believer in Christ has in himself all the divine graces together. But since by our laziness we are far from having an active love for Him (which manifests to us the divine treasures in us), reasonably enough we suppose that we have no part in the divine graces.

70. If—so the divine Apostle—*Christ dwells in our hearts by faith* and *all the treasures of wisdom and knowledge are hid in Him,*[231] then all the treasures of wisdom and knowledge are hid in our hearts. They are made manifest to the heart in proportion to each one's purification by the commandments.

71. This is the treasure hidden in the field of your heart, which you have not yet found because of laziness. For if you had found it, you would therefore have sold all and acquired that field.[232] But now you leave the field and go after things nearby, in which there is nothing to be found but thorns and brambles.

72. Therefore the Savior says: *Blessed are the clean of heart, for they shall see God.*[233] They will then see Him and the treasures in Him, when by love and self-mastery they purify themselves, and the more fully the further they press the purification.

73. Therefore also He says: *Sell what you possess and give alms; and behold, all things are clean unto you.*[234] Such people no longer devote their time to things for the body, but hasten to purify the mind of hate and intemperance (the mind the Lord called heart). For these things that stain the mind do not permit it to see Christ dwelling in it by the grace of holy baptism.

74. Scripture calls the virtues ways; and the best of all ways is charity. Therefore the Apostle said: *I show unto you yet a more excellent way*[235]—one which would persuade to despise material things and prefer nothing temporal to the eternal.

75. Love for God is opposed to concupiscence, for it persuades the mind to abstain from pleasures. Love for neighbor is opposed to anger, for it makes it scorn fame and money. These are the two pence that the Savior gave to the host that he might take care of you.[236] So then, do not show yourself inconsiderate, joining up with the robbers, lest you be once again beaten and be found not half but fully dead.

76. Cleanse your mind of anger, grudges, and shameful thoughts. Then you will be able to know the indwelling of Christ.

77. Who illumined you with the faith of the holy, consubstantial, worshipful Trinity? Or who made known to you the incarnate dispensation of one of the Holy Trinity? And who taught you about the natures of incorporeal beings and the reasons of the beginnings and consummation of the visible world? Or about the resurrection from the dead and eternal life? Or about the glory of the kingdom of the heavens and the dread judgment? Was it not the grace of Christ dwelling in you, the pledge of the Holy Spirit?[237] What is greater than this grace? What is better

than this wisdom and knowledge? Or what is more exalted than these promises? If then we are lazy and careless and do not cleanse ourselves from the passions, which check and blind our mind, so as to see more clearly than the sun the natures and reasons of these things, at least let us blame ourselves and not deny the indwelling of grace.

78. God, who has promised you eternal goods and placed in your heart the pledge of the Spirit, commanded you to tend with care your manner of life that the inner man, freed from the passions, might begin here and now to enjoy those goods.

79. You, to whom have been granted divinely exalted contemplations, take the greatest care for charity and self-mastery, that by keeping your sensitive part undisturbed, the soul's splendor may be unfailing.[238]

80. Check the soul's irascible element with charity; the concupiscible reduce with self-mastery; and wing its rational part with prayer. And at no time will the light of your mind be darkened.[239]

81. These are examples of the things that break charity: dishonor, loss, calumny—either against the faith or one's manner of life—beatings, stripes, and so on, whether they happen to oneself or to one's relatives or friends. He who breaks charity for one of these, has not yet learned what the purpose of Christ's commandments is.

82. Be eager to love every man as much as you can. If you are unable to do this, at least hate no one. And you cannot even do this unless you despise the things of the world.[240]

83. So and so has slandered. Do not hate him, but the slander and the demon who brings on the slander. If you hate the slanderer, you have hated a man and transgressed the commandment and do in deed what he had done in

word. If you keep the commandment, show marks of love and, if you can in any way, help to free him from the evil.

84. Christ does not want you to have hate for any man or grief, or anger, or grudges in any way whatsoever at all or for any temporal thing whatsoever. And this surely the four Gospels proclaim with loud voice.

85. We talkers are many, doers there are few. No one then ought to falsify the word of God by his own negligence; rather one should confess his weakness and not cover up God's truth, lest we be guilty of false interpretation of the word of God as well as of the transgression of the commandments.

86. Love and self-mastery free the soul from passions; reading and contemplation deliver the mind from ignorance; the state of prayer places it with God Himself.

87. When the demons see us despising the things of the world, lest for such things we hate men and fall from charity, then they incite calumnies against us, in order that, not bearing the grief, we hate the calumniators.

88. There is no trouble more grievous to the soul than calumny, whether faith be its object or one's manner of life. And no one can scorn it, save only he who, as did Susanna, looks to God, who alone is able to rescue in need, as He did her, to give men, as in her case, satisfaction, and to comfort the soul with hope.

89. As much as you pray from your heart for your calumniator, so much too God makes the truth known to those who were scandalized.

90. God alone is good by nature, and only the imitator of God is good through conformity of will. His purpose indeed is to join the wicked to the good by nature that they may become good. Therefore, reviled, He blesses them; persecuted, He endures; slandered, He entreats; put

to death, He intercedes. He does everything in order not to fall from love's purpose.[241]

91. The commandments of the Lord teach us to use means reasonably. The reasonable use of means purifies the soul's condition; a pure condition begets discernment and discernment begets detachment, from which perfect love is begotten.[242]

92. He does not yet have detachment who is not able, in case of temptation, to overlook the fault of a friend, whether it be real or apparent. The roused passions in his soul blind his intelligence and do not permit him to look into the rays of truth nor to distinguish the good from the bad. Neither then does such a one possess perfect charity that casts out the fear of judgment.[243]

93. *Nothing can be compared to a faithful friend.*[244] Indeed he takes his friend's misfortunes as his own and endures with him in hardships until death.

94. The number of friends is great, but only in good times; in time of trial you will scarce find one.

95. Every man is to be loved from the soul; our hope is to be placed in God alone; He alone is to be served with all our strength. For so long as He preserves us, all our friends treat us with respect and all our enemies are impotent against us. But should He desert us at any time, all our friends turn from us and all our enemies prevail against us.[245]

96. There are four general kinds of dereliction. One is in the Dispensation, as with the Lord, that through the apparent dereliction, the deserted may be saved. Another is for trial and proof, as with Job and Joseph, that they may be manifest as pillars—one of courage, the other of chastity. The third is for spiritual education, as with the Apostle, that in humility he might keep the superabundant treasure

of grace. The fourth is a turning away, as with the Jews, that in punishment they might be bowed down to repentance. All these ways are saving and full of the divine goodness and kindness.[246]

97. Only the strict observers of the commandments and the genuine initiates in the divine judgments do not desert their friends suffering divinely-permitted trials. People who disregard the commandments and are inexperienced in the divine judgments, take pleasure with their friend in prosperity, but in the hardships of trial they desert him, or even, it may be, side with his opponents.

98. The friends of Christ love all sincerely, but are not loved by all; the friends of the world neither love all nor are loved by all. The friends of Christ preserve the bond of charity until the end; the friends of the world until they are in conflict with one another for things of the world.

99. *A faithful friend is a strong defense.*[247] For in prosperity he is a good counselor and an intimate collaborator, and in hardships truly a genuine helper and a most sympathetic ally.

100. Many have said much about charity. Looking for it only among the disciples of Christ will you find it, for they alone held the true Charity, the Teacher of charity, of which it is said: *If I should have prophecy and should know all mysteries, and all knowledge, . . . and have not charity, it profiteth me nothing.* He then that possesses charity, possesses God Himself, for *God is charity.*[248]

To Him be glory through the ages. Amen.

NOTES

BIBLIOGRAPHY

In the following list of select bibliography note also the abbreviations used to eliminate unnecessary repetition in the references.

Balthasar, H. Urs von: *Die 'Gnostischen Centurien' des Maximus Confessor* (Freiburg 1941) [*Die Gn. Cent.*

—— *Kosmische Liturgie. Maximus der Bekenner: Höhe und Krisis des griechischen Weltbild* (Freiburg 1941)=*Liturgie cosmique. Maxime le Confesseur* traduit de l'allemand par L. Lhaumet et H.-A. Prentout (Paris 1947)
[KL followed by the German and the French pagination

Caspar, E.: 'Lateransynode von 649,' *Zeitschr. f. Kirchengeschichte* 51 (1932) 90 ff.

Dalmais, I.-H.: 'L'oeuvre spirituelle de s. Maxime le Confesseur,' *Vie Spirituelle, supplém.* 6 (1952) 216–26

—— 'La théorie des 'Logoi' des créatures chez s. Maxime le Confesseur,' *Rev. des sciences phil. et théol.* 36 (1952) 244–49

—— "La doctrine ascétique de s. Maxime le Confesseur d'après le *Liber asceticus*," *Irénikon* 26 (1953) 17–39

—— 'Un traité de théologie contemplative: Le commentaire du Pater Noster de s. Maxime le Confesseur,' *Rev. d'asc. et myst.* 29 (1953) 123–59

Devreesse, R.: 'La vie de s. Maxime le Confesseur et ses recensions,' *Anal. Bolland.* [=AB] 46 (1928) 5–49

—— 'Le texte grec de l'Hypomnesticon de Théodore Spoudée,' AB 53 (1935) 49–80

—— 'La fin inédite d'une lettre de saint Maxime,' *Rev. de science rel.* [=RevSR] 17 (1937) 25–35

Epifanovitch, S. L.: *Materials to Serve in the Study of the Life and Works of St. Maximus the Confessor* (Kiev 1917)—in Russian. See the table of contents in: *Rev. d'hist. ecclés.* 24 (1928) 802 f.
[Epifanovitch

Grumel, V.: 'Notes d'histoire et de chronologie sur la vie de s. Maxime le Confesseur,' *Echos d'Orient* [=EO] 26 (1927) 24–32

—— 'Recherches sur l'histoire de monothélisme,' EO 27 (1928) 6–16 and after

—— 'Maxime le Confesseur,' in *Dict. de théologie cath.* 10 (1928) 448–59

Hausherr, I.: *Philautie, de la tendresse pour soi à la charité, selon saint Maxime le confesseur* (Rome 1952)

—— 'Massimo il confessore,' *Enciclopedia cattolica* 8 (1952) 307

Loosen, J.: *Logos und Pneuma im begnadeten Menschen bei Maximus Confessor* (Münster i. W. 1941)

Pegon, J.: *Maxime le Confesseur: Centuries sur la charité* (Sources chrétiennes 9, Paris 1945)   [Pegon

Pierres, I.: *S. Maximus Confessor—princeps apologetarum synodi Lateranensis a. 649—pars historica* (diss. Gregoriana, Rome 1940); see B. Altaner, *Theol. Revue* 41 (1942) 50   [Pierres

Sherwood, P.: *An Annotated Date-list of the Works of Maximus the Confessor* (Rome 1952)   [Date-list

—— *The Earlier Ambigua of St. Maximus the Confessor and His Refutation of Origenism* (Rome 1955)   [The Earlier Ambigua

Viller, M.: 'Aux sources de la spiritualité de saint Maxime: les oeuvres d'Évagre le Pontique,' *Rev. d'asc. et myst.* 11 (1930) 156–84, 239–68, 331–36
                        [Viller, followed by number of page or note

The references to Maximus' text are all given according to the column numbers of the Migne reprint of the Combefis edition (Paris 1675) and of the Oehler edition (for the *Ambigua*, Halle 1857). For brevity's sake these column numbers are added directly to the abbreviation of the individual work referred to. The volume of Migne is indicated in the following list. Only four works are found in volume 91. For the *Centuries* I cite only by Century number and chapter, thus: Char 1.15.

Migne, *PATROLOGIA GRAECA*

90:		91:	
Vita et certamen	VC	*Opuscula theologica et*	
Relatio motionis	RM	*polemica*	TP
Disputatio Bizyae	DB	*Epistulae*	Ep
Quaestiones ad Thalassium	Thal	*Mystagogia*	Myst
		Ambiguorum liber de variis	
Quaestiones et dubia	QD	*difficilibus locis Sancto-*	
In Psalmum 59	Ps 59	*rum Dionysii Areopa-*	
Orationis Dominicae expositio	PN	*gitae et Gregorii theologi*	Amb
Liber asceticus	LA		
4 Centuriae de charitate	Char		

Capita 200 theologica et oeconomica	ThOec
Quaestiones ad Theo-pemptum	Theop

Evagrius I have cited thus: Evagrius, *Practicos* 1.26; *De oratione* 1.32; *Centuries* 1.86 (Frankenberg 122). The *Practicos* and the *De oratione* may be found in Migne's Greek Patrology, respectively in volume 40.1221–52 and 79.1165–1200. Lists of Evagrius' works are given in I. Hausherr's article in *Rev. d'asc. et myst.* 15 (1934) 34 f. and in R. Draguet's in *Rev. d'hist. ecclés.* 41 (1946) 323 f.

Abbreviations not listed above:

CSEL Corpus scriptorum ecclesiasticorum latinorum
GCS Die griechischen christlichen Schriftsteller der ersten drei Jahrhunderte
Mansi Sacrorum conciliorum nova et amplissima collectio
MG Migne, Patrologia graeca
ML Migne, Patrologia latina
OCP Orientalia christiana periodica
RE Realenzyklopädie der classischen Altertumswissenschaft

INTRODUCTION

(For the abbreviations used see the Bibliography immediately
preceding)

[1] See *The Earlier Ambigua*, esp. ch. II, *Excursus* I for Pseudo-Denis.
[1a] Cf. KL 4/13.

[2] According to E. Caspar, "Lateransynode von 649," *Zeitschr. f.
Kirchengeschichte* 51 (1932) 75–137, canons 10 and 11 of the Lateran
Council are the work, principally, of Maximus.

[3] Amb introd.–1033A; Ep 15–549A.

[4] Amb 42–1341A.11 ff.; TP 28–320D; cf. also Char 4.77. For the
same phenomenon in the west see J. de Ghellinck, *Le mouvement théologique du xiie siècle* (2 ed. Paris 1948) 474 ff.

[5] For example, I. Hausherr, 'Ignorance infinie,' OCP 2 (1936)
361, and the review of KL in the same periodical, 8 (1942) 221.

[6] Thus one reduces Thomistic theology to God, as the supreme
mystery of *Being*. See R. Garrigou-Lagrange, *De Revelatione* (3 ed.
Rome 1931) 1.31.

[7] R. Devreesse, AB 46 (1928) 44.

[8] See the first two articles of Devreesse in the bibliography; the
documents in question are the following:

1. *Relatio motionis*, 655, before the palace tribunal, reported by
Anastasius the monk MG 90.109–129.

2. Letter of Maximus to Anastasius the monk, on an incident of
the above process MG 90.132 f.

3. Letter of the monk Anastasius to the community of monks at
Caglari MG 90.133–36.

4. Dispute at Bizya, August–September 656, reported by Anastasius the monk MG 90.136–72.

5. Letter of Anastasius the Apocrisary to Theodosius of Gangres,
before 666 MG 90.171–78.

6. *Hypomnesticon* of Theodore Spoudaeus, about August 668
Latin MG 90.193–202; Greek AB 53 (1935) 66–80.

[9] The greater part of Maximus' known works have been reprinted
in MG 90, 91 from the edition of Combefis (Paris 1675) and from that
of Oehler (Halle 1857, for the *Ambigua*). Of this corpus the following
are generally reckoned dubious or spurious:

The Five Centuries   MG 90.1177–1392
Other chapters (243)   90.1401–61
A fragment   90.1461
On the soul   91.353–61
5 Dialogues on the Trinity mentioned but not
  printed in MG 91
  Loci communes   MG 91.721–1017
  Hymns   91.1417–24

The remaining works, save for the interspersed scholia, may be considered on the whole genuine, though some of the letters and little tracts may have to be denied to Maximus (so Loosen, XI, XII).

The above listed works I have entirely neglected; the same must be said for the scholia on Denis, of which only a few scant marginal notes come from Maximus (so von Balthasar, 'Das Scholienwerk des Johannes von Skythopolis,' Scholastik 15 [1940] 37).

[10] Grumel, EO 26 (1927) 24–32. The following pages on the life of St. Maximus have served as the narrative portion of my Date-List.

[11] On this general education (ἐγκύκλιος παίδευσις) see P. Koukoulès, Vie et civilization Byzantines 1.1 (Athens 1948) 105–137; on the schools at Constantinople see F. Dvornik, Photius et la réorganization de l'Académie patriarcale (AB 68 [1950] 108–119, esp. 110 f.). In both the imperial and patriarchal schools the general education was given, in the former, however, no theology.

[12] For a more detailed account of Maximus' life up to the time of his establishment in Africa, see my article 'Notes on the life and doctrine of Maximus the Confessor,' Am. Benedictine Review 1 (1950) 347–56.

[13] Ep 2–396C, TP 1–33A.

[14] Amb 7–1076C.

[15] Amb introd.–1064B.

[16] Amb 7 and KL 97/81.

[17] The authenticity of these two centuries (MG 90.1084–173) as a work of Maximus has not yet been fully accepted. See for example the review of von Balthasar's Die Gn. Cent. in OCP 8 (1942) 222. In both my Date List (item 37) and The Earlier Ambigua (3 f.) I failed to notice the contemporary reference to Maximus' works contained in the piece Adversus Constantinopolitanos (MG 90.204B), found in the 12th century manuscript Coisl. 267 fol. 514 f.

[18] In von Balthasar's analysis of these centuries 94 are given as of Origenistic motif, 36 Evagrian, a total of 130 against 70 assigned to opposed motifs drawn from Denis the Mystic and others.

[19] KL 42/40.

[20] *Die Gn. Cent.* 23.

[21] That there are just ten chapters in this group is not fortuitous. Elsewhere in Maximus we find such groups—TP 13–145, TP 23–260–64B.4, TP 25–269, and the 17th item published by Epifanovitch 66 f. Even therefore should it prove necessary to reject Maximian authorship for these two centuries, I would retain it for this initial group of ten.

[22] The detailed substantiation of the position I am here maintaining is out of place in an introduction. I hope later to give proof for what I am now asserting.

[23] St. Thomas Aquinas has done something similar for Aristotle's doctrine of substance. The doctrine and its terminology has been retained and transposed intact to a context in which the distinction of essence and existence is primordial. See E. Gilson, *Being and Some Philosophers* (Toronto 1949) 166, also 160–62.

[24] See Letters 28–31, also Letter 8 which seems to me also addressed to John despite the ascription to Sophronius in *Vat. gr.* 504 f. 150v (Devreesse, RevSR 17 [1937] 34 f.) and in *Vat. gr.* 507 f. 148 (Epifanovitch 84). Combefis and *Coisl.* 90 read *to the same*. The preceding letter, Ep 7, is inscribed *to John the priest* (Combefis) or *to Jordanes the priest* (*Coisl.* 90). In his note Combefis clearly prefers a bishop for the correspondent, though he does not exclude a simple priest or superior from the possibilities. Grumel proposes simply to take over the reading of *Coisl.* 90 for Ep 7, *Jordanes*.

[25] RevSR 17 (1937) 31 ff. Devreesse speaks of Maximus' departure from Chrysopolis. The same event, however, is sufficient to explain the dispersion of St. George's monastery at Cyzicus.

[26] TP3—49C. Maximus does not indicate the time of this stay; but as there is nowhere a hint that once in Africa he was again in the eastern Mediterranean before his arrest, it is more reasonable to assign this stay to the year 626–27.

[27] Ep 21–604; as to the importance of this town, see RE 11.2306.

[28] A letter is addressed to Marinus the monk (Ep 20), an opusculum to Marinus the deacon (TP 7), and several to Marinus the priest (TP 1–3, 10, 19, 20). I am inclined to suppose only one Marinus, with whom he would have become acquainted while on the island.

[29] See below n. 64.

[30] See n. 25.

[31] TP 12–142A.4 ff.

[32] Ep 12–461A.8 ff. John Moschus was also surnamed *Eucratas* (H. Delehaye, AB 45 [1927] 6). The Sophronius of Maximus is certainly

the patriarch; this surname connects him with Moschus. Delehaye (*loc. cit.*) apparently does not consider this in declaring the identity of the Sophronius of Moschus and the patriarch as still uncertain.

³³ Cf. the MS inscriptions to Letter 8 cited in n. 24.

³⁴ Ep 13–533A.

³⁵ See von Balthasar, *Die Gn. Cent.* 155 f.

³⁶ Ep 8–445A. On Ep 8 as addressed to Sophronius see above, p. 9 and n. 24.

³⁷ Ep 31–625C ult.

³⁸ TP 1–9–12. See below, p. 23 and n. 88.

³⁹ RM 1–112AB, *strategos* of Numidia; for Peter's other movements see Ep 13–509C, 512BC, 533A.

⁴⁰ Ep 14–536A.4.

⁴¹ TP 12–141–46. It may be that Peter was sent again to Africa after the recall of George.

⁴² Ep 1–364 ff.

⁴³ Ep 12. The sequence of events is not too clear. Aside from Ep 12, Ep 18,1,44,B (Epifanovitch 84 f.), and 45 pertain to this affair. See my comments on each of them in *Date-List*, 33, 66, 67, 69, 70.

⁴⁴ So Grumel, EO 26 (1927) 30.

⁴⁵ TP 28–332B ff.

⁴⁶ L. Duchesne, *L'Église au vi^e siècle* (Paris 1925) 394, gives this year.

⁴⁷ Aside from the historians of the Church and of dogma, encyclopedia articles, and the like, one may read Grumel's studies: *Recherches sur l'histoire du monothélisme* in EO for 1928, 1929, 1930.

⁴⁸ VC 5–72D.

⁴⁹ *Die Gn. Cent.* 152; KL 42 f./40.

⁵⁰ The more so that Maximus assures us of its complete orthodoxy (TP 9–132C.9).

⁵¹ Ep 19–592C.5.

⁵² EO 27 (1928) 13; the text is taken from Mansi 11.536E–537A.

⁵³ The passages are: from the letter to Honorius, Mansi 11.533CD, from the *Ecthesis*, Mansi 10.993E–96AB (=C. Kirch, *Enchiridion fontium historiae ecclesiasticae antiquae* 6.ed. 1070–73). The variants are of no substantial import. Further, Sergius prefaces the passage in his letter to Honorius with these words: "We wrote to the patriarch of Alexandria . . . that he, rightly promoting the union with the former dissidents, no longer permit any one to say one or two operations of Christ our God. . . ." The parallel begins with the word *permit*.

⁵⁴ RM 10–126AB.

⁵⁵ Ep 19–592B–C.7.

[56] Sergius to Honorius, Mansi 11.536B; *Dispute with Pyrrhus,* TP 28-349C.

[57] Ep 19-593A.2 f.

[58] Ep 19-593B.1-5.

[59] Ep 19-596B.

[60] See TP 28-330C-332B.2, where six interpretations are attributed to Sergius. Perhaps all of them are not Sergius' own personal interpretations; but they would be at least of his entourage.

[61] See below p. 19 and *n.* 66.

[62] TP 20-228-45.

[63] TP 20-244C ff.

[64] TP 20-245C. Who might this bishop be? Combefis suggests Arcadius. Maximus, in his letter to Peter (TP 12-143B), refers to this Arcadius as already dead. TP 12 was written probably in the latter part of 643; we know Sergius and other bishops of Cyprus wrote Pope Theodore a joint letter in May 29, 643 (Mansi 10.913-16). As this letter does not appear to be a synodical letter on the occasion of Sergius' election, we are left with no sure determination of the date of Arcadius' death or of Sergius' election.

[65] Mansi 10.996BC (Kirch, *Enchiridion* 1072, 73).

[66] Grumel (EO 29 [1930] 24) gives this date. The delay in consecration could only have been due to the detention of the apocrisaries at Constantinople.

[67] See R. Aigrain in Fliche-Martin, *Histoire de l'Église* 5.400 n. 6.

[68] We have only the Latin version preserved in the *Collectanea* of Anastasius (ML 129.583D f.; printed also in Mansi 10.677 f.).

[69] Ep 12, relating this affair to John the Chamberlain, with a refutation of the Monophysite position of Severus; Ep 1 to George at his departure, Ep 44 and 45 again to John, commending George to him; Ep B (Epifanovitch 84 f.) to Stephen at Constantinople to insure the correct transmission of an important document. Cf. above n. 43.

[70] Mansi 10.996D ult.

[71] John wrote in defence of Honorius and for the removal of the *Ecthesis* to Heraclius' son Constantine, who died in May, 641 (the letter is in Mansi 10.682-86 and ML 129.561). L. Bréhier seems to have slipped (Fliche-Martin, *Hist. de l'Église* 5.143 n. 5) in gathering from this letter that Pyrrhus was already no longer patriarch. He was deposed only September 29, 641 (see E. W. Brooks, *Byz. Zeitschr.* 6 [1897] 53 f.), several months after Constantine's death.

[72] Letters to Paul of Constantinople in response to his synodical letters; to the consecrators of Paul, and a short statement against the innovations of Pyrrhus and the *Ecthesis*. They are to be found in Mansi

10.702–708 and ML 129.577 ff. They must date from the end of 642 or the beginning of 643, as Paul had been patriarch of Constantinople from October 1, 641, a full year before Theodore's consecration.

[73] Mansi, 10.704D.

[74] *Ibid.* 705A and 704A; 707C.

[75] TP 12–144AB and D f. It is only in Anastasius' version that we have fragments of this letter (a *defloratio*). From these excerpts (esp. 144A.11–13, 144D.7) it appears that this Peter is a man of authority, presumably in Africa. He is probably to be identified with the Peter, *strategos of Numidia*, mentioned in RM 1–112A, 2–113A, the same to whom Ep 13, 14 and the *Computus Ecclesiasticus* are addressed. If in 633 (see above, 12) he was *strategos* of Numidia, what office did he hold ten years later, the time of the letter about Pyrrhus? Was he the successor of George, eparch of Africa? V. Laurent, 'Une effigie inédite de s. Augustin sur le sceau du duc byzantin de Numidie Pierre,' *Cahiers de Byrsa* 2 (1952) 88 would reckon Peter's *strategos*-ship as ten years later (643 instead of 633). But we must still reckon with Ep 13 and 14. See my comments on these in *Date-List.*

[76] See above n. 44.

[77] See above p. 17.

[78] I note some of these opuscula (the column number in parentheses is where explicit mention of two wills is to be found): TP 6–65; TP 7–69 (77D); TP 8–89 (109D); TP 14–149; TP 16–184; TP 24–268; TP 25–269; TP 26–276.

[79] The text of this dispute (TP 28–287–354) has come to us through manuscripts copied at Rome as the scribe's colophon indicates (353A.11–B.4).

[80] These letters may be found in Mansi 10.919, 925, 929. It is uncertain whether there were actually three councils or but one composed of the three groups—from Numidia, Byzacenus, Mauretania.

[81] There is, so far as I know, no direct proof of the time of Maximus' arrival in Rome or whether he came there with Pyrrhus. There is only the inference from the second accusation recorded in RM 2–112C ff. This supposes Maximus to have been in Rome nine years before—a supposition he does not call into question. But nine years before 655 is 646 (or only 647?). If then in Rome by 646, Maximus was there contemporaneously with Pyrrhus.

[82] Its extent is remarkable. Combefis prints three portions of it: TP 1–9–37 (which is certainly the beginning, see below); TP 2–40–45 with TP 3–45–56 are numbered chapters 50 and 51 respectively. This is not all. Epifanovitch (62 f.) prints three fragments labeled chapters 58, 59, and 92. The content is as definitely dyothelite as anything

Combefis has printed. The remaining chapters are lost, at least their identity is lost, among the other lesser opuscula.

[83] *Die Gn. Cent.* 153. It is clear that von Balthasar thinks only of the years 646–53.

[84] TP 10–133–7.

[85] TP 10–137B.7.

[86] The analyses of acts of the soul extend to TP 1–21C; the rest of TP 1 as well as TP 2 and 3 are all on related topics. Letters 6 and 7, both treating of the soul, cannot be considered as satisfying the reference; neither are addressed to Marinus, neither gives any suggestion of such a late date.

[87] Maximus refers to the *Ecthesis* (136D.7) of which he knew only in 640 (see above, p. 19 and n. 66) and to the 'synodicals of the present pope' (133D.3, 4). This might be John IV or Theodore (scarcely Martin, as Combefis says in his *Monitum* [col. 140]; there is no mention of the *Type*). But John IV (640–42) is improbable as being too early for such a developed stage of the controversy, as is evident in TP 1. The date must therefore be between November, 642 (Theodore's consecration), and Maximus' departure from Africa (645–46) as he writes from Carthage (137C). The more likely date without doubt is 645–46.

[88] With 'extending the motion of thy desire to the infinity' (9A.8), compare Amb 15–1220C where the infinity that surrounds God is represented as the limit of all mutation. See below, pp. 31 f., nn. 129, 134. With 'eon and time' (9A.6) compare ThOec 1.5. With the assigning of virtues to reason and contemplation, better union (I would not accept Combefis emendation—knowledge for union—the scholiast also read our text) to mind, compare the magnificent development of the general motion of the soul in Amb 10–1112D ff., 1113D. On the joining of virtue and contemplation together with goodness and truth compare Myst 676A, 677D.

[89] See preceding note, all of Thal 61–628A ff.; also von Balthasar, KL 24,127 f./27,103.

[90] RM 2–112C.7. The accusation necessitates Maximus' presence in Rome nine years before. It was then 655: cf. RM 6–120C.3; to take the interlocutors here literally, the discussions between Maximus and Pyrrhus would also have occurred at Rome. Cf. n. 81.

[91] L. Duchesne, *L'Église au vie siècle* (Paris 1925) 439 f., supposes the whole of Pyrrhus' double change of face to be connected with Gregory's revolt in Africa. The revolt a failure, Pyrrhus quickly reconciles himself with the imperial position. L. Bréhier, in Fliche-Martin, *Histoire de l'Église* 5.163 n. 3, reckons this as mere conjecture.

[92] TP 9. The letter is addressed to 'the superiors . . . in Sicily here.'

The phrase, 'after the man's (Pyrrhus') complete deviation' (132C.9), seems best understood of his reversion to the imperial fold.

93 See the extra chapter edited by Devreesse, AB 46 (1928) 18, line 24 ff.

94 RM 4–113D ff.

95 The *Typos* was promulgated in September, 647, as Devreesse has pointed out (AB 46 [1928] 44; cf. also W. M. Peitz, *Hist. Jahrbuch* 38 [1917] 219). Most authors continue to give 648.

96 See the material assembled in Pierres.

97 TP 28–333A.

98 Ep 13–532D f. Monenergism is not properly in question in this letter. Properly therefore it provides no evidence with regard to an anti-Monenergistic *florilegium*.

99 Mansi 11. 532D, 533B.

100 See above n. 53.

101 The Greek runs thus: Christ in both His natures is θελητικὸν καὶ ἐνεργητικὸν τῆς ἡμῶν σωτηρίας. See TP 28–320C.13; canon 10 of the Lateran Council, Mansi 10.1153E; see the discussion in Caspar (*art. cit.* [cf. above, n. 2] 90).

102 Caspar (*art. cit.* 120), in view of the dependence of canons 10 and 11 on Maximus, considers his presence at the council as certain. This is further confirmed by the subscriptions. The oriental monks, resident in Rome at that time, petitioned (*art. cit.* 84 f.) that a Greek version be made of the acts. Among the 36 signatures (*art. cit.* 84 n. 19) in third from last place occurs: *Maximus monachus similiter* (Mansi 10.910—the subscriptions are wanting in the Greek text). It is curious to note that an *Anastasius* follows.

103 The *Hypomnesticon* dates the troubles of Maximus from the 11th year of the indiction, that is from September, 652–August, 653 (AB 53 [1935] 75 n. 17).

104 The date *post quam* is certainly the consecration of Pope Eugene (August 10, 654), as his apocrisaries have just arrived (RM 6–121B) in Constantinople. But the alleged communion of these apocrisaries with the patriarch took place on Sunday the 18th, Pentecost, that is, May 18, 655. The whole process therefore took place in May, 655. The patriarch in question is Peter. This Peter ascended the throne in May/June 654. So Devreesse (AB 46 [1928] 48 f.) against E. W. Brooks, May/June, 655 (*Byz. Zeitschr.* 6 [1897] 53 f.).

105 Bréhier, Fliche-Martin, *Histoire de l'Église* 5.171,173, draws attention to the tribunal before which both Martin and Maximus were tried, that namely of the patriarchal *sacellarius*, to whom was committed the disciplinary jurisdiction of the patriarch. In other

words, the crime in question was merely political, the ecclesiastical tribunal being necessitated by the clerical character of the accused. The *sacellarius* would not have been competent in a doctrinal case.

[106] RM 6–11.

[107] The documents for the above account are:

1. Deposition of Macarius of Antioch at the 6th council, 681, concerning the Monothelite council against Maximus: Mansi 11.357C.

2. Fragment of this council: Mansi 11.73; MG 90.169C ff. (with Greek text).

3. Letter of Anastasius the apocrisary to Theodosius of Gangres: MG 90.171 ff.

4. *Hypomnesticon* 1: AB 53 (1935) 67.

On the order and value of these documents see Devreesse (AB 46 [1928] 38 ff.). A succinct account of the whole affair is given by P. Peeters in the *Propylaeum ad Acta Sanctorum Decembris* (Brussels 1940) 336 f.

[108] The death of Maximus is related in Anastasius' letter to Theodosius (MG 90.174A.12 ff.) and in the *Hypomnesticon* 5 (AB 53 [1935] 75).

[109] RM 6–120C.

[110] Cf. J. Heintjes, 'De opgang van den menschelijken geest tot God volgens Sint Maximus Confessor,' *Bijdragen der Nederlandsche Jezuieten* 6 (1943–45) 123.

[111] For a brief history of this doctrine see M. Lot-Borodine, 'La doctrine de la déification dans l'Église grecque jusqu'au xie siècle,' *Rev. d'hist. des rel.* 105 (1932) 1–43, 525–74; 106 (1933) 8–55.

[112] Ep 24–609C. The same finality dominates all the Christological doctrine, however technical it may be. The end is always man's salvation. See TP 28–320C.13 (text cited at n. 101). This salvation is the scope of the Incarnation, see LA 1–912A; Thal 61–632A.

[113] It is clear that I cannot attempt to give a complete analysis of Maximus' doctrine. This can only be done after special analyses have been made of the *Ambigua* and the *Quaestiones ad Thalassium*. In the meanwhile the studies of Loosen and of Heintjes are most valuable; the synthesis of von Balthaser is very suggestive, but does not give adequate attention to the Holy Spirit, the Church, the sacraments.

[114] Myst 5—esp. 677C; cf. TP 1–12A.

[115] Char 1.25.

[116] *Practica* 2.100=MG 40.1252B.

[117] W. Bousset, *Apophthegmata* (Tübingen 1923) 307; R. Draguet, 'L'histoire lausiaque, une oeuvre écrite dans l'esprit d'Évagre,' *Rev. d'hist. ecclés.* 41 (1946) 358.

[118] Ep 2–401D.

[119] *De div. nom.* 4.1; 2.1–MG 3.693B, 636.

[120] Amb 10–1196B.

[121] Thal 40–396C; Char 4.9.

[122] ThOec 2.2 f.

[123] See von Balthasar, *Die Gn. Cent.* 141. St. Thomas places it at the beginning of his treatise on God, *Summa theologica* 1.3.

[124] See Heintjes, *Bijdragen* 6 (1943–45) 121 f.

[125] Myst prooem.–664C.

[126] ThOec 1.7.

[127] Amb 10–1133C; Char 1.96; Thal 13–296A; ThOec 1.9.

[128] Amb 15–1220C.

[129] Char 1.100; TP 21–249B; cf. Char 1.12 and n. 8.

[130] See V. Lossky, *Essai sur la théologie mystique de l'Église d'Orient* (Paris 1944) 83.

[131] Char 4.7.

[132] See 2 Peter 1.4; also, for example, the Roman preface for the Ascension.

[133] To support the Palamite distinction of divine nature and un-created energies with the authority of Denis the Mystic is to betray the true thought of Denis. So E. von Ivanka, 'La signification historique du Corpus Areopagiticum,' *Rech. de sc. rel.* 36 (1949) 5–24, esp. 22 ff.

[134] Char 1.100 and Gregory, *Orat.* 38.7=MG 38.317BC.

[135] TP 1–9A.8, 24; C f.; cf. Amb 7–1089B.

[136] Amb 15–1217C. In line C.10 I suggest reading παύεται for the impossible ποιεῖται. This is confirmed by the MSS; see *The Earlier Ambigua* 43.

[137] KL 68 f./60.

[138] ThOec 2.1; Myst 23–700D ff.; PN–892D ff.

[139] KL 70 f./61.

[140] See n. 138.

[141] Amb 10–1193D ff.

[141a] This historic Revelation is clearly recognized by Maximus: see Amb 23–1261B. Cf. below, no. 183.

[142] Amb 10–1185C.8.

[143] Amb 1–1036B. Von Balthasar (KL 69/80) declares on the basis of this text that the Trinity, as belonging to the negative theology, is not, properly speaking, the object of a theological science. Understood in the context of Maximus the statement is true. The Greek concept of science (whose contrary was opinion) had not yet been transposed to the data of Revelation. Any theological thought on the revealed mysteries could not then rightly be called αἰτιολογία; it remained

therefore that it was pious opinion. This was inadequate, surely; but not false. Understood in a modern context, and this is von Balthasar's intent, the statement is gravely misleading; the question had not yet been posed.

[144] For this distinction see the following section.

[145] Amb 1–1036C.10. Maximus here uses ἔκφανσις, manifestation. It is a Neoplatonic and Dionysian word, used also as a synonym for πρόοδος, procession, but without, in the Dionysian use, implying a production of the inferior orders of being. Cf. R. Roques, L'Univers Dionysien, structure hiérarchique du monde selon le Pseudo-Denys (Paris 1954) 77 n. 6, 135 n. 3. A close study of such elements of Dionysian vocabulary in Maximus would be a sure gauge of the extent of the Dionysian influence.

[146] Amb 10–1188A.3 = De div. nom. 13.3 = MG 3.980D.3.

[147] The fullest exposition of this distinction is found in Amb 42–1341D ff. Examples of its application may be found in Char 4.9; TP 16–192C; TP 28–308D; TP 1–24D f. See the full treatment of this distinction in The Earlier Ambigua, ch. iv. Φύσις alone generally retains a concrete sense. See below, n. 287.

[148] According to G. L. Prestige, God in Patristic Thought (London 1936) 245, St. Basil introduced this form of logic into theological use.

[149] This is Prestige's criticism, op. cit. 278.

[150] TP 21–249B; Amb 40–1304A.

[151] PN–876CD; Thal 63–624BC.

[152] PN–877A; 384C.9 ff.

[153] PN–876D.2 f.; 892B.3 and C.12; Amb 23–1260D.9; Thal 15–297D.

[154] TP 10–136AB. The importance of this passage has recently been emphasized. See V. Rodzianko in The Christian East (1953) or in Eastern Churches Quarterly (1953) 177–91.

[155] Thal 63–672C.10 ff. Cf. Prestige, op. cit. 253. A further Trinitarian text, connecting the divine Persons in diverse ways with our salvation, is found in Amb 10–1140D, when the lacuna is correctly filled in. See The Earlier Ambigua, 41.

[156] Amb 10–1168A (not 1161, as von Baltshasar gives it, KL 69/60).

[157] Rom. 1.20.

[158] Thal 13–293D f.

[159] Thal 13–296B.

[160] The word I have twice rendered 'objectively existent' clearly implies the personal existence of the second and third Person of the Trinity. The distinction λόγος φύσεως and τρόπος ὑπάρξεως underlies this passage. See above 35 and n. 147.

¹⁶¹ Thal 13–296C.

¹⁶² Amb 10–1133 ff.

¹⁶³ Origen's erroneous theories are found above all in his *De principiis* 1.6.2; 2.9.5,6; 3.1.13,17=GCS 22 (Origen 5) 79.9–80.14; 168.12–170.17; 218.9–13; 228.14 f. Koetschau.

¹⁶⁴ Amb 10–1136BC.

¹⁶⁵ The *Selecta in Psalmos* are commonly attributed to Origen; von Balthasar esteems them to be from the *Hiera* of Evagrius (see *Zeitschr. f. kath. Theol.* 63 [1939] 86–106, 181–206). The passage in question is found in MG 12.1661CD.

¹⁶⁶ MG 3.816C; see also *De div. nom.* 2.3, 5, 7–MG 3.640B.6; 644A.4; 645A.14.

¹⁶⁷ See the text in E. R. Dodds' edition (Oxford 1933): and the commentary 252 f.

¹⁶⁸ Other instances of triadic arrangements are: Char 1.96, 100; Amb 10–1192B; ThOec 1.10; 2.1. It may be worthwhile remarking that the goodness of God, so characteristic in Denis' and Maximus' thought, is for Origen the motive of God's creation and providence. Origen even has a triadic arrangement, though not as providing some trace of the Trinity: In hac enim sola trinitate, quae est auctor omnium, bonitas substantialiter inest; ceteri vero accidentem eam ac decidentem habent, et tunc sunt in beatitudine, cum de sanctitate et sapientia ac de ipsa deitate participant (*De princ.* 1.6.2=GCS 22 [Origen 5] 80.11–14).

¹⁶⁹ Amb 7–1088A; also 10–1196A.

¹⁷⁰ See K. Holl, *Amphilochius von Ikonium* (Tübingen 1904) 176. This trace of the Trinity is to be found again towards the end of the 6th century in the Pseudo-Eulogius of Alexandria, published by Bardenhewer (*Theol. Quartalschrift* 78 [1896] 364), but perhaps to be ascribed to Epiphanius II of Cyprus (*Rev. d'hist. Ecclés.* 24 [1928] 802).

¹⁷¹ *Comm. in Ioann.* 1.38 (42)=(GCS 10 [Origen 4] 49); ThOec 2.22. See the texts in von Balthasar, *Die Gn. Cent.* 27.

¹⁷² I Cor. 14.14.

¹⁷³ *Orat.* 23=MG 35.1161C.

¹⁷⁴ Amb 7–1088C.

¹⁷⁵ G. Verbeke, *L'Evolution de la doctrine du Pneuma du Stoicisme à s. Augustin* (Louvain 1945) 385.

¹⁷⁶ Amb 10–1196B.

¹⁷⁷ *Orat. theol.* 3.2–MG 36.76B.

¹⁷⁸ Amb 23–1257C–60B.

¹⁷⁹ *De div. nom.* 4.14–MG 3.712C.1–5.

¹⁸⁰ *Ibid.* 4.10–MG 3.708B; see also G. Horn, 'Amour et Extase,' *Rev. d'asc. et myst.* 6 (1925) 284 f.

15

[181] Amb 23-1260C.7-10.

[182] Amb 23-1260D. We have seen above that in these triads wisdom is connected with distinction, while the third member is connected with motion. These are very similar to the fundamental moments of the Neoplatonic triadic world-structure—identity, difference, reversion. The similarities of Maximus' doctrine with such triads is undeniable; the differences are no less profound. See for instance Proclus' propositions 31-35, 46 in his *Elements of Theology*. Any study of Proclus and Maximus would have to include Denis. I have found no evidence that Maximus knew Proclus directly. But even in that case, not at all improbable, Maximus' understanding of Proclus would have been colored by his own knowledge of Denis.

[183] Amb 23-1261A. As a rule Maximus pays no attention to the historical aspect of things, even of the Incarnation. All things are viewed from on high, so that the historical process is overlooked. It is therefore the more interesting to note this recognition of a development in Scripture. It is unfortunate that von Balthasar overlooked this 23. Difficulty.

[184] Amb 1-1036C. See above 34, 42 f.

[185] Amb 1-1036B.13-C.5.

[186] Prestige, *God in Patristic Thought* 249; see also 301.

[187] Myst 20-696C.

[188] ThOec 1.5.

[189] Amb 7-1077C; 10-1188BC.

[190] For Maximus every being is composite, at least of substance and accidents. Char 4.9; TP 21-249A.4.

[191] Amb 42-1345A-C. Cf. *De div. nom.* 5.8 (=MG 3.824BC). It must be admitted that the syllogism begun at 1329B.9 for the eventual rejoining of body and soul (resurrection) is so loosely phrased as to comprehend any mortal creature.

[192] Amb 15-1221AB.

[193] Amb 7-1068D f. On this Origenism see *The Earlier Ambigua*, esp. ch. I.

[194] Amb 7-1072B.10 ff.

[195] Amb 15-1220A.

[196] Amb 7-1069B.

[197] Amb 15-1220D.3.

[198] This triad is of the utmost importance. It permits the rational explanation of motion and is integral to the defense of two wills in Christ. On the origin and use of the triad see *The Earlier Ambigua*, ch. II, 103 f.

[199] TP 1-33B.9 ff.

200 Amb 2–1037C.12 ff. See what Prestige, *God in Patristic Thought* 278 f., has to say on the sense of οὐσία changed from signifying a concrete whole to signifying essence, the change being occasioned by the Christological controversies.

201 A created end, as for example a merely analogous knowledge of God, would never have entered Maximus' head.

202 Amb 7–1076C.

203 Amb 7–1076D.1. See Viller, n. 134.

204 Amb 10–1112D.7 ff.; 1113B.2 ff.

205 *Ibid.*

206 *Contra Nestorianos et Eutychianos* 1=MG 86.1281B. See also V. Grumel, 'La comparaison de l'âme et du corps et l'union hypostatique chez Léonce de Byzance et s. Maxime le confesseur,' EO 25 (1926) 393–406.

207 Ep 12–488D.9–14.

208 Amb 7–1100D.2–1101A.4; Ep 13–529B.3–5.

209 This polemic against the Jews who said that the soul came to the body only with the fortieth day after conception, that is, at the time of the ritual purification, is of less importance; the arguments against pre-existence are equally valid against postexistence, especially as they are founded on the necessary simultaneity of the parts.

210 Amb 7–1101B.

211 Amb 42–1321D.8–1324A.8.

212 TP 13–145B.12–14; Ep 15–552D.13 ff.

213 See TP 16–192C; Ep 12–504A; Amb 42–1333AB, 1341AB. Maximus is not always original in these points; in some of them he is following out a line indicated by Gregory of Nyssa. See *The Earlier Ambigua* ch. V n. 41.

214 KL 173–75/136 f.

215 Metaphysicize—by this I mean the (illegitimate) essential predication of qualities or other predicates which may nonetheless be legitimately predicated of the thing in its concrete existence. The underlying distinction is that between essence and fulness (integrity); it is illustrated in the ambiguity of von Balthasar's phrase *Truth of the creature* (*Die Wahrheit der Kreatur*); this may mean all and only that which pertains to the creature's metaphysical definition or all that pertains to its fulness, whencesoever it may come.

216 See Prat, *Origène* xxix f. I have given another treatment of freedom in *The Earlier Ambigua* ch. v D : SELF-DETERMINATION.

217 Ep 6–425B.

218 Ep 7–436C.

219 TP 28–301A–C.

[220] TP 28-324C.11 ff.; 304B.

[221] TP 26-277C; cf. TP 28-301C. Diadochus wrote: 'Self-determination is a willing of the rational soul, readily moved to whatever it might will; which we believe to be a readiness only as to the good, that ever with good thoughts we may exhaust the memory of evil' (Diadochus' *Liber asceticus* ch. 5). It is from Diadochus that Maximus takes over the identification of self-determination and will (θέλησις). He takes over only the definition; the connection of the free will with good and evil he omits entirely in these two places, as not pertaining, it would seem, to the essence of the will.

[222] TP 1-17D.

[223] Amb 42-1345D ult.

[224] Ep 6-432A ult.

[225] TP 28-352AB. This was one of the fundamental errors of Monenergism and Monothelitism. Because in Christ the divine Person was necessarily and obviously active, therefore in contradistinction, the human could only be passive.

[226] Ep 6-428D.4-429A. This passage, which we have just summarized, occurs in almost the only writing of Maximus in which he deliberately sets aside Scriptural and patristic arguments. One could wish a further precision of that in which the veracity of predicating being and so on of the inferior member of the analogy consists. His last word is μεθεκτῶς, by participation, and then he adds: 'unlesss one would prefer to say, which is quite true, that the Divine is above nature and things.'

[227] TP 20-236D.

[228] Amb 7-1072B.13.

[229] See *The Earlier Ambigua* ch. v, C: FIXEDNESS, and Amb 10-1196AB; Amb 7-1076B.12 ff.

[230] Maximus had himself noticed 28 different senses of γνώμη in Scripture and the Fathers: TP 28-312B.

[231] Ep 6-428D. Γνώμη is related to διάθεσις as the habit to the act initiating it. See TP 1-17C and the index under will (=γνώμη) and intention (=διάθεσις).

[232] Ep 6-432AB. See the treatment of mutability in *The Earlier Ambigua* ch. v, C: FIXEDNESS.

[233] Ep 2-396D; 400A. On the natural equality of worth of all men see Ep 10.

[234] Char 1.70, 71; cf. TP 14-152C.

[235] Char 3.80, the divine and angelic γνώμη.

[236] PN-893B, 901, 904D f.

[237] PN-877D.

²³⁸ Amb 10–1116B; Amb 7–1073C.

²³⁹ Amb 7–1076B. Fixity in good is developed in Ep 1–365B, 368A, D, where γνώμη also enters the picture.

²⁴⁰ See Thal 6–280 f. and Thal 64–724C ff. Ep 14–533B, 541C, adds nothing new.

²⁴¹ TP 14–152C.

²⁴² TP 24–268B.

²⁴³ TP 7–80A; this repeats the statement of PN cited above, n. 237.

²⁴⁴ TP 16–193A, 192A. This latter (192A), as to the defectibility of γνώμη, recalls Ep 6, possibly Maximus' first work.

²⁴⁵ As an indication of this see the same list of acts of the volitive faculty in TP 28–293B.10 ff. and TP 1–21D f.

²⁴⁶ TP 28–308C.

²⁴⁷ TP 1–17C.

²⁴⁸ See references at n. 245.

²⁴⁹ TP 1–17C.9.

²⁵⁰ TP 1–24B; TP 28–329D.

²⁵¹ TP 28–312BC.

²⁵² See especially TP 2–40–45; TP 16–192C.

²⁵³ TP 28–313B.

²⁵⁴ TP 16–192C; TP 28–308D.

²⁵⁵ Note how Maximus preserves here what earlier he had less felicitously expressed as one will.

²⁵⁶ I have condensed Maximus' text in TP 1–24C.6 ff.

²⁵⁷ Not only is the antithesis Adam-Christ Pauline, but the whole movement of this Thal 61 corresponds with that of St. Paul's chapters 5 and 6 to the Romans.

²⁵⁸ The chief passages are: Amb 10–1156C–1160A; Amb 42–1321B; Amb 48–1361–65; Thal prol.–253B–D.

²⁵⁹ Thal 61–628A; cf. Amb 48–1361A.

²⁶⁰ Maximus does not speak much of the paradisiacal state. For the first act of man was that by which he fell. If, however, the paradisiacal state was not an historical fact extended in time, still Maximus everywhere supposes it as a reality. God did not make man to place him in his present circumstances of corruption and death. See Thal 61–629A; Amb 10–1156D; Amb 42–1321A.

²⁶¹ Ep 10–449B.

²⁶² Thal 61–628A.14: ἅμα τῷ γενέσθαι—see n. 260. In Amb 42–1321B.1 the same phrase is used, but with the further indication that the defective movement was due to the deceit of the devil.

²⁶³ Thal 61–628AB.

²⁶⁴ Thal prol.–253C.3.

[265] Thal prol. 253C; Amb 10–1157A.

[266] Thal 61–628A.

[267] Thal prol.–256.

[268] Thal prol.–260A.

[269] See above 56.

[270] Thal 61–628A.

[271] See above 51 ff.

[272] Amb 7–1100A.10–14; Amb 42–1337B.9–13.

[273] Thal 1–269A. See Gregory of Nyssa, De hom. opif. 18=MG 44. 192. This is Gregory's doctrine of a double creation; see below n. 279.

[274] Ep 12–488D.9–14.

[275] Thal 61–628B.3–7.

[276] Thal prol.–253C.7–11; D.2–4.

[277] Ep 7–436D f.

[278] Thal prol.–260A.14 ff. See also above 50, on the *composite motion* of the soul, n. 204.

[279] Gregory of Nyssa, De hom. opif. 16–18=MG 44.177 ff. See the résumé of this doctrine in J. Daniélou, *Platonisme et théologie mystique* (Paris 1944) 56 f.

[280] Amb 42–1340BC; 1341C. An outright statement of the idea of a non-sexual condition in Paradise is found in Amb 41–1309A. For Gregory of Nyssa one may read the remarks of Daniélou, *op. cit.* 51 ff. The idea is also known to St. Augustine. See De bono coni. 2 (CSEL 41.188–190) and De Gen. ad litt. 9.5–8 (CSEL 28.1.273–76).

[281] Matt 22.30, and Gregory, *op. cit.* 16=MG 44.188C (cf. Daniélou as in n. 279). This is of the type of Origen's argument for the henad: the end is like the beginning; we know the end: *that all may be one* (John 17.21); therefore the beginning of creatures is the same (Origen, De princ. 1.6.2=GCs 22 [Origen 5] 79.19 ff.). See J.-F. Bonnefoy, 'La méthode théologique d'Origène," *Mélanges Cavallera* (Toulouse 1948) 113 f. I do not affirm that Gregory, Maximus, and others who argue from heaven to Paradise are all guilty of this same error of principle as Origen. To have noted the parallel, however, is to have given a caution.

[282] Thal 61–636B.

[283] Amb 42–1321A.

[284] Thal 61–628B.

[285] Thal prol.–256B; *ibid.* 64–724CD; Ep 10–449, 452A; Ep 2–396D.

[286] Thal prol.–256B–D.

[287] Φύσις is a very plastic word in Greek. In Christological and Trinitarian contexts it seems with Maximus to have undergone the same shift as οὐσία from a concrete object to an abstract universal (see the

definition given in TP 26–276A; and the equation of *common,* οὐσία, φύσις as against *particular,* ὑπόστασις, *person* in Ep 15–545A; Prestige, *God in Patristic Thought* 279, has criticized this interpretation); yet in an anthropological context, such as is our present one, Maximus preserves throughout the sense given it by his master in these matters, Gregory of Nyssa. This Father conceived nature as a *concrete universal* (see von Balthasar, *Présence et Pensée* [Paris 1942] 22 f.). As to Adam, in him was the *whole of humanity,* the reason being that the image of God which is in man according to Genesis is only in the whole (*De hom. opif.* 16=MG 44.185BC–cf. Daniélou, *op. cit.* 57 f. n. 279). The most manifest instance of this use in Maximus occurs in Thal 61–637A.5: 'The saints, through many sufferings, free *the nature that is in them* from the condemnation of death on account of sin.' Loosen (52 n. 15) gives a bibliography on this question; note especially E. Malevez, 'L'Église dans le Christ,' *Rech. de sc. rel.* 25 (1935) 257–91, 418–40.

[288] This is the theme of the whole 61st question so often cited; see particularly 628CD, 632D, 633B; for the last details, 632A.

[289] Ἐνανθρώπησις, of more frequent use, and (ἐν)σάρκωσις are mostly represented in Latin theology and the derivative English theological vocabulary by *incarnatio.* The former term more fully represents the mystery, though less immediately Scriptural. If it be worthwhile adding it to our theological vocabulary, one may either borrow another Latin word, *inhumanatio,* whose sense would not be so immediately apparent to all, or make an English equivalent as in the text or else forge a new term on the analogy of embodiment. Thus one could have in English this triplet: enfleshment, embodiment, en*man*ment.

[290] Thal 61–636D. The antithesis *generally for nature* (κατὰ φύσιν) . . . *particularly in act* (κατ᾽ἐνέργειαν) is instructive. A very common correlative of *in act* is *in potency,* which is here also suggested by the words *generally, particularly.* Yet what Maximus says is *for nature,* which here must have that concrete general sense that I have just explained (n. 287).

[291] TP 28–309C f. *Natural* must here be understood in its full sense, so that the sense is: the virtues stand out in their paradisiacal perfection.

[292] The practical identification of deification and salvation in Maximus is evident in the *Liber asceticus.* The whole first part is given over to making clear the scope of the Incarnation—salvation; in the conclusion (43) he speaks of deification. In Thal 61–640A he qualifies salvation as 'that completest grace of deification given by God to the worthy.' He realizes, however, that there is some difference. In the same question (632A) he connects deification 'above nature' directly

with the Incarnation, while the various factors of our restoration are connected with privations, suffering, death; the word salvation does not there occur. See the text cited at n. 295.

[293] 1 Cor. 2.9.

[294] 2 Peter 1.4.

[295] Ep 24–609C.

[296] The slip is in Amb 7–1076C; the correction in TP 1–33B.

[297] Amb 7–1097C; LA43–953B.

[298] Thal 64–725C. Cf. above the antithesis *Adam–Christ.*

[299] Amb 7–1088C; this immutability is the pair of (sinful) mutability of which we have spoken above (58)—ἀτρεψία–τροπή).

[300] Thal 25–333A; Myst 5–680B.

[301] Thal 64–725C; Ep 2–405A.

[302] Thal 6–281A; Thal 15–297D.

[303] See above 37 n. 155.

[304] Amb 7–1088, 1097, 1100. In 1088A he adduces the simile as a development of his own on the doctrine of Gregory, whose text he is explaining.

[305] Ep 18–584D; for the Pauline context see Amb 7–1097.

[306] Zach. 4.2; Thal 63–665 ff.

[307] The Church of which Maximus speaks is simply the Church on earth; I have found no indication that he makes a distinction of militant and triumphant Church, or the like.

[308] I refer chiefly to the first chapter (664 f.); much could be drawn from this work as to the sacramental nature of the Church, but it would require a special study.

[309] DB 28–165A.

[310] RM 13–128C: 'We have a command to hate no one; I love the Romans as of the same faith, the Greeks as of the same tongue.' So Maximus replied in the first Process to the accusation of loving the Romans and hating the Greeks, because of his refusal to communicate with the emperor, who still maintained the condemned *Type.*

[311] End of Ep 8; Devreesse, RevSR 17 (1935) 35. Maximus has in mind the forced baptism of the Jews in 632.

[312] Ep 10.

[313] RM 4–117B. Elsewhere (Ep 31–625A) Maximus, speaking in a Dionysian way (cf. *Hier. Eccl.* 1, 2–MG 3.372D ff.), says that the end of the priesthood is 'to be deified and to deify.'

[314] 1 Cor. 12.28 (modified).

[315] RM 9–124A.

[316] Modern exegesis generally understands the *apostles* not merely of the Twelve, but of that larger group of which Barnabas, Silas,

Apollo were members. The *prophets* likewise are those of the New Testament. The doctors similarly belong to the ministry of the first-century Church whose office was not simply the antecedent of any one of the subsequent hierarchical orders. Maximus doubtless identifies the *apostles* with the Twelve, the *prophets* with those of the Old Testament, the *doctors* with bishops. Similarly for Augustine the *doctores ecclesiae* are the bishops. Yet the position of *doctor* continued for some time apart from the episcopal office. Origen was doctor (διδάσκαλος) and apparently considered his position to have its authority from the text of the apostle. Cf. J. Daniélou, *Origène* (Paris 1948) 57–63.

[317] TP 28–320BC.

[318] TP 28–300C.

[319] DB 12–148AB.

[320] DB 17–153C.

[321] See above 20 and n. 75.

[322] TP 12–144C.4–12.

[323] TP 11–137D ff.

[324] It would be interesting to know what influence the Africans may have had, for contact with them Maximus must have had, in the formation of this unequivocal teaching concerning the Roman See.

[325] The chief references to baptism are found in the following: LA 44–956A; PN–877A; Myst 24–712B; Thal 6–280C ff.; Thal 61–636D; ThOec 1.87; 2.63.

[326] See above 70 and n. 290.

[327] Thal 6–280C f. On the sense of γνώμη see above 58.

[328] Thal 61–632A; Amb 7–1097C.

[329] Thal 61–636C.11.

[330] ThOec 1.87.

[331] Thal 61–636D f.; LA 34–940B.11. These texts place this participation of the faithful, especially of the saints, in the redemptive work of Christ in relation with baptism only, not with the monastic life. But as the latter is but the utmost of the Christian life flowing from baptism, this participation would be eminently realized therein. Consequently it is not only in the 12th century that a monastic 'awareness of this redemptive task' comes into the clear, as Dom F. Vandenbroucke (*Le moine dans l'Église du Christ* [Louvain 1947] 157 f.) supposes.

[332] ThOec 1.87; death voluntarily accepted must be understood in the light of Christ's death, and so the Christian's, being in condemnation not of nature but of sin.

[333] See LA 44–953D f.; Char 2.41; 3.55; Thal 10–289B.4.

[334] La 44–956A.

[335] G. E. Steitz, "Die Abendmahlslehre der griechischen Kirche in

ihrer geschichtlichen Entwickelung," *Jahrb. für deutsche Theologie* 11 (1866) 229–38; W. Lampen, 'De Eucharistie-Leer van S. Maximus Confessor,' *Studia Catholica* 2 (1926) 373–83.

[336] The texts pertaining to the Eucharist so far as I have noted them are the following: QD 40–818CD (priesthood); QD 41–820A (communion); Ep 31–625A (priesthood); Ep 21–604D (priesthood); PN–877C, 897A (communion); Amb 48–1361 ff. (communion), 1364B (sacrifice); Amb fin.–1417C (sacrifice); Myst 21,24–697A, 704D f. (communion); Thal 35–377B (communion); Thal 36–380D f. (communion); RM 4–117B (priesthood).

[337] Myst introd.–660D f.

[338] These various senses of feeding on the Word, though distinct, compenetrate, and precisely on the Word, the *Logos*, who is always the God-man, as axis. In these texts Maximus can only be understood against the background of Origen and Gregory of Nyssa. See H. de Lubac's recent study, *Histoire et Esprit, l'intelligence de l'Écriture d'après Origène* (Paris 1950) 355–73, and J. Daniélou, *Platonisme et théologie mystique* (Paris 1944) 259 ff.

[339] QD 40–818D.

[340] Ep 21–604D.

[341] Ep 31–625A.

[342] Ep 21–604D.

[343] Thal 36–381B.

[344] Heb. 9.11; 5.14.

[345] PN–897BC. I rather think these reasons for diversifying the gift of deification will finally, also for Maximus, be the degree of charity. His last remark in Amb (1417C) is that only one sacrifice is demanded of us, love (φιλανθρωπία) for one another. And for that matter, that there should be diversities of deification, that is, of the manner in which God is enjoyed, not of the hierarchical position among the blessed, due to the peculiar diverse imitative capacities, native and acquired, of each one for the Word of God, is neither strange nor objectionable.

[346] Amb 48–1364B ff.

[347] This correspondence of the Eucharist with the paradisiacal tree of life is established in PN–897A ff.

[348] Pegon designates the last two sections of his introduction *la technique* and *le sens*. The larger aspects of the nature of man that he treats under this head, I have already considered. It remains for me to treat chiefly of the virtues, vices, natural contemplation and prayer.

[349] I say *separate* deliberately; the schematization which we find in Maximus of the powers of the soul, the virtues, vices, natural con-

templation, and so on, is largely taken from Evagrius and has in the process been separated from Evagrius' metaphysical suppositions. The schematization is therefore *separable*; but Maximus has welded it into a new whole, so that in him it is wrong to speak of it as separate or even separable in his thought from the whole context in which he placed it.

[350] For Gregory of Nyssa, cf. Daniélou *Platonisme et théol. myst.* 260; it seems very obvious for Denis.

[351] LA 42–953B; that our salvation is an affair of γνώμη, is evident on every page of Maximus: the λόγος of our nature is immutable, our fall, and so also our restoration, will be a change of the mode; and this is the field of γνώμη; that it is likewise a realization of our nature, follows from the antithesis of Adam and Christ; more explicitly Maximus affirms that the virtues are *natural*, the point of asceticism being to eradicate the vices impeding their natural blossoming (TP 28–309C f.).

[352] See the notice in the *Downside Review* 68 (1950) 252–54 on P. Glorieux' article in *Mélanges de science religieuse* for November, 1949, on the fundamental orientation of the soul at death. In a similar sense J. B. Manyà has written *Theologumena II: De ratione peccati poenam aeternam inducentis* (Barcelona 1947). See the review in *Theol. Studies* 10 (1949) 118–22.

[353] A. Nygren, *Eros et Agape, la notion chrétienne de l'amour et ses transformations* (Paris 1944). I have only the French version available. See L. Bouyer, *Irénikon* 17 (1940) 24–49; J. Daniélou, *Platonisme et théol. myst.* 212–20; H. C. Graef in *La vie spir.* Suppl. 4 (1950) 99–105; Char 3.67,71. Nygren's analysis is useful, but proceeds under the influence of his Lutheran theology.

[354] Char 2.13.

[355] See Amb 10–1157C; Ep 9–609D.

[356] After the article of Viller no one has doubted of the indebtedness of Maximus to Evagrius. But it is one thing to note such an indebtedness and another to determine its nature and extent. Bousset has remarked that compared with Origen, Evagrius' ability is especially 'in the field of practical piety' (W. Bousset, *Apophthegmata* [Tübingen 1923] 304, repeated by R. Draguet, *Rev. d'hist. Ecclés.* 42 [1947] 40). This is the area of Maximus' greatest indebtedness; for metaphysical views and theological positions Maximus rather refutes Origen and follows other masters. But even in his indebtedness to Evagrius he has been able to alter not a little some cardinal points, as to the nature of love for neighbor and self-love. Also there is in Maximus a closer cohesion of the ascetic with the sacramental and liturgical life of the Church. Viller's method and purpose did not permit him to draw

attention to such things. In the notes attention is drawn to these divergencies from strict Evagrianism. For further notes on the same subject see *The Earlier Ambigua* ch. IV.

[357] See R. Draguet, *Rev. d'hist. ecclés.* 41 (1946) 333, and Viller 160 ff.

[358] Char 4.44; Amb 10–1116A.

[359] Amb 10–1196C ff., an elaborate division and subdivision of the passible part of the soul.

[360] See the marshalling of vices under pleasure and pain in Thal introd.–256B f.

[361] See Viller nn. 71, 72; Evagrius, *De oratione* 27, says: 'If you are armed against anger, you will never tolerate concupiscence; for the latter furnishes food for anger, and the former disturbs the eye of the soul by spoiling the state of prayer.' I. Hausherr in his comment (*Rev. d'asc. et myst.* 15 [1934] 64) cites *Practicos* 2.99 (MG 40.1252B): 'Another monk said: For this reason I do away with pleasures, that I may cut off the excuses of anger; for I know that it is always battling for pleasures, upsetting my mind and driving out knowledge. . . .' Maximus takes the same point of view, as to anger and desire, in Char 1.66,79; 4.80; also LA 20.

[362] Compare the passages cited in the preceding note. Maximus is not so much a theorician that he cannot speak of desire and anger as also hindering prayer (Char 1.49); yet this is not his main theme.

[363] The role of meekness (πραότης) in Evagrius has been noted especially by Draguet (*Rev. d'hist. ecclés.* 41 [1946] 328 ff.); cf. *De oratione* 14 (Hausherr, *art. cit.* 55).

[364] PN–885B, 888B, 893B; Ep 4–417B; Ep 5–421C; Ep 13–509D; Char 1.80. Viller (173 f.) is misleading in his treatment; to be sure, he says meekness (*douceur*) is a form of charity, but he notes in no way the reason why Maximus should have preferred charity to meekness. It is not only the commandment and example of the Lord, which LA makes incontrovertibly clear, but also the relation of charity to the good and its unitive quality; this will be made clear farther on.

[365] LA 23–929A f.

[366] The relation of self-mastery and detachment are illustrated in Christ: in Him self-mastery has no place inasmuch as it implies an active restraint of disordered passions, a choice between following them or rejecting them. TP 1–29D, 32A.

[367] H. E. White has drawn especial attention to this: *The History of the Monasteries of Nitria and of Scetis* (New York 1932) 14; see a text in Palladius' *Historia Lausiaca* 18 (ed. Butler, 2 [Cambridge 1904] 50, or MG 34.1052C).

[368] See particularly Char 2.84.

³⁶⁹ Viller n. 102; Char 2.71. The following are some of the chapters referring to demons: Char 2.13,18,22,31,67,85,90.

³⁷⁰ LA 19; Draguet (*Rev. d'hist. ecclés.* 41 [1946] 335 n. 21; also 42 [1947] 5 n. 138) draws attention to the fact that anger is the demon's passion *par excellence*.

³⁷¹ Char 4.75 pairs love of God off with concupiscence, love of neighbor with anger. This too is the thought underlying LA—the temptation of Our Lord in the desert against the love for God and those in His ministry against love for neighbor. The inference is therefore that it is love of neighbor which chiefly conquers anger.

³⁷² See above 39, 50.

³⁷³ LA 24–929C.

³⁷⁴ Ep 2–401C–404A. For a like reticence or silence concerning 'natural contemplation' see also Ep 4, 5, 24, also addressed to seculars, and Ep 9 and 20, which, though addressed to religious, are elementary.

³⁷⁵ This last sentence should be understood in the light of Char 1.100. See von Balthasar's comment on this passage in KL 340 ff./256 ff.

³⁷⁶ Amb 10–1113A.1, B.2 f.

³⁷⁷ 1 Cor. 11.3; Thal 25–329.

³⁷⁸ Thal 25–332C.11: Ὁ τὴν ... ὑπερέχουσαν ἑαυτοῦ τε καὶ τῶν ὄντων ... θεοποιὸν στέρησιν συνασκούμενος νοῦς. I take this to refer to the efforts of the individual rather than to the divine action alone capable of producing ἔκστασις.

³⁷⁹ Thal 25–333D. This is clearly in the realm of apophatic theology; 'natural contemplation,' however, necessarily pertains to kataphatic theology. This is the case with the passage on the five ways of 'natural consideration' cited at n. 162.

³⁸⁰ See in addition to the passages already cited Char 2.61, 62; LA 19–928A.

³⁸¹ See above 30.

³⁸² See Char 3.97 and the note there.

³⁸³ See Hausherr, 'Ignorance infinie,' OCP 2 (1936) 358.

³⁸⁴ *Theologia myst.* 1.1 (=MG 3.997B fin. f.).

³⁸⁵ See n. 383; for von Balthasar's critique of this article see KL 31–5/32–4.

³⁸⁶ See above 39 f.

³⁸⁷ Amb 10–1112D fin., 1113A.1 f., and 1113B.2–C.3; Thal 25–332C.11, 63–673D; Myst 5–676CD.

³⁸⁷ᵃ 'To the unknown,' 'ad ignotum,' so Scotus and *Vat. gr.* 1502 against Oehler: πρὸς τὸ γνωστόν.

³⁸⁸ Ep 2–393C.1.

³⁸⁹ Viller 239. In n. 118 Viller notes how Clement of Alexandria

(*Strom.* 4.22.136) could oppose, theoretically only, eternal salvation and knowledge of God with a preference for the latter. In Maximus it is always salvation and deification which hold the place of end and final cause; charity is the deifying virtue *par excellence*, and thereby is at once given an importance above knowledge, though in some of its aspects it is conducive to knowledge.

390 See above 85.

391 The word ἀπάθεια is common in the ascetical writers; it must be understood in the sense they give it, not in that of its English equivalent with a sense taken over largely from the Stoic use. I have rendered (*calm of*) *detachment*, Pegon, *liberté intérieure*. See its use in Char 1.25, 36; 2.89; 3.35,98; 4.42,48,53,54,58,91,92; Ep 1–364B f., and the article of Bardy in the *Dictionnaire de spiritualité ascétique et mystique* 1 (1937) 727–46 (on Maximus, 742). Cf. H. Graef in ACW 18.187 n. 68.

392 See Char 1.77,91; 2.22,30,34; 4.42,57.

393 See Char 1.25.

394 Char 2.25.

395 Char 4.30; 1.29.

396 Ep 2–402D.

397 Evagrius, *Practicos* 2.100 (=MG 40.1252B).

398 The requirement of equal love is found in Char 1.17,24,25,61, 71; 2.10,30. In Char 1 there are 20 chapters on fraternal charity, 5 in Char 2, 3 in Char 3, 21 in Char 4. Over a quarter therefore of these chapters refer to or are devoted to fraternal charity.

399 Char 1.61.

400 Char 1.25.

401 Char 1.71; 2.30. See also Ep 2–397D f.; Thal prol. –245D; Thal 64–724D, 725C; Ep 25–613A.

402 John 15.13 and Thal 64–725C.

403 See above n. and Thal 61–632A; PN–877C; Ep 2–405A.

404 1 Tim. 2.3; Char 1.61; Thal 6–281A. But see the use of ἐπίγνωσις as a technical term in *The Earlier Ambigua*, 215–20.

405 Ep 2–404A.12; PN–877C; Ep 25–613D.

406 See above 29–31.

407 Char 4.8,9.

408 Amb 10–1185C ff.; Myst 5–680B, 681B; 21–696D.

409 Thal 25–333A.

410 *De div. nom.* 2.1; 4.1 (=MG 3.636C, 693B). The divine goodness is also a commonplace with the Alexandrians and with the Neoplatonists; only Denis makes more of it than they.

411 Amb 7–1069C.

412 Amb 7–1076BC and Gal. 2.20. In *De div. nom.* 4.13 (MG3.712A)

Denis introduces this text as said by Paul 'in the grip of the divine *eros* and its ecstastic power.'

⁴¹³ TP 1–33A referring to Amb 7–1076C.10 f.

⁴¹⁴ Amb 7–1073C.11 f. Here *love* represents the root used in *eros*.

⁴¹⁵ Amb 7–1076C. Cf. ThOec 1.81; also *The Earlier Ambigua*, ch. IV.

⁴¹⁶ For this last see Amb 7–1088C.

⁴¹⁷ The conclusion comes in 1077B.

⁴¹⁸ KL 33/33.

⁴¹⁹ Amb 15–1220AB; ThOec 1.82; 2.2; cf. Myst prooem.–664C.

⁴²⁰ Ep 2–396B–D.

⁴²¹ Viller (n. 122) notes that *door of knowledge* is an Evagrian phrase. Given the other Johannine figures here for Our Lord (way, vine), there is no need to insist on an Evagrian dependence, though of course it is not excluded.

⁴²² Ep 2–401D, 404AB.

⁴²³ Myst 5–672D, 673A–C.

⁴²⁴ TP 1–9A.15 ff. The sense of the first concise phrase is that Marinus' outward life has manifested the Godward direction of his mind; and correspondingly his mind has inspired his life—in an harmonious whole.

⁴²⁵ Char 3.25; Amb 7–1092B, 1096A, 1097C. This use of *image* is not constant. Loosen (42 n. 27) has collected a number of references to image, but from a broader point of view.

⁴²⁶ Thal prol.–253C.

TEXT

The Ascetic Life

[1] Salvation is at the very heart of Maximus' thought, ascetic and dogmatic; it is the grace of deification (Thal 61–640A); it enters the very formula for expressing two energies and two wills in Christ (see text cited in n. 101 of Introduction). Note how here and again in TP 24 (268A) Maximus' starting point is the creed: 'for us men and for our salvation.'

[2] For a fuller description of man's condition after the fall, see Introd. 63.

[3] Luke 1.79.

[4] Cf. Heb. 2.14.

[5] 1 Cor. 15.22.

[6] The observance of the commandments is the first of the three ways of the spiritual life (c.f Char 4.47). LA is written for beginners in the monastic life, the observance of the commandments forms the chief object of the dialogue; but love is also numbered among the commandments, and love is deifying (cf. Ep 2–405A). Maximus even speaks of deification as directly the result of faithful observance of the commandments (LA 43), with not a word in the immediate context of the detailed means (self-mastery and prayer).

[7] Matt. 28.19 f.

[8] Ps. 118.128.

[9] Imitation can be said to be one of the central themes of Maximus' spirituality. Here there is question of imitating the humble, suffering Lord. Hausherr has written especially on this aspect in his article, 'L'imitation de Jésus-Christ dans la spiritualité byzantine,' *Mélanges Cavallera* (Toulouse 1948) 246–51. But there is more. In this imitation of Christ there is also the imitation of the divinity, especially of the firmness of the will in the good. Whence there is that imitation of God's goodness and charity which effect a likeness of the Trinity. See the Introd. 29, 30, 42. In LA imitation is also mentioned in 15 and 34; imitation of the saints, in 18 and 45; of both the Savior and the saints, in 30; cf. Char 1.24,61; 4.55.

[10] Matt. 19.27.

[11] Luke 10.19.

[12] 1 Cor. 11.1.

¹³ Rom. 8.1,4.

¹⁴ Gal. 5.24.

¹⁵ *Ibid.* 6.14.

¹⁶ Ps. 90.1 f.

¹⁷ *Ibid.* 90.13,11.

¹⁸ Matt. 10.37.

¹⁹ *Ibid.* 10.38.

²⁰ Luke 14,33.

²¹ On the demons see Introd. 86. In addition to the references of n. 369 see also below LA 10,13,15,16.

²² Cf. Mark 12.30 f.

²³ Matt. 6.24.

²⁴ *Ibid.*

²⁵ This strong emphasis on renunciation can, especially in a thought world where the material is slighted as in the Platonic and Neoplatonic philosophies, give specious support to a dualist view. See the open rejection of Manichaeism cited in the Introd. 68. For that matter, Maximus might have in mind some influence of the Paulicians, a dualist sect coming into evidence about that time (Cf. R. Janin, *Dict. de théol. cath.* 12 [1933] 56–62; T. Nersayan, *Eastern Churches Qu.* 5 [1944] 403–412).

²⁶ Cf. John 14.15.

²⁷ *Ibid.* 15.12.

²⁸ Cf. Rom. 13.10.

²⁹ In the Introduction renunciation is not set in any relief. Maximus seldom uses the word. As to the sense of the doctrine, it is everywhere in Maximus, and no more so than here. Renunciation is necessary to self-mastery, it is a necessary sign of love for God; it is even love for God, inasmuch as it is the preference of Him to creatures. This is in full accord with Stolz's doctrine: 'The fundamental idea of all Christian asceticism would be in our opinion separation from the world in order to give oneself more freely to God': A. Stolz, *L'ascesi cristiana* (2 ed. Brescia 1944) 5.

³⁰ On the origin of pain for Maximus see Introd. 64, 70. 'Self-love crossed by pain begets anger, envy, hate, enmity...'; Thal prol. 256C.

³¹ Matt. 5.44.

³² This tendency to bestiality was one of the chief results of the primordial immersion in sense. See Introd. n. 265; Char 2.52. Its antidote, fraternal charity, is urged below in 41.

³³ Cf. Gal. 4.4.

³⁴ Cf. Matt. 22.37–40.

16

[35] The words here rendered by 'egg on' and 'Instigator' are forms of ἐνεργέω which in the present passive participle, ἐνεργούμενος, became a technical term for the possessed, for the demoniacs and as such has passed into Latin (cf. the admonition of the bishop to exorcists: 'accipitis itaque potestatem imponendi manum super *energumenos*'); but in our text the devil's activity has not reached the stage of possession. The Scribes and Pharisees were not possessed.

[36] Phil. 2.5.

[37] 2 Cor. 13.4.

[38] Heb. 2.14.

[39] 2 Cor. 12.9.

[40] Eph. 6.12.

[41] Cf. *ibid.* 6.11–17.

[42] I Cor. 9.26 f.

[43] *Ibid.* 4.11.

[44] 2 Cor. 11.27 f. In St. Paul's text this last phrase belongs to the following verse; here it is a senseless pendent.

[45] I Cor. 4.12 f.

[46] Cf. Rom. 12.21.

[47] Luke 23.34.

[48] James 4.7. 'God's brother' (that is, Christ's cousin): ἀδελφόθεος.

[49] Soberness (νῆψις). The term has Scriptural authority (1 Peter 5.8; 1 Thess. 5.6) of which Maximus is aware as he twice joins it with vigilance (LA 45–956B; Ep 5–424B), as in St. Peter's text; but it has more than Scriptural connotations. Philo had already spoken of 'sober drunkenness,' an idea that was to be taken up by some of the Fathers (Origen, Gregory of Nyssa, Ambrose, Augustine: see the study of H. Lewy, *Sobria ebrietas* (Giessen 1929 = *Zeitschr. f. d. Nt. Wissenschaft*, Beih. 9). It later became a technical term of the Hesychast spirituality, used, more or less synonymously with several others, to indicate that custody of the heart which is the entrance to contemplation and continual prayer. Maximus was reckoned among the Hesychast fathers by Nicodemus the Hagiorite, who included Char and ThOec in his *Philocalia* (Venice 1782). The work had small success in Greek, but in Russian a most phenomenal vogue. It is *the* book of the Pilgrim: see 'The Way of a Pilgrim' in G. P. Fedotov, *A Treasury of Russian Spirituality* (New York 1948). But this is a posterior development; in Maximus νῆψις already appears as a special term, always connected with St. Peter's text, and represents a virtue or condition that is proximate to continual prayer. In the present context it has occurred six times: LA 16–924D.4, *sober-minded* (νηφεῖν); LA 17–925A.4, *soberly* (νηφόντως); LA 18–925B.2, *soberness* (νῆψις); LA 18–925B.12,

be sober 1 Peter 5.8; LA 18–925C.6, *soberly* (νηφόντως); and LA 18–925D.2, *sober-minded* (νηφόμενος). It is found also in Char 2.11,59.

⁵⁰ Thoughts (νοήματα, more often λογισμοί). The whole of the ascetic struggle turns in a way about thoughts. The doctrine is common in Evagrius and in Maximus. One must distinguish between the thing, the memory of it or the thought, and passion towards it. Thoughts are evil or passionate, when to the mere thought is joined the disordered desire for the thing. The man in the world deals especially with the things; they are the source of his temptation. The monk is removed from their presence; he retains their memory, through which the demons can instigate him to desire them. The occurrence of these terms is so frequent that it is useless to give more than a typical reference, Char 3.42 f. For the confrontation of Evagrius and Maximus, see Viller, index under λογισμός; cf. also n. 21 and references there.

⁵¹ Ps. 53.9.

⁵² 1 Peter 5.8 f.

⁵³ Matt. 26.41.

⁵⁴ Eccles. 10.4.

⁵⁵ 2 Cor. 10.3–6.

⁵⁶ Mind (νοῦς). The doctrine of the mind, here and in 24 briefly alluded to, is thoroughly after the manner of Evagrius, as an ascetical and mystical doctrine; as to the psychological and physiological presuppositions, one must recognize a vast difference. See note on Char 3.97.

⁵⁷ The arrangement is triadic. One might have expected here, inasmuch as the third member is pure prayer, the triad: sense, reason, mind (explained in the Introd. 50). The present triad of virtues however is built on this other triad equally well known to Evagrius and Maximus: the irascible, concupiscible, reason (here: mind). The result is that in this little treatise for beginners nothing is said of natural contemplation.

⁵⁸ Self-mastery (ἐγκράτεια). Continence is a more usual version of the Greek term, but it has acquired in English a too narrow connotation, namely restraint as to things of sex. The virtue indicated restrains the subject from any excessive activity of desire. See, for example, Char 1.64–66; 2.56.

⁵⁹ Ecclus. 1.29 f.

⁶⁰ 2 Kings 16.10.

⁶¹ Job 2.10.

⁶² Mental (νοητά). It was commonplace for Byzantine writers, especially those influenced by the Neoplatonic Denis, to speak of a sense-perceptible world and a mental world, of which the latter had a

greater share of reality as being a world of things perceived by the mind alone, whether in their existence such things be independent of matter or not. This mental world, then, is not the subjective world of man's ideas, but the objective world of things capable of being understood completely.

[63] On the mind in prayer see Introd. 89.
[64] 1 Thess. 5.17.
[65] Rom. 8.35,38.
[66] 2 Cor. 4.8-10.
[67] *Ibid.* 12.9,10.
[68] On compunction see Introd. 100 f.
[69] Deut. 32.22 f.
[70] *Ibid.* 32.41.
[71] Isa. 33.14 (Sept.).
[72] *Ibid.* 50.11.
[73] *Ibid.* 66.24.
[74] Jer. 13.16.
[75] *Ibid.* 5.21 f.
[76] *Ibid.* 2.19,21 (Sept.).
[77] *Ibid.* 15.17 (Sept.).
[78] Ezech. 7.8 f., 4.
[79] The constant insistence in LA on judgment and the consequent punishment does not permit any question as to Maximus' belief in their regard. Yet in the texts where the salvation of nature is spoken of, there is no indication at all of there being any individual exceptions, so that the Origenist doctrine of universal restoration (ἀποκατάστασις) seems to be implied. See the treatment of the question in *The Earlier Ambigua* ch. VI: *Apocatastasis.*
[80] Dan. 7.9 f.
[81] *Ibid.* 7.13-15.
[82] Ps. 61.12 f.
[83] Eccles. 12.13 f. (Sept.).
[84] 2 Cor. 5.10 (Rom. 14.10).
[85] Jer. 31.10 (Sept.)=48.10 (Vulg.).
[86] Matt. 7.13 f.
[87] *Ibid.* 25.41.
[88] Exod. 20.13-15.
[89] Matt. 5.20.
[90] Jer. 9.1.
[91] Deut. 32.15.
[92] Mich. 7.1-3 (Sept.).
[93] Ps. 11.2.

94 Rom. 3.12–14,16–18.
95 2 Tim. 3.1–4.
96 John 8.41,44.
97 Rom. 8.14.
98 *Ibid.* 8.6.
99 Gal. 5.22 f.
100 John 3.6.
101 Gen. 6.3.
102 James 2.19.
103 *Ibid.*, conflation of 2.17 and 26.
104 Gal. 2.20.
105 This is an unmistakable recognition of the social and redemptive character of the Christian life, and a tacit interpretation of Col. 1.24. See Introd. 78 and n. 331.
106 1 Cor. 4.12 f.
107 Luke 6.27 f.
108 Cf. 1 Cor. 3.16 f. and John 2.16.
109 Cf. Matt. 21.13.
110 Cf. 1 Peter 2.9.
111 Cf. Isa. 1.4.
112 *Ibid.* 1.5 f. (Sept.).
113 *Ibid.* 1.8.
114 Rom. 1.28–32.
115 *Ibid.* 1.24.
116 *Ibid.* 1.18.
117 Matt. 23.37 f.
118 Isa. 1.10–15 (Sept.).
119 1 John 3.15.
120 Matt. 15.8 (Isa. 29.13).
121 *Ibid.* 23.4.
122 *Ibid.* 23.5.
123 *Ibid.* 23.6 f.
124 Cf. Luke 11.52 and Matt. 23.13
125 Matt. 23.15.
126 *Ibid.* 23.24.
127 *Ibid.* 23.25.
128 Luke 11.42.
129 *Ibid.* 11.44 and Matt. 23.28.
130 Cf. Matt. 23.29.
131 Cf. Lam. 4.2,1.
132 Cf. *ibid.* 4.7 f.
133 Cf. *ibid.* 4.5 f.

[134] Cf. 1 Thess. 5.5.

[135] Ps. 81.6 f.

[136] Cf. Dan. 3.32.

[137] Cf. Heb. 10.29.

[138] Here begins the prayer that continues to the end of §39.

[139] Dan. 3.34 f.

[140] This phrase has fallen out of the Greek text in Migne, as Cantarella indicates.

[141] Ps. 78.8 f.

[142] Cf. *ibid.* 54.2 and 43.23.

[143] Cf. Dan. 9.18.

[144] Cf. Ps. 50.13,2,3.

[145] 1 Cor. 12.6.

[146] Isa. 63.15-19 (Sept.), with additions.

[147] *Ibid.* 63.19-64.4 (Sept.).

[148] *Ibid.* 64.4-12 (Sept.).

[149] This is but another application of the principle St. Paul enunciates (1 Cor. 10.6,11) concerning the passage of the Red Sea and baptism. The historical quality of the Old Testament events is in no way impugned; rather it is necessary so that they may serve as types. Cf. Thal 16-380D.

[150] Ps. 78.4.

[151] *Ibid.* 37.5.

[152] Matt. 19.26.

[153] Ps. 94.2,6 f. (Sept.).

[154] Isa. 30.15 (Sept.).

[155] *Ibid.* 59.1 f. (Sept.).

[156] *Ibid.* 1.16-20 (Sept.).

[157] Joel 2.12 f.

[158] Ezech. 33.10 f.

[159] 3 Kings 21.19,23.

[160] *Ibid.* 21.27-29 (shortened).

[161] Ps. 31.5 f.

[162] Matt. 4.17.

[163] *Ibid.* 18.21 f.

[164] Cf. 1 Cor. 9.27.

[165] 2 Cor. 7.1.

[166] Cf. Heb. 10.24.

[167] Eph. 4.25.

[168] 1 John 2.1 f.

[169] Ps. 144.18.

[170] *Ibid.* 49.14 f.

[171] Isa. 58.6–10 (shortened).

[172] This is the first of evils consequent on the Fall, though it receives less attention from Maximus than self-love (Thal prol.–253C).

[173] Cf. Rom. 12.17.

[174] Luke 6.37.

[175] Matt. 6.14.

[176] *Ibid.* 5.7.

[177] *Ibid.* 7.2.

[178] Cf. John 1.12. This provides a Scriptural basis for Maximus' doctrine of renewal of powers. Cf. Thal 61–632A and the following note.

[179] Salvation and deification are God's gift, yet they require of us the right use of our renewed powers. See Introd. 71, 79, 81 f.

[180] Ps. 80.14 f.

[181] *Cf. ibid.* 54.23.

[182] *Ibid.* 43.7 f.

[183] Matt. 7.15.

[184] See Introd. n. 391.

[185] Προγονικὴ ἁμαρτία. The term is unusual (occurring only here and in LA 1–912B.13). The whole of Thal 61 (cf. Introd. 64, 78) is concerned with the sin of Adam, but there we find only 'Adam the forefather' ('Αδὰμ ὁ προπάτωρ—Thal 61–632B.1) or the 'disobedience' or 'sin of the forefather' (632C.1; 633D.8). Or again, we find: 'those who have their being from Adam' (636B.10) receive necessarily the damnation of death. By baptism we are freed from death as penalty for sin. Thal 61 then provides a full commentary of this passage in LA. It would be tempting to translate προγονικὴ ἁμαρτία by *original sin*. But this latter term would introduce a whole series of theological connotations foreign, so it seems, to Maximus. The term *original* sin implies controversies as to the mode by which sin is transmitted; but for Maximus such a question can scarcely arise, given his sense of human nature as a 'concrete universal' (see Introd. n. 287). The more literal rendering, 'ancestral sin,' is therefore to be preferred.

[186] Gal. 5.16.

[187] Phil. 3.13.

[188] Heb. 12.14.

[189] Note the plural. The fiction of dialogue is forgotten; Maximus is simply addressing his fellow monks.

[190] Τὸν κοσμοκράτορα: the devil, the lord 'of the rulers of the world of this darkness' (Eph. 6.12). Cf. J. Dölger, *Die Sonne der Gerechtigkeit und der Schwarze* (Münster i.W. 1918) 49 ff.

THE FOUR CENTURIES ON CHARITY

[1] Cf. Evagrius, *Centuries* 1.86 (Frankenberg 122): 'Love is an exalted state of the rational soul in which it is impossible to love any thing of this world more than knowledge of God.' Maximus has enlarged and heightened the antithesis; he has furthermore changed *state* to *disposition*, thus giving greater prominence to the gnomic quality of charity. He can, however, refer to the state of charity (Char 4.30). For the similar placing of knowledge of God as end of charity, see Char 1.4, 9, 27 and Introd. n. 389.

[2] On detachment see Introd. n. 391. This same series is repeated in the inverse order in the next chapter. Note that it contains the three theological virtues. Of hope he writes in Ep 2–396B: 'Hope is the strength of the extremes, I mean charity and faith; through itself it indicates the trustworthy and lovable (quality) of both and teaches the contest to be made for it.' There is an Evagrian parallel (*Practicos* introd.–1221BC), which however joins hope with patience and goes on from love to the gate of natural knowledge, to θεολογία and the ultimate blessedness. See also Char 1.81.

[3] The mind is reckoned as the highest part of the soul. See the division, Introd. 84. Purified, it is at home in the state of pure prayer (Char 2.61). Cf. Char 1.97; 3.97, 99 and the n. to 3.97.

[4] For this insistence in regard to one's own body, see LA 8.

[4a] Cf. 1 Cor. 13.13.

[5] Of ἔρως I have briefly spoken in the Introd. 83. It occurs in the following chapter and in Char 2.6,47,48. Cf. also Amb 48–1361A.13. The connection of ἔρως with desire is particularly marked in the passage from Amb and Char 2.48. Ἔρως and ἀγάπη are distinguished therefore, but in a human mode, as responding to desire and anger. Ἀγάπη however prevails over ἔρως and itself 'embraces the ultimate in desire' (Ep 2–396C). The more proper notes of ἀγάπη are its unifying power and equality.

[6] This term (ἐκδημία, a being abroad, that is, in a foreign country) occurs here and in Char 2.28; 3.20. It is used rather of the Evagrian introspection. See Introd. 89.

[7] *Ravished*, the term occurs again in this connection in Char 2.6 and Amb 10–1113C.1; Amb 10–1237C.4. In chapters 2 and 3 Maximus in effect elaborated the triad, faith, hope, charity, not continuing from charity to divine knowledge. Here this latter again comes to the fore; but note that knowledge effects its seizure only through charity. If charity is a means, it is not merely preparatory, but integral with the seizure.

⁸ *Infinity* (ἀπειρία) occurs frequently in this rather special sense of the goal of contemplative effort—the limitless reaches about God rather than God Himself. The attaining of this ἀπειρία is the entrance into contemplation. In Maximus the word does not have the connotation of inexperience (likewise ἀπειρία) as Hausherr affirms for the Byzantine mystical vocabulary, OCP 2 (1936) 353: 'In mystical vocabulary ἀπειρία might mean the oblivion of all sense impressions, the being lifted up above all concepts, and so entrance into intuitive contemplation.' See Char 1.100; 2.27 and n. 49 of chap. I of *The Earlier Ambigua.*

⁹ Isa. 6.5 (Sept.). Note the effect of desire and love satisfied, an access of humility. This chapter and its citation seem to terminate the first group of chapters, on love itself.

¹⁰ This is the first chapter on fraternal charity. A bit of statistics I have given in the Introd. n. 398. It is useless to give a complete list of chapters touching on this theme. Note the extreme practical tone of this first chapter.

¹¹ John 14.15 (modified); 15.12.

¹² See Introd. n. 398.

¹³ Cf. Rom. 13.14.

¹⁴ Cf. Rom. 1.25.

¹⁵ Maximus often speaks of grief in the *Centuries* and especially in Ep 4–413 ff. There are two griefs, according to God and worldly, as St. Paul teaches 2 Cor. 7.8 ff. It is sometimes joined with pain and so paired with pleasure, as one of the two fundamental movements of the soul in its present fallen state. See Introd. 64, 85, and Index under 'grief.'

¹⁶ Viller cites Evagrius, *Practicos* 1.9. Maximus' tone is less absolute; both authors, of course, have monks in mind. Cf. above, n. 10.

¹⁷ One of the more important chapters. It makes charity an imitation of God and illustrates this with a reminiscence of Matt. 5.45. The giving of alms is the equivalent of charity in our modern sense. The relative place of almsgiving is indicated in ch. 26. Maximus' idea of charity was quite practical. Cf. Char 1.79, where almsgiving is again used where charity could stand.

¹⁸ *Word of God:* this must be taken in as many senses as ways in which the divine Word has manifested Himself to us, after the manner of Origen. See Introd. 79 and n. 338.

¹⁹ Cf. Jer. 17.16.

²⁰ Cf. Char 4.30.

²¹ For vainglory see Char 1.46,80; 3.59–62,75,77,83,84; 4.43.

²² Faith, charity, knowledge—the triad is of Clement of Alexandria; see Viller n. 123.

²³ Cf. Char 1.90; Viller n. 124.

²⁴ Cf. Char 3.71. Such a movement is illustrated in Char 2.16; 3.42. See Viller n. 56.

²⁵ See Introd. n. 391. All human ἀπάθεια is by γνώμη (Char 1.25). It is a state allowing the soul to develop towards God, because freed from attachments to lesser things.

²⁶ Cf. Luke 23.34.

²⁷ Cf. 1 Cor. 13.4,7.

²⁸ Cf. John 4.8.

²⁹ Cf. Jer. 7.4.

³⁰ James 2.19.

³¹ 2 Cor. 7.8; cf. above, n. 15.

³² The statement is universal, but the practices indicated are monastic. The very term *angelic life*, in fact, would be enough to indicate some form of monastic life.

³³ See Evagrius, *Practicos* 1.4.

³⁴ Peace here holds the role of ἀπάθεια. So also in Char 1.69.

³⁵ The phrase *holiness in chasteness* occurs also in LA 45–956B. Chasteness (σωφροσύνη) has an ampler connotation than is associated with the customary English equivalent, especially in its more Latin form of chastity. As peace in the preceding chapter, with which the present is in strict parallel, so chasteness is closely connected with ἀπάθεια. Cf. also *soberness*, LA n. 49.

³⁶ See Evagrius, *Practicos* 1.21. For other instances of vainglory see above n. 21.

³⁷ Gen. 18.27.

³⁸ Cf. Evagrius, *Practicos* 1.22. Maximus adds the elements of fear and thanksgiving; charity replaces ἀπάθεια.

³⁹ Listlessness (ἀκηδία) is a spirit of restlessness and incapacity for applying oneself to any task. See the article of Bardy in the *Dict. de Spiritualité* 1 (1937) 166–69. Cf. Evagrius, *Practicos* 1.14; Char 1.52,67.

³⁹ᵃ See below n. 178.

⁴⁰ This and the following chapter (1.51,52, as also 1.68) speak of a 'fleeing' or 'leaving.' In this there is great similarity with Evagrius, *Practicos* 1.13,19. Without question the substance of the thought is identical in both authors; the presuppositions as to the monastic milieu, however, are diverse. Pegon (83 n. 2 and 79 n. 1) would take the ἀναχώρησις of *Practicos* 1.13 as withdrawal from the cenobitic to a more eremitic life. It is in this sense that he would understand the ὑποχώρησῃ of Char 1.68. However *Palat. gr.* 49 reads ἀποχώρησῃ. And in fact Maximus may better be understood as speaking of withdrawal

from the religious profession. Such is Combefis' interpretation of Char 1.68.

[41] Cf. Matt. 5.24. This chapter (1.53) is the first of a series (1.53–63) explaining the Scripture commandment of charity. Thus in themselves these chapters are applicable to any Christian, and only subsequently to monks. This double interpretation fits 1.59 very well.

[42] I Cor. 13.1–3. The phrasing of the latter part repeats Char 1.43. The gifts of the Holy Spirit are treated largely in Thal 63–672B ff. Cf. Joseph a Spiritu Sancto, O.C.D., 'The Seven Gifts of the Holy Ghost in Early Greek Theology' (that is, in effect, in Maximus), *Hom. and Past. Rev.* 26 (1926) 820–27, 930–38. Cf. Char 4.69.

[43] Rom. 13.10. On eternal judgment cf. LA n. 79.

[44] James 4.11.

[44a] See above, n. 41.

[45] Luke 6.27,28 and Matt. 5.44 (conflated).

[46] On the imitation of God see LA n. 9.

[47] I Tim. 2.4.

[48] Matt. 5.39–41.

[49] On the part of memory cf. Char 1.84,91; Viller n. 92.

[50] Cf. Evagrius, *Practicos* 1.24. I use both self-control and self-mastery to render ἐγκράτεια.

[51] Cf. Evagrius, *Practicos* 1.26 and *De oratione* 27. Char 1.66 is effectively the theme of the first part of LA.

[52] Luke 21.19. For *listlessness* see Char 1.41 n. 39.

[53] 'May go away,' see above, n. 40; 'divine familiarity,' see below, n. 178.

[54] Of the present group, 70–75, treating of perfect charity, this chapter is the fullest and is clearly of the same thoroughly Christian temper as the LA. Note the final reference to glory and punishment, for which each fits himself. Cf. LA n. 79; also Char 2.49; 4.16,91.

[55] Rom. 8.35–39.

[56] *Ibid.* 9.1–3.

[57] Cf. Exod. 32.31 f.

[58] Cf. Char 1.66.

[59] Ps. 24.18.

[60] Here the object of the five contemplations are named: God (the Holy Trinity), the invisible creation (that is the angels—see Char 1.90), the visible creation, providence, judgment. See Viller nn. 130, 132. It is above all necessary to understand these contemplations in the light of Maximus' own doctrine; see the Introd. 39, and 87 ff., where I have seen reason to distinguish sharply between the natural contemplation

and pure prayer. In the *Centuries* see the following: Char 1.79,96,99, 100; 2.27; 3.33.

[61] Here almsgiving and fasting take the place of the master virtues, charity and self-control.

[62] Matt. 11.29.

[63] For *meekness* and its role in Evagrius see Introd. 85 and nn. 363, 364. There seems to be no immediate literary dependence. On *vainglory* cf. Char 1.30 and n. 21.

[64] On the two fears there is the whole of Thal 10–288 ff.

[65] Prov. 15.29 and 1.7.

[66] Ps. 18.10 and 33.10.

[67] Col. 3.5.

[68] Cf. Rom. 8.6.

[69] This must refer to Col. 3.5 cited in the previous chapter.

[70] On this chapter see also Evagrius, Ep. 39 (Frankenberg 593 *init.*).

[71] I.e. the angels. Cf. Char 1.32; Viller n. 124; Char 1.78.

[72] Cf. Char 3.3. One must remember that though nature does have its λόγος and τρόπος, its τρόπος is often taken according to its maximum capacity, so that that is natural which fulfils the capacity of man as he was before the fall. See *The Earlier Ambigua*, ch. IV, 165. Thus the ascetical life may be viewed as but the removal of vices that impede the flowering of nature in its virtues (TP 28–309 f.).

[73] Evagrius, *Practicos* 1.36, gives the same sign. There is no immediate literary dependence.

[74] Here one θεωρία is left behind or put off to make way for the next; in Char 1.86 there is passage through one to the next. This is not a contradiction. However, if there is a continuity between the contemplations, there is equally a disjunction. This I have pointed out especially for the various contemplations and pure prayer or the summit where the soul is joined to God. See Introd. 87 f. There is no ironclad scheme; the terms, the phrases vary. See Viller nn. 133, 134.

[75] 'Essences' = λόγους. See Amb 10–1113A. The λόγος-theme recurs in Char 1.98,99.

[76] This chapter reminds us that the distinctions of the kataphatic and apophatic theology are always valid. Our knowledge of God from contemplation of things belongs to the first category. Note the Trinitarian allusion.

[77] This is a parallel of Char 1.94.

[78] Cf. Gregory Naz., *Orat.* 38.7 and 45.3 (MG 36.317C and 628A).

[79] This chapter serves as conclusion to the series beginning with 85, but more especially with those dealing with the pure mind (from 94). They proceed on a different line from those devoted to perfect charity

(Char 1.70–75). The accent falls again on the apophatic theology (cf. 96). It seems from the initial phrase ('placed in God'—see also Char 2.26 (61),100; 3.97; Viller n. 7; and Amb 7—1089B) that here we have to do with the summit of the spiritual life. This life has its distinctions: natural contemplation is not pure prayer (cf. Char 2.26); yet it remains an integral whole. On *infinity* see Char 1.12 n. 8; also Char 3.23.

[80] The first seven chapters of the second *Century* concern pure prayer. This first chapter applies to prayer the lessons of the opening chapters of the first *Century* on separation from worldly things to adhere to God.

[81] For 'reading,' cf. LA 25, Char 4.44. Though seldom mentioned in the *Centuries*, reading formed a necessary part of the monastic discipline. Both reading and the contemplations prepare one for pure prayer.

[82] The active (or practical) way and the contemplative are effectively described in the foregoing chapter. Evagrius, *Practicos* 1.50,51, gives this definition of the practical way: 'The practical is a spiritual way, purifying the passible part of the soul.' The ignorance mentioned by Maximus would be ignorance of God, which is the fundamental disease of man consequent upon the fall (Thal prol. 253C).

[83] On these two states of prayer see the development I have given the question in the Introd. 87 at n. 372 ff. Von Balthasar comments KL 340 ff.–256 ff. Some elements of this chapter I have already commented: 'burning love' (ἔρως), above, Char 1.10 n. 5; 'rapt' Char 1.12 n. 7. The action of the contemplations is implied as already having attained their effect in the 'maximum purification' (Char 2.5); but they are not active in the pure prayer itself. These two states of prayer may be put in two words: presence, illumination.

[84] 'Self-love' (φιλαυτία) has been explained in the Introd. 65 at nn. 268,269. It occurs mostly in the second and third *Centuries* (2.8,59, 60; 3.7,8,56,57); cf. also Thal prol.–253D, 260A,D; Ep 2–397; Ep 25–613D. It is defined in terms of attachment for the body, but pride and vainglory are among its first offspring (Thal prol.–256C; Char 3.57). Pegon (note on Char 3.57) has well characterized it: 'It (φιλαυτία) is that fundamental lack of balance which makes the center of gravity of the human composite fall from the mind to the lower, sense faculties. The first impulse of nature was turned to God and, therefore, ecstatic; it has been folded back on itself. The "body" is the ego as bound to matter.' See also Hausherr's summary of Maximian spirituality, as seen under this formality, in his essay: *Philautie* (Rome 1952).

[85] Cf. Char 2.50; and Evagrius, Ep 18 (Frankenberg 578).

[86] Ps. 36.27.

[87] On 'soberness' cf. LA n. 49; *dressing* and *keeping*, Gen. 2.15. Evagrius, *De orat.* 48, explains the text: 'Cultivate the fruits of prayer and preserve them.' It was a tag, current in the desert; Abbot Poemen, in the *Apophthegmata Patrum* (Poemen 39: MG 65.332), is reported as saying: 'Sorrow is twofold: one (must) dress and keep.' I have these references from Hausherr, *Penthos* (Rome 1944) 137.

[88] In part this chapter runs parallel with Evagrius, *Practicos* 1.5; but the whole comparison, the Lord's temptation and ours, is Maximus' own. See LA 10,11.

[89] Ps. 36.15. On the part of the devil see references at LA n. 21.

[90] Evil and its origin was one of the chief problems set for treatment in the prologue to Thal (cf. Char 3.29); the affirmation of the ontological goodness of things occurs not infrequently (see especially Amb 42–1340B f.), it is supposed in the doctrine of misuse, as explained in the following chapters.

[91] Passion is defined or explained in the following chapters, Char 1.35; 3.42,71.

[92] Vice here is the equivalent of passion.

[93] Ps. 16.11; 31.7. To this group of chapters on demons (18–22) join Char 2.13,14,31,71,90; 3.41; Introd. 86 at n. 367. Cf. Evagrius, *Practicos* 2.48.

[94] 'Him in his retirement,' ἡσυχάζοντι, the term is nearly technical, for that withdrawal from full community life for the sake of a more thorough campaign against the devil and a completer dedication to contemplation. Hesychasm was an institution already known in sixth-century Palestine (cf. Cyril of Scythopolis [ed. E. Schwartz, Leipzig 1939], esp. the life of John the Hesychast; cf. also the latter part of the article 'Esicasmo' in *Enciclopedia Cattolica* 5 [1950] 579–80; and the article 'Hésychastes' in *Dict. d'Archéologie chr. et de Liturgie* 6 [1925] 362–65). Its later history is joined with the work of Simeon the New Theologian, Gregory of Sinai, Gregory Palamas, and, in modern times, with Nicodemus the Hagiorite, compiler of the *Philocalia* (see 'Hagiorita,' *Lexikon f. Theologie u. Kirche* 4 [1932] 786 f.) Cf. below, Char 3.20,37.

[95] Cf. Ps. 6.11. Cf. also Evagrius, *Practicos* 2.48.

[96] See above what was said on the preisthood—Introd. 79. Its scope, to be deified and to deify, is in a way an abridgement of what Maximus here borrows from Denis (*Eccl. Hier.* 5.3–7 [MG 3.504–509]).

[97] Ps. 9.4.

[98] The *divine judgments* (κρίματα), here as in LA 22, indicate rather the involuntary afflictions of this life, such as are mentioned in Char

2.66. Κρίσις (judgment or discernment) refers to this life or the next and implies something definitive. Cf. Char 2.39,42,44,46; 4.97.

⁹⁹ Ps. 16.4. Cf. Char 1.77.

¹⁰⁰ Viller finds precedent in Clement of Alexandria (*Strom.* 7.10.55.7–57.4—GCS 17.41.7–42.9) for placing charity after knowledge. In the passage indicated there is question of passage from unbelief to faith and from faith to knowledge, and then consummation in charity wherein is found the communion of friends. For Clement the central element remains *gnosis*, the development of faith; charity seems rather to pertain to the final communion, the κληρονομία. This chapter (2.25) of Maximus cannot then be cited as a witness to Maximus' systematic shift of emphasis to charity (as suggested in the Introd. 92), but is an indication that also the Alexandrians perceived that knowledge effected the communion of known and knower—the proper effect of charity. The systematic shift must be sought in the comparative enhancement of the good and the impulse to it through love in relation with the emphasis given by the gnostic doctors (Clement, Origen, Evagrius) to knowledge.

¹⁰¹ 'Grace of theology': here and in the following chapter (2.27), as also in 4.64, Maximus speaks of 'theology.' This is the state of pure prayer, conversation with God, above and beyond the lower stages of the spiritual life: practice of the commandments, contemplation of nature, contemplation of the intelligible world (cf. Char 1.94). It is the 'being in God' (Char 1.100 and n. 79). Pegon annotates these chapters (2.26,27) at length, developing especially the comparison with Evagrius. See also Viller, n. 39.

¹⁰² For these 'things about God' (His attributes) cf. Char 1.100.

¹⁰³ On the union of πρᾶξις and θεωρία see the last two paragraphs of the Introd. On this 'departing for God' see Char 1.10, n. 6.

¹⁰⁴ John 10.30,38. 'Tritheists': The tritheism here in view should be that resulting, in the doctrine of John Philoponus (6th cent.), from the meeting of Aristotelian thought and monophysite doctrine. Person and nature were declared to be identical; hence as there are three persons in God, so there are three natures. This position, however, was intended rather to affirm the identity of nature and person in each of the three hypostases of the Godhead than to establish a plurality of divine being. For that matter Philoponus did not deny the numerical unity of the divine essence. See M. Jugie, *Enciclopedia Cattolica* 5 (1950) 1349.

¹⁰⁵ Pegon suggests *Orat.* 39 (MG 36.349CD).

¹⁰⁶ Cf. Char 1.70–75, a series on perfect love. 'Neither Greek nor Jew,' see Gal. 3.28 with Eph. 1.23; cf. PN–892 f.; Amb 41–1309A.15 ff.

This is a loose citation of St. Paul. The reference given to Amb 41 shows that the 'in Him,' in the present chapter without antecedent, refers to Christ. The text from Gal. is one which serves as support for Gregory of Nyssa's and Maximus' view on the primitive state of man. See Introd. 68.

[107] Matt. 24.15.

[108] The relation of the literal and allegorical interpretation is here illustrated.

[109] For this and 33 cf. Char 3.93; also Thal 15–297D; Evagrius, *Practicos* 1.65; and Viller n. 96 for references in regard to the 'natural tendencies' (φυσικὰ σπέρματα). These can be nothing else than that primitive desire or drive on which the whole life of man depends— Introd. 64. 'Holy Powers' (ἅγιαι δυνάμεις)—Pegon renders 'les bons anges.'

[110] James 4.3.

[111] 'Intention' (σκοπός). The whole first part of LA is devoted to the Lord's σκοπός in the Incarnation. Cf. Char 2.37,73,84; 3.19,47,48,76; Amb 7–1097. The doctrine of intention is allied to that of use and misuse.

[112] Ps. 61.13.

[113] John 15.5. On 'pride' and 'vainglory' cf. Char 1.10 n. 21.

[114] I Cor. 11.31 f. Cf. Char 1.22 n. 15.

[115] Notice the distribution of virtues between desire and anger and the further distinction between those that merely hinder and those that actively reduce the passion. Thus, for anger, meekness belongs to the first group, charity to the second. Cf. Char 1.80 n. 63. Cf. Evagrius, *Practicos* 1.6,11.

[116] See Char 1.10 n. 5. Ἔρως indubitably here is the primordial desire of man directed properly to God (cf. Char 3.64,67). It proceeds in the line of its natural tendency; the irascible, however, must be changed that it become divine charity. 'Illumination' (ἔλλαμψις): Gregory Nazianzen (*Orat.* 39–MG 36.341D,344A) uses this term, which use was known to Maximus (Amb 40–1301D f.). In both the illumination is at the summit of the spiritual life.

[117] Cf. Char 1.70–75.

[118] Matt. 6.21.

[119] Bestiality: see LA n. 32. Here there is clearly question of moral qualities. For connection with Evagrius' epistemology see Char 3.97 n. 187.

[120] I John 2.15 f. (modified).

[121] Cf. Gen. 46.34. See Char 2.5,44,68. The distinction of practical and contemplative is known; here *gnostic* takes the place of the latter.

The chapter is redolent of the Alexandrian exegesis, as also the use of the term *gnostic*, less frequent in Maximus' time. See Char 2.90.

[122] 'Philosopher,' not at all to be understood in our modern sense, but in that ancient use in which the ascetic was the lover of wisdom. Cf. Char 3.96; 4.30,47. See the study of V. Warnach in: *Vom christlichen Mysterium* (Düsseldorf 1951) 135-51: 'Das Mönchtum als "Pneumatische Philosophie" in den Nilusbriefen.'

[123] Cf. Rom. 13.14.

[124] See Introd. 80, 95; also Viller 250 f.; Hausherr, 'Le traité de l'oraison d'Évagre,' *Rev. d'asc. et myst.* 15 (1934) 114. In Maximus cf. LA 19, 24; Char 2.6,26,28,90,100; 3.97; 4.42. It is interesting that here in one of the capital chapters Maximus reminds us ('they say'—cf. also Char 2.67) that the *Centuries* make no pretension to originality. Prayer 'without ceasing' was a constant concern of the monks. It is the perfect prayer. See also LA 24 end; Char 1.4,19,34. The 'undistracted' prayer of Char 2.1,4,5,6, does not seem to indicate the same degree of perfection.

[125] On demons see Char 2.18 and n. 93.

[126] This 'condition and temperament' is the κρᾶσις of the body referred to more fully below (Char 2.92). The character and disposition of a man were considered as largely dependent on the proportion of elements and humors in his body. Aquinas refers to this generally as *complexio* (Cf. *Summa theol.* 2.2.156). It was a doctrine common in antiquity. As to the role of memory in prayer, cf. Evagrius, *De orat.* 44-46.

[127] See this question of right use treated in LA 7; see also Char 2.17, 73,76,78,82,84; 3.3,4,86; 4.14,66; Amb 7-1097C; Ep 1-369A; Ep 10-449B. 'Their accidents,' that is, the knowledge or ignorance and the like perfecting the human faculties, which are the primary gifts of God to man.

[128] I Cor. 15.49.

[129] John 14.6; Matt. 7.14.

[130] Above, Char 2.67, there is a list of five reasons why attacks of demons are permitted. The contemplations are likewise five. In Char 2.32,33 there are given motives for the good and for the bad, but in sets of three.

[131] The *rational* element and the *Word* in Greek have a perfect verbal correspondence. The subjection of the rational element to reason is expounded, as of the natural law, in Thal 64-724C. See also Char 4.15 and Pegon's note.

[132] Exod. 20.13-15; 12.3 f.

[133] Cf. Heb. 10.34.

17

134 Matt. 19.22.

135 On demons cf. Char 2.18 n. 93 ; on prayer Char 2.61 n. 124. Cf. Viller nn. 89,90.

136 Luke 14.33 and 21.19.

137 'Temperament,' cf. Char 2.74 and above, n. 126. 'Soul' here stands for the passible part.

138 1 Cor. 15.56; John 14.6.

139 Cf. Ps. 22.2. This psalm is commented in the following chapters: Char 2.95,96,99; 3.2 Viller (p. 261) shows that it was a traditional Alexandrian interpretation. Pegon refers to Evagrius' comment, *Selecta in Psalmos* (MG 12.1260C f.). Maximus interprets the same psalm again in Ep 8–441B.12–D.7.

140 Ps. 22.4a.

141 *Ibid.* 22.4b.

142 *Ibid.* 22.5 f.: *Thou hast prepared a table before me against them that afflict me. Thou hast anointed my head with oil; and my chalice which enebriateth me, how goodly is it! And Thy mercy will follow me all the days of my life. And that I may dwell in the house of the Lord unto length of days.*—Here Maximus presents a threefold division: active life, natural contemplation, knowledge of God, to which is added the Word. Cf. Char 4.47. The reference to St. Paul is verified in Phil. 3.12.

143 See Char 2.75 n. 127.

144 *De div. nom.* 4.23 (MG 3.724 f.).

145 Eph. 5.29 conflated with 1 Cor. 9.27.

146 Rom. 8.8 conflated with Gal. 5.24.

147 Cf. Rom. 13.14.

148 The ground of such a doctrine of stewardship is found in the New Testament, Matt. 22.45; 25.4 ff.; Acts 4.35; Eph. 4.22. Maximus does not attend to the means of earning money but to the intention, the σκοπός. See Char 2.36 n. 111.

149 On the 'flights' (more properly 'departure') of prayer see Char 1.10 n. 6. The causes of thoughts are here elaborated on a plan indicated above, Char 1.7. For 'solitary' cf. Char 2.19 n. 94.

150 The chapters 21–33 form a distinct group, that serves to place the spiritual doctrine of the *Centuries* against the fuller background of God and the relations of creatures to Him. (Is it mere chance that there are 13 chapters? Epifanovitch 64 f. [from the MS *Vat. gr.* 507 f. 127v–128] prints '13 chapters on the wills, that is, against those who speak of one will of Our Lord and God and Savior Jesus Christ'; cf. also the group Char 4.1–13). The first chapters (21–24) dealing with God's knowledge of Himself and by His creatures, clearly distinguish God from His creatures. The 25th establishes a basis for distinguishing image and likeness, the one depending on the metaphysical structure of the creature, the other on his free activity. There follows (26) the division of rational creatures into angels and men, and each of these into the good and the wicked. Chs. 27 and 28 return to the distinction of God and creatures, but now on the ontological basis of there being for God no contrary whatsoever, while in creatures there is always the possibility that the opposite be realized. This possible privation of good explains ignorance and evil (29,30). The inanimate and merely animate creation are then brought into the synthesis (31,32). In 33 there is the binding together of creation by the higher angels who share their greater knowledge and virtue with the lesser and with men. See Pegon's note to this group.

151 Wisdom here refers to the Word of God. This is indicated by the following 'through which and in which' (cf. Rom. 11.36 and Col. 1. 16), and confirmed by the conclusion of 24 affirming that the wisdom in things is not substantial (hypostatic).

152 The series of three, 'eternal, infinite, immense,' occurs in Char 1.100, where goodness and wisdom (found here in the next chapter) are joined to them. The other triplet, 'being, well-being, ever-being,' is one not always interpreted identically. The uncertainty is due to the tacit assumption that eternal being is the same as eternal well-being. This is excluded just below, in 25, and also in 4.13. In Amb 42 (1325B f. and 1348D) eternal being is joined with the resurrection. In Amb 7 (1073C) the end of creaturely motion (in the full sense) is said to be everlasting well-being. In Amb 10 (1116B) it is stated that it is only the well-being, dependent on our own efforts, which permits either the being or the everlasting being to be strictly predicated. In Thal 64 (728A) everlasting well-being is attributed to the law of grace. Though the word 'image' there occurs, Maximus does not think to contrast it with 'likeness.'

153 'Aptness' (ἐπιτηδειότης): the concept is explained in the dispute with Pyrrhus (TP 28–313A f.); it cannot be ascribed to Christ (cf. 27). He therefore always had eternal well-being, or well-being in full act. The gnomic character of this term is underlined in the following chapter, 'fitness of will and judgment' (γνωμικὴ ἐπιτηδειότης). 'Goodness' and 'wisdom': cf. Char 1.100 and the Introd. on the traces of the Trinity, 40. The final qualification of wisdom as seen in creation as non-substantial is doubtless in contradistinction to the hypostatic Wisdom of 22.

154 On 'likeness' (ὁμοίωσις) see the references given for 'image' (εἰκών) in the Introd. n. 425.

155 Of these two sets of distinctions one is clearly ontological, the

other moral. It was the lack of this distinction that permitted Origen to divide spiritual beings ontologically by the degree of their moral purity. Cf. Introd. 39.

[156] For this and chapter 30, Viller (258), whom Pegon follows, cites Evagrius, *Centuries* 1.1,2,4 (Frankenberg 49,51). Between Char 3.30 and Evagrius 1.4 there is great similarity, yet Maximus' fulness of treatment is not due to Evagrius, who merely states: 'everything that comes to be is either receptive of contraries or made up of contraries.' In ch. 28 it is rather the pagan doctrine that is rejected. Evagrius does not at all say that created substances have a contrary, namely, not to be.—For the Scriptural allusion see Rom. 11.29.

[157] This chapter is a strict consequent of the preceding. The contrary of substance, not-being, is explained by the better known ideas of evil and ignorance as privations of good and of knowledge (cf. Thal prol.–253AB). See also Char 2.15,17; 4.14.

[158] 'Imperishable and immortal': this constitutes the image and pertains to the λόγος; imitation of goodness and wisdom constitutes the likeness and pertains to man's free activity.

[159] Ps. 91.9. The communication of knowledge is according to the five contemplations met with above, Char 1.78 n. 60. Pegon, 135 n. 1, denies any Dionysian influence in the entire chapter, preferring to emphasize the importance of angelic illumination in Evagrius and Origen. This latter influence, however, does not exclude all possibility of the former.

[160] Chapters 34–36 depend on the tripartite distinction of man, spoken of in the Introd. 84.

[161] What difference there is between this sentence and the Terentian dictum (*Heaut.* 77): 'Homo sum: humani nil a me alienum puto'!

[162] Cf. Char 2,18, n. 93.

[163] Cf. Evagrius, *Practicos* 1.71.

[163a] Cf. Evagrius, *Cent.* 1.87.

[164] Matt. 5.3 ff. For the doctrine of intention illustrated here and in the next chapter, see the references at Char 2.36, n. 111.

[165] Ps. 91.12.

[166] John 5.22; Matt. 7.1 with Luke 6.37.

[167] I Cor. 4.5 and Rom. 2.1.

[168] Jer. 2.12.

[169] Ps. 4.3 (modified).

[170] Cf. Gal. 2.2.

[171] Cf. Evagrius, *Practicos* 2.31. For other chapters on vainglory see Char 1.30 n. 21.

[172] 'Secret exercise,' that is, of the virtues. Cf. Char 4.43.

¹⁷³ Chapters 63–72 (note, a group of 10) treat of the relation of knowledge and desire. Mere, bare knowledge is not enough; there must be the 'blessed passion (πάθος) of holy charity' (67, cf. 71). Along with this theme is that of the precarious nature of our contemplation and knowledge, due to its being now in figure and enigma—a situation which permits the passage from (mere) knowledge again to earthly passions. The figured and enigmatic nature of our knowledge makes it the special thing it is, an acquired habit of understanding the figures of Scripture and nature (69).

¹⁷⁴ For chapters 63,64 cf. Evagrius, *Practicos* 1.21; also Char 1.1. This chapter makes peculiarly clear that desire is not extinguished but must be put on the right track. Cf. Char 2.48 and n. 116, also 71 below.

¹⁷⁴ᵃ Cf. 2 Peter 2.22.

¹⁷⁵ 2 Cor. 5.7.

¹⁷⁶ See Char 3.19.

¹⁷⁷ Viller 241. In such common sentiments to indicate parallels or even a dependence signifies little.

¹⁷⁸ 'Free-speech' (παρρησία) is primitively the freedom of speech which Athenian citizens claimed as their right. Here, as often, it refers to that familiarity with God which is the due of sons in His presence, or to the familiarity of brothers one with the other. See Char 1.50,68; 4.32; Thal 10–289C; Ep 32–628A. Cf. the observations by H. Graef, ACW 18.183 n. 26.

¹⁷⁹ 'Departure' (ἔξοδος) is to be understood of the departure of death, not of pure prayer (ἐκδημία—cf. Char 1.10 n. 1). Death is the sense in Char 4.33 and Ep 12–612A.

¹⁸⁰ On knowledge of self as means to further knowledge (of God) cf. Thal 63–673D and Introd. 90.

¹⁸¹ 'Prudence' here equals worldly wisdom.

¹⁸² Prov. 12.28; 21.24 (Sept.).

¹⁸³ Rom. 12.15.

¹⁸⁴ Cf. Char 2.32 and n. 109.

¹⁸⁵ Cf. Char 2.56 and n. 122.

¹⁸⁶ See Char 1.100 and n. 79.

¹⁸⁷ This chapter requires a critique of the relations of Evagrian and Maximian doctrine. Viller (249) in commenting this chapter supposes the theory of knowledge of Evagrius and Maximus to be the same. Hausherr expounds this theory in his comment on the 50th chapter of Evagrius' *De oratione* (MG 79.1177). The Evagrian text runs thus: 'Why do the demons wish to rouse in us gluttony, fornication, greed, wrath and the recollection of wrongs, and the rest of the passions?

In order that the mind, coarsened by these, may not be able to pray as is fitting; for as the passions of the irrational part of man dominate, they do not allow it to be rationally moved to seek the Word of God.' Hausherr comments upon this as follows. The coarsening or thickening of the mind recalls the Origenist speculations on the fall of the spirits in diverse degrees of matter (see Introd. 47). The ultimate in man is then his intellect, his mind. 'A great principle dominates all, though it is nowhere formulated as a general axiom: knowledge is a real assimilation of the knower to the known.' And in the footnote: 'One could get a perfect formulation of this principle by inversion of what Evagrius says of God (Letter 8, of Basil, n. 7): 'God knows what He is'; the created intellect is what it knows' (Hausherr, 'Le traité de l'oraison d'Évagre le Pontique,' *Rev. d'asc. et myst.* 15 [1934] 82). In view of the terminology of our present chapter (the mind being patterned after, conformed to each object of contemplation) is there any ground for Viller's supposition? It seems to me that there is none. I have already pointed out (Introd. 39) how Maximus can take over an Evagrian passage, explicitly insisting on certain distinctions which avoid completely the confusion of the moral and ontological orders. The same error underlies the Evagrian theory of knowledge as sketched by Hausherr. But elsewhere Maximus is very definite in his refutation of Origen's theory of spirit's progressive embodiment according to the degree of sin (see Introd. 51). He allows that there is a real intellectual knowledge originating in sense knowledge (Introd. 66). Now it is noteworthy that Maximus does not speak of the mind as being 'coarsened' or the like. This 'patterning after,' this 'conforming to,' are illustrated in another chapter (Char 2.52), where obviously the effect of the 'patterning' is moral, not ontological. Once again therefore Evagrius and Origen have been corrected and the confusion of the moral and ontological orders avoided.

[188] See Introd. 89 and nn. 383–85,418,419. Viller (248) confronts with Evagrius, *Centuries* 3.15 (Frankenberg 199). In the Introduction my critique of Hausherr's article on this chapter implied that his conclusion—the Dionysian vocabulary is merely superimposed on the Evagrian thought—is not accurate. What then are we to say? The Dionysian and Evagrian 'techniques' are diverse and in tension, but God remains the goal of either. That Maximus' underlying thought is wholly Evagrian has not been proved. As to 'providence' and 'judgment,' it is not Evagrian; as to theory of knowledge (see preceding n.), it is not Evagrian; as to knowledge of God, that is here the question. But is there really excluded the possibility that the modalities of the two techniques are here deliberately juxtaposed in view of the pro-

founder harmony? For a more extensive study of these relations, see
The Earlier Ambigua ch. IV.

189 I Cor. 13.13. 'Time' (χρόνος) is dealt with in ThOec 1.5. The
threefold division here in view is doubtless that of the law of nature,
in writing, and of grace (Thal 64-724C ff.). The second part of the
chapter refers not to time but to eternity.

190 Ps. 144.3. The chs. 1-13 (14?) form a group; cf. Char 3.21-33.
There is an undertone of polemic against the pagan ways more pro-
nounced than in the group Char 3.21-33, but at the same time our
present group shows a greater wonder and awe at the divine work of
creation and at the divine transcendence. In either group οὐσία is used
throughout whether for the divine or for the created beings; φύσις
does not occur. Char 4.14 follows so closely in thought on 4.13,
that one may be not justified in making this initial group close with
4.13.

191 This and the following chapters touch an important question.
The Good is diffusive of Itself: how then is creation not necessary or
at least eternal? Maximus responds here by affirming creation as resulting from the divine Will, the impossibility of eternal coexistence for
the perfectly infinite and the finite, the inscrutability of the divine
Wisdom. These replies are all very good, but they do not satisfy the
difficulties inherent in the doctrine of the good naturally diffusive of
itself. Later Maximus, in contrast to Denis, saw this need for diffusion
satisfied in the intra-trinitarian life (Introd. 43), but at the time
of writing the *Centuries* he had apparently not yet developed this
point.

192 'Eternally pre-existent knowledge of things': in this phrase is
implied Maximus' doctrine of pre-existent λόγοι. See Introd. 46.

193 'Recently': this is equivalent to saying in time, not eternally.

194 Combefis gives two general references to Gregory Nazianzen.
I have been unable to find there anything that satisfies Maximus' text.
The citation might be from Gregory of Nyssa.

195 This is the fundamental distinction of the negative theology. Cf.
Char 1.100.

196 'Mutability': on its role in the human drama, see Introd. 58.

197 The degrees of being participated and participation are integral
to the hierarchy and distinction of beings. On being and well-being
see Char 3.23 n. 152.

198 See Char 3.29 and n. 157.

199 This chapter and Char 2.83 should be read together. It then
appears that the soul well regulated by reason (λόγος) is fully subjected
to the Word (the Λόγος); and that this condition is 'according to

nature.' One might perhaps term this the optimum that the mode of nature may attain, the full development of its capacities. The essence or λόγος of human nature is of course immutable.

²⁰⁰ For other chapters on perfect charity see Char 1.71 n. 54.

²⁰¹ John 11.52. This unity of man in faith and charity is most fully described by Maximus in Myst 1–665C. As with Origen, the purpose of Providence is unity; with him it proceeded through successive purgations to the matterless unity of the primitive henad, with Maximus it proceeds through the trials of this life to unity in faith and charity now, to unity of knowledge and charity hereafter.

²⁰² 1 Cor. 13.4.

²⁰³ Prov. 14.29.

²⁰⁴ Rom. 6.22.

²⁰⁵ John 17.3.

²⁰⁶ Lev. 19.17.

²⁰⁷ 'Charitable dispositions': cf. Char 1.29; 'philosophic': see Char 2.56 and n. 122.

²⁰⁸ 'Freedom': see Char 3.80 and n. 178.

²⁰⁹ Matt. 6.14 f.

²¹⁰ Matt. 22.40.

²¹¹ 1 Cor. 12.3.

²¹² See Char 2.61 and n. 124.

²¹³ 'Vainglory': see Char 1.30; for the remedy, Char 3.62.

²¹⁴ The remedies for the passible part of the soul are more fully given in Ep 12–612A. 'Reading': cf. Char 2.4; LA 25.

²¹⁵ See Char 2.83, 4.15 and n. 199.

²¹⁶ Soul here is used for the passible part of the soul only; see Introd. 84. Ignorance and knowledge have their character as evil and good, even as sickness and health. As the first evil was ignorance of God, so the corresponding knowledge is divine knowledge. Char 3.63–72 give an idea of this knowledge now to be had.

²¹⁷ 'Philosopher': cf. Char 2.56 and n. 122.

²¹⁸ Not infrequently Maximus speaks of the mind as of the only thing that matters, the sum of man. See Char 3.94–99. For Evagrius this was quite so; see n. 187 to Char 3.97. Here Maximus places *mind* in the Pauline context of outer and inner man. The relations between them in regard to contemplation are illustrated in Char 3.63–72.

²¹⁹ Evagrius, *Practicos* 2.60 speaks of imperfect detachment; Maximus will speak of four degrees of detachment (Thal 55–544C), and here of partial detachment, according to the several objects to which one may be attached.

²²⁰ Matt. 7.20; John 14.15. 'Imitates': see LA 3 and n. 9. 'These three,' namely benefaction, patience under rebuff, the passion. They may be discerned also in LA 12.

²²¹ 'Splendor': Evagrius, *Practicos* 1.36, speaks of the proper splendor of the mind as a sign of detachment. Cf. Char 4.79. This splendor of soul would also be connected with self-knowledge; see Char 3.81 and n. 180.

²²² 'Humility': this virtue occurs rather infrequently in Maximus, though it be one of the fundamental virtues. See Char 1.76; 3.14,87; PN–888B, 893B; Ep 2–396A; Ep 4–417AB; Ep 5–421C; Ep 13–512A. In Ep 2 it is called 'the first ground of the virtues.' In Ep 4 it is introduced as a fruit of grief according to God (compunction) and defined as that 'by which the pious man reckons himself truly the least of all and sets human weakness the measure of his prudence, in which weakness all who share the same nature are equally included.' It is joined with meekness in the verse, *I am meek and humble of heart* (Matt. 11.29), and therefore has place in the exposition of meekness (see Introd. 85 and nn. 363 f.). How is it that this virtue takes so little part in Maximus' spirituality, when in others, as St. Benedict, humility serves as the means whereby the whole ascent to God is described (Rule of St. Benedict, ch. 7)? The ground of the difference would seem to be in the way the fall is considered. For Maximus it is first of all immersion in sense, hence the remedy, self-mastery, detachment, love; for St. Benedict it is disobedience (prologue), which would be the first step of a human exaltation or pride, hence obedience is the first step of humility (ch. 5) or of true exaltation to heaven. But cf. LA 13 (obedience).

²²³ 1 Cor. 8.1. Viller (242) remarks that St. Paul's text has here dictated the exegesis. Knowledge (γνῶσις) does not have with Maximus the exclusive sense of perfection and sanctity as with the Alexandrians, but rather a fuller gamut of senses, sacred and profane. That the dictation of which Viller speaks was not to an unwilling scribe, is clear in that Maximus develops the thought in the next chapters (59–62). In fact he has been quite careful to determine the relation of knowledge, the passions and love in Char 3.63–72. Here he returns to the same subject but, as it were, from the outside.

²²⁴ Cf. Phil. 3.12.

²²⁵ 1 Tim. 4.8.

²²⁶ Gal. 5.16. 'Theology': see Char 2.26 and n. 101. This chapter is a complement to 59–62, as the man of the inner life is known by the notes of charity (1 Cor. 13) and so attains to theology.

²²⁷ See Char 2.75.

[228] Therefore the monastic life is also a state of penance for past sins.

[229] Cf. Luke 12.35.

[230] On the charismata see Char 1.54 and n. 42. Chapters 69–78 form a group of 10 (I see no reason to include 79 and 80 as does Pegon; see his note) on the indwelling Christ as source of wisdom and knowledge. A sense of carelessness is noted in 69 and 77, reminiscent of the plaints in LA.

[231] Eph. 3.17 and Col. 2.3.

[232] Cf. Matt. 13.44.

[233] *Ibid.* 5.8.

[234] Luke 12.33; 11.41.

[235] 1 Cor. 12.31.

[236] Cf. Luke 10.35.

[237] The fact of the indwelling Christ is dear to Maximus. I have noted this in the Introd. 4. It is perhaps the Christological conflicts that have contributed to this emphasis. On the indwelling of the Holy Spirit see Thal 15–297D.

[238] See above, Char 4.56 and n. 221.

[239] 'Check': cf. Evagrius, *Practicos* 1.26. On the relation of anger and love see Introd. 85. Cf. Char 1.66,79, and LA 20.

[240] On the requirement of equal love see Introd. n. 398. In most chapters Maximus insists on the ideal, here he allows that it will not always be realized.

[241] 'Good by nature': cf. Char 1.25; 'imitator of God': cf. LA n. 9; 'He blesses': the Greek of Combefis gives the subjunctive; *Pal. gr.* 49 the indicative; I have translated as an indicative. Who is the subject of this latter part, God (that is Christ) or the imitator of God? In either case Christ's ministry and passion as recounted in LA are here recapitulated. The sentence is more coherent if the same subject (Christ) be retained throughout.

[242] On right use see Char 2.75 and n. 127. On perfect love, Char 1. 70–75. Of discernment Maximus makes very little.

[243] Cf. 1 John 4.18.

[244] Ecclus. 6.15; cf. Char 3.79.

[245] The whole chapter is Biblical reminiscence: Mark 12.30 and the Psalms; but the reminiscence is too vague for exact reference. It is further a reproduction almost verbatim of LA 43–953C.9–D.2.

[246] Maximus' treatment of dereliction is fuller than that of Evagrius, *Gnosticos* 132 (Frankenberg 551); *De oratione* 37.

[247] Ecclus. 6.14.

[248] 1 Cor. 13.2 f.; 1 John 4.8. This chapter is clearly intended as

conclusion to the whole work; it tacitly refers the reader to those chapters where charity and knowledge are shown in their mutual relations, so that charity retains a pre-eminence (Char 3.63–72; 4.59–62). It is these chapters which should be taken as giving a norm of interpretation for Maximus' mind. See also Char 1.38.

INDEX

INDEX

Note: in referring to LA the section number is given and the page; to Char, the Century and chapter numbers are given, without the page number, thus: demons, 86; LA 15: 111 f.; Char 1.91. . . .

Note further: the entries of this index pertaining to the translation form a word index based on the Greek text. But a single Greek word is represented by several English words, and one English word may render a variety of Greek words. To circumvent this difficulty, I have gathered all references to one Greek word under the prevailiang English equivalent. The minor renderings are entered in their due place with a reference to the chief word; and at this chief entry these minor renderings are repeated in parentheses after the Greek word whose instances are there listed. See the entries *charity* and *love*. A noun and its corresponding verb are sometimes given together in a single entry.

Abraham, Char 1.47

abuse (κακολογέω), Char 4.30, 31, 35, 42, 43

act of love (ἔργα), *see* works

action (πρᾶξις: deed, active life), Char 1.44; 2.28, 31, 90

active (πρακτικός: practical, *as substantive*), Char 2.6, 26, 55; 3.68; active life, *see* action

Adam, human nature in, 69, 82; Char 2.93; type of Christ, 63 f.; the new, LA 12: 110

affection (φιλία: love), Char 2.16; 3.8, 42, 57

Africa, councils in, *see* council; Maximus' arrival in, 11

Aigrain, R., 218

alike (ἐξ ἴσου), *see* equally

alms (ἐλεημοσύνη: almsdeeds), Char 1.24, 79; 2.34, 47. *See also* mercy

almsgiving, 249, 252

Ambigua, the conception of the, 8

Anastasius the Apocrisary, 18, 27

Anastasius the Librarian, 19, 22

Anastasius the monk, 7, 27, 221

angelic, Char 3.34, 92; 4.36; — life, Char 1.42; — nature, Char. 3.26

angels, Char 2.69, 92. *See* powers

anger, 84 ff., 92, 237; (θυμός: temper, irascible element), Char 1.51, 75, 80; 2.28, 47–49, 69, 70; 3.5, 20, 35. *See* irascible

anger (ὀργή : angry, wrath). Char 1.29, 61; 2.2, 8; 3.13, 56, 59, 66, 96; 4.76, 84; (ὀργίζομαι), Char 2.33; 4.65

angry (ὀργή), *see* anger

anthropology, 45, 53

ἀπάθεια, *see* detachment

apocatastasis, 39, 244

Arcadius, 10, 218

Aristotle, 33; hylomorphism of, 53

artificer (δημιουργός), *see* creator

ascetic exercises (ἄσκησις), *see* exercise

asceticism, 69 ff.; the technique of, 81–87

attachment (πάθος), *see* passion; (προσπάθεια), Char 1.1; (σχέσις), LA 5: 106; to material things (φιλοϋλία), Char 3.20; without (ἀπαθής), *see* detached

attitudes, *see* intention

attributes, divine, Char 2.52; 3.25

Augustine, St., 230

αὐτεξούσιον, 55. *See* freedom

authority in the Church, 75–77

avarice (φιλαργυρία), Char 1.75; 2.9, 59; 3.4, 7, 56, 76, 83

avaricious (φιλάργυρος), Char 2.68

bad (ἐμπαθής), *see* impassioned

bad bargains (τῶν χρημάτων ζημία), *see* money

Balthasar, H. U. von, 4, 9, 37, 96, 215 f., 217, 220, 223, 237, 253; on Origenist

280 INDEX

passion, of, passionate (ἐμπαθής), see impassioned; without, passionless (ἀπαθής), see detached
passions, 66, 69, 84, 86; (πάθος: lust, attachment, passionate motion), LA 1: 103; Char 1.13, 27, 34, 35, 51, 65–67, 76, 83, 84, 94; 2.2, 3, 5, 8, 11, 15, 16, 19, 22, 23, 30, 31, 33, 34, 44, 47, 60, 68, 69, 84, 85, 100; 3.6, 12, 13, 40, 41, 44, 50, 56, 57, 59, 60, 68, 70–72, 75, 78, 81, 87, 88, 90, 93; 4.47–49, 52, 53, 77, 78, 86, 92; baser (τὰ ὑπογάστρια), Char 3.64
distinguished, of soul and body, Char 1.64; from thing and representation, Char 3.42; in laudable sense, Char 3.66, 67, 71
patience (ὑπομονή), LA 45: 135; Char 1.2, 40, 67, 81; (μακροθυμία), see long-suffering
pattern after (μετασχηματίζομαι), Char 3.97
Paul, St., LA 13: 111; Char 1.40; 3.2
Paul, patriarch of Constantinople, 22, 218
Paulicians, 241
peace, Char 1.44, 69; 4.34–36
Peeters, P., 222
Pegon, J., 101, 238, 253, 255, 257, 258, 266
Peitz, W. M., 221
penance, sacrament of, 78 f.; (μετάνοια: penance, repentance), LA 44: 134; Char 2.41; 3.55; 4.96. See repent
perfect (τέλειος), said of charity, Char 1.61, 70–74, 82; 2.10, 30, 49; 4.16, 39, 42, 91, 92; of detachment, LA 44: 134; Char 4.54; of the mind, Char 3.99; of the soul, Char 3.98
person, distinguished from nature, 35, 82
Peter the Illustrious, 12, 219
Pharisees, LA 11: 110; Char 2.13
Philo, 33
Philocalia, the Russian, 101
philosopher, 257; (φιλοσοφ-έω, -ία), Char 2.56; 4.30, 47
φύσις, sense of, 230
pleasure, 64 f., 67; (ἡδονή), Char 1.72, 75; 2.17, 41, 56, 58, 63, 65, 76; 3.16, 63, 65, 72, 77

poor (ἀκτήμων: without possessions), Char 2.88; 3.83; (πτωχοί), Char 3.47
poverty (ἀκτημοσύνη: possess nothing), LA 45: 135; Char 3.85; 4.67; (πενία), Char 1.72
power, the divine, Char 1.96, 100; 2.27
powerful, Char 2.52
Powers (Δυνάμεις), Char 2.32; 3.21–23, 93, 94; faculties, Char 4.10
practice (ἄσκησις), see exercise
Praxis and Theoria, 87, 92, 98
prayer, 87 ff., 94, 248, 253, 257; (προσευχή—plural, Char 2.6), and contemplation, LA 19: 114; 24: 116; Char 1.79; 2.47, 70; 3.11; 4.15, 44, 68, 80; continual, Char 1.53; 2.19; 3.87; 4.43; departure of (ἐκδημία), Char 3.20; and psalmody, Char 1.45; 2.35, 54; 3.50; 4.48; pure, Char 1.11, 49; 2.6, 7; 3.44; 4.51; state of, Char 2.6, 14, 52, 61; 3.95; 4.86; time of, Char 1.68, 88; 3.49; 4.33, 42; (προσεύχομαι), Char 1.42; 2.1, 4, 5, 62, 90, 100; 3.90; 4.35, 64
pre-existence of souls, 51 f.
Prestige, G. L. 44, 231
presumption (οἴησις), Char 3.14, 61, 70, 81; 4.61
pride (ὑπερηφανία), Char 2.38, 40, 43; 3.56, 57, 59, 61, 62, 84, 87
priest (πρεσβύτερος), Char 2.21
priesthood, 79, 254
privation (στέρησις: stripping, loss), Char 2.89, 91; 3.5, 29
procession in the Trinity, 37, 41
Proclus, 6, 40
procreation before the Fall, 68
promises, Char 2.24
property, (ὕπαρξις), see existence
providence (πρόνοια: provision, forethought), purpose of, LA 1: 103; Char 4.16–18; 264; in relation with the temporal judgments of God, Char 2.41, 46, 74, 91; 4.16–18; ontological, 39; 1.96; 2.98, 99; 3.18; 4.9; of the flesh, Char 1.20; 2.60; 3.12. See also judgment and providence
provision for the flesh, see providence
prudence (φρόνησις), Char 2.26; 3.3; 4.1
psalmody, see prayer and psalmody

ANCIENT CHRISTIAN WRITERS

The Works of the Fathers in Translation

Edited by

J. QUASTEN, S.T.D., and J. C. PLUMPE, PH.D.